1992

Foucault and education

Foucault's work continues to have an enormous cross-disciplinary influence. This book is the first to explore his key ideas and concepts in relation to educational contexts and issues. It argues that schools, like prisons and asylums, are fundamentally concerned with moral and social regulation and provides excellent case studies related to Foucault's concern with the technologies of power and domination and the arbitrariness of modern institutions.

The essays in the collection approach the subject in different and original ways. Three use historical material to explore aspects of the constitution of modern education. Three examine the role of discourse about education in the contemporary politics of education – the discursive work of the New Right is of particular interest. Other contributions consider the theoretical relevance of Foucault's work to assessment and educational research. This is an original and challenging book, and will be of great interest to students and lecturers of educational theory as well as to those interested in critical theory and the history of thought.

Stephen J. Ball, the editor, is Professor of Education in the Centre for Educational Studies, King's College, University of London.

Foucault and education
Disciplines and knowledge

Edited by
Stephen J. Ball

London and New York

First published in 1990
by Routledge
11 New Fetter Lane, London EC4P 4EE

Simultaneously published in the USA and Canada
by Routledge
a division of Routledge, Chapman and Hall, Inc.
29 West 35th Street, New York, NY 10001

Reprinted 1991

Typeset by LaserScript Limited, Mitcham, Surrey

Printed and bound in Great Britain by
Biddles Ltd, Guildford and King's Lynn

British Library Cataloguing in Publication Data
Foucault and education: disciplines and knowledge.
   1. Education. Theories of Foucault, Michel, 1926–1984.
   I. Ball, Stephen, 1950–,
   370′.1
   ISBN 0-415-04710-2
   ISBN 0-415-05004-9 pbk

Library of Congress Cataloging in Publication Data
Foucault and education : disciplines and knowledge/edited by
   Stephen J. Ball
     p.   cm.
   Includes bibliographical references.
   ISBN 0-415-04710-2.—ISBN 0-415-05004-9
   1. Foucault, Michel. 2. Education—Philosophy.
   3. Education—Social aspects. I. Ball, Stephen J.
   LB880.F682F68 1990
   370.1—dc20   89–49384
                                             CIP

Contents

Contributors

Stephen Ball is Professor of Education in the Centre for Educational Studies, King's College London. He is author of *Beachside Comprehensive* and *The Micropolitics of the School* and is currently researching education policy making.

Ian Dowbiggin is currently a postdoctoral fellow at the Faculty of Education of the University of Western Ontario. He received his Ph.D. in history in 1986 from the University of Rochester, New York and has taught modern European history there and at the University of Dallas. His current interests include the social history of professional knowledge in the modern era.

Ivor Goodson is Professor of Education at the University of Western Ontario, London, Canada. He is author of *School Subjects and Curriculum Change*, and *The Making of Curriculum* and numerous papers and articles on curriculum history and life history methods.

Keith Hoskin was educated at the Universities of Oxford and Pennsylvania, and is currently Lecturer in Accounting and Finance, Business School, University of Warwick. His main concern is the way in which educational practices have constructed power–knowledge relations over the course of western history. He is currently writing on the genesis of modern managerialism, and on the development of 'education power' in the United States, from this perspective.

Dave Jones has a Ph.D. in political theory from the London School of Economics and is currently completing a second in education at King's College. He ran a truancy project in Brent from 1980–88.

Richard Jones is a biology teacher at Woodway Park School and Community College, Coventry. He was awarded an M.A. for research in the history and philosophy of science and has published work on the historiography of science. Having recently completed entries on the biological sciences and the philosophy of science for the forthcoming *Oxford Companion to Science*, he is currently carrying out research for a Ph.D. thesis on the philosophy of human nature.

Jane Kenway has taught at all levels of the education system and is currently senior lecturer in Social and Administrative Studies at Deakin University in Victoria, Australia. Her current research is concerned with the refinement and use of hegemony theory as a means of exploring the multifaceted relationship between social class, gender, and education. A particular focus of her research has been the educational and social ascendancy of high-status private schools in Australia.

John Knight lectures in the sociology of education at the University of Queensland. His particular interest is the impact of religious fundament-alism and the New Right on curriculum content and education policy. He is co-author of *Understanding Schooling: An Introductory Sociology of Australian Education* (London: Routledge, 1988).

James Marshall was born in Timaru and educated at Waitaki B.H.S., New Zealand, Dartmouth Royal Naval College, and Bristol University from which he obtained a doctorate in philosophy in 1973. He has been a naval officer, a secondary school teacher, and lecturer in teacher training in England, and has taught in universities in England and New Zealand. His present position is Professor and Head of Department of Education, University of Auckland. His books are *What is Education?*, *Positivism or Pragmatism: Philosophy of Education in New Zealand* and *Why Go to School?* He has published widely in international journals concerned with the philosophy of education, programme evaluation, policy analysis, public administration, and education in general. He was co-founder of the New Zealand educational journal *Access*.

Judyth Sachs is senior lecturer in education at the Gold Coast College of Advanced Education. Her particular interests are cultural theory and teacher culture.

Richard Smith is Professor in Social and Cultural Studies at the James Cook University. His research interests are the sociology of education and cultural studies.

1 Introducing Monsieur Foucault

Stephen J. Ball

Michel Foucault is an enigma, a massively influential intellectual who steadfastly refused to align himself with any of the major traditions of western social thought. His primary concern with the history of scientific thought, the development of technologies of power and domination, and the arbitrariness of modern social institutions speak to but stand outside the main currents of Weberian and Marxist scholarship. In an interview in 1982, in response to a question about his intellectual identity, Foucault characteristically replied:

> I don't feel it is necessary to know exactly what I am. The main interest in life and work is to become someone else you were not in the beginning. If you knew when you began a book what you would say at the end, do you think you would have the courage to write it?
>
> (Martin *et al.* 1988: 9)

Foucault's playfulness and elusiveness seem to have stimulated fascination and exasperation in equal measure. None the less, his work has been taken up or has impacted upon a wide range of disciplines – sociology, history, psychology, philosophy, politics, linguistics, cultural studies, literary theory, and so on.

At the centre of his work, over a 25-year period, has been a series of attempts to analyse particular ideas or models of humanity which have developed as the result of very precise historical changes, and the ways in which these ideas have become normative or universal. Foucault has set himself staunchly against the notion of universal or self-evident humanity. Again in interview he explained:

> My role – and that is too emphatic a word – is to show people that they are much freer than they feel, that people accept as truth, as evidence, some themes which have been built up at a certain moment during history, and that this so-called evidence can be

criticized and destroyed. To change something in the minds of
people – that's the role of an intellectual.

(Martin *et al.* 1988: 10)

Foucault has identified certain knowledges – human sciences – and
certain attendant practices as central to the normalization of social principles and institutions of modern society. Among these are psychological, medical, penitential, and educational knowledges and practices.
Our concern here is with the role of the latter, education, and its inter-
relationship with politics, economics, and history in the formation and
constitution of human beings as subjects. By normalization Foucault
means the establishment of measurements, hierarchy, and regulations
around the idea of a distributionary statistical norm within a given
population – the idea of judgment based on what is normal and thus what
is abnormal. The various chapters in this book employ a Foucauldian
perspective for the analysis of aspects of the history of education and of
some of the discourses and disciplinary disputes currently being formed,
developed, and re-formed in the educational field.

Discourse is a central concept in Foucault's analytical framework.
Discourses are about what can be said and thought, but also about who
can speak, when, and with what authority. Discourses embody meaning
and social relationships, they constitute both subjectivity and power
relations. Discourses are 'practices that systematically form the objects
of which they speak. . . . Discourses are not about objects; they do not
identify objects, they constitute them and in the practice of doing so
conceal their own invention' (Foucault 1974: 49). Thus the possibilities
for meaning and for definition, are preempted through the social and
institutional position held by those who use them. Meanings thus arise
not from language but from institutional practices, from power relations.
Words and concepts change their meaning and their effects as they are
deployed within different discourses. Discourses constrain the possibilities of thought. They order and combine words in particular ways
and exclude or displace other combinations. However, in so far as
discourses are constituted by exclusions as well as inclusions, by what
cannot as well as what can be said, they stand in antagonistic relationship to other discourses, other possibilities of meaning, other claims,
rights, and positions. This is Foucault's 'principle of discontinuity': 'We
must make allowance for the complex and unstable powers whereby
discourse can be both an instrument and an effect of power, but also a
hindrance, a stumbling block, a point of resistance and a starting point
for an opposing strategy' (Foucault 1982: 101).

Discourse lies between the level of pure atemporal linguistic
'structure' (*langue*) and the level of surface speaking (*parole*): it

expresses the historical specificity of what is said and what remains unsaid.

[D]iscourses are composed of signs, but what they do is more than use these signs to designate things. It is this move that renders them irreducible to the language and to speech. It is this 'move' that we must reveal and describe.

(Foucault 1974: 49)

The issue in discourse analysis is why, at a given time, out of all the possible things that could be said, only certain things were said: 'how is it that one particular statement appeared rather than another' (Foucault 1974: 27). Further it is essential to reveal the 'density' and 'complexity' within discursive practices, to go beyond the boundaries of structure, or utterances, *langue*, and *parole*. The world is perceived differently within different discourses. Discourse is structured by assumptions within which any speaker must operate in order to be heard as meaningful. Thus the concept of discourse emphasizes the social processes that produce meaning.

We are concerned here with educational sites as generators of an historically specific (modern) discourse, that is, as sites in which certain modern validations of, and exclusions from, the 'right to speak' are generated.

Educational sites are subject to discourse but are also centrally involved in the propagation and selective dissemination of discourses, the 'social appropriation' of discourses. Educational institutions control the access of individuals to various kinds of discourse.

But we know very well that, in its distribution, in what it permits and what it prevents, it follows the lines laid down by social differences, conflicts and struggles. Every educational system is a political means of maintaining or modifying the appropriateness of discourses with the knowledge and power they bring with them.

(Foucault 1971: 46)

Above all, the distribution and appropriateness of discourses in education is mediated by the examination, that 'slender technique' in which is to be found 'a whole domain of knowledge, a whole type of power'. Indeed, Keith Hoskin in Chapter 3 argues that the examination is a key concept in understanding the nexus of power–knowledge relations. The act, the process of examining, embodies and relates power and knowledge in technological form.

Foucault's history is the history of the different modes by which, in our culture, human beings are made subjects. (Foucault in Dreyfus and Rabinow 1982: 208). That is the objectification of the subject by processes of classification and division. The latter, what Foucault called

3

'dividing practices' are clearly central to the organizational processes of education in our society. These divisions and objectifications are achieved either within the subject or between the subject and others. The use of testing, examining, profiling, and streaming in education, the use of entry criteria for different types of schooling, and the formation of different types of intelligence, ability, and scholastic identity in the processes of schooling are all examples of such 'dividing practices'. In these ways, using these techniques and forms of organization, and the creation of separate and different curricula, pedagogies, forms of teacher–student relationships, identities and subjectivities are formed, learned and carried. Through the creation of remedial and advanced groups, and the separation of the educationally subnormal or those with special educational needs, abilities are stigmatized and normalized.

These dividing practices are critically interconnected with the formation, and increasingly sophisticated elaboration, of the educational sciences: educational psychology, pedagogics, the sociology of education, cognitive and developmental psychology. These are the arenas in which 'truth games' about education are played out. For example, the development of the sociology of education in the 1960s and 1970s was organized around and informed and reinforced the 'problem of working-class underachievement'. The sociological findings of the period constructed a sophisticated and powerful social pathology of working-class family life as deficient and culturally deprived – abnormal. The problem of underachievement was defined as beyond the control and capabilities of the teacher, and as culturally determined and inevitable. Teachers were provided with a rich, pseudo-scientific vocabulary of classifications and justifications for the inevitability of differences in intellectual performance between the social classes. Individuals drawn from the undifferentiated mass of school students could be objectified in terms of various fixed social class or other social indicators (Sharp and Green 1975) instituted in the school's spatial, temporal, and social compartmentalizations. Knowledge and practices drawn from the educational sciences provided (in Foucault's terms) modes of classification, control, and containment, often paradoxically linked to humanitarian rhetoric of reform and progress: streaming, remedial classes, off-site units and sanctuaries, informal or invisible pedagogies (Bernstein 1975).

In the processes of schooling the student is compiled and constructed both in the passive processes of objectification, and in an active, self-forming subjectification, the latter involving processes of self-understanding mediated by an external authority figure – for our purposes, most commonly the teacher. For example, this is apparent in the increasing use of profiling and records of achievement in schools (Hargreaves 1986).

As indicated already, the key concepts in Foucault's exploration of the problem of the subject are those of power and knowledge, or more precisely that of power–knowledge, the single, inseparable configuration of ideas and practices that constitute a discourse. Power and knowledge are two sides of a single process. Knowledge does not reflect power relations but is immanent in them.

One text of Foucault's *Discipline and Punish*, is key reading for much of the analysis and argument contained in this volume. Several of the chapters make extensive reference to this work and both Marshall and Hoskin discuss its significance and implications at some length. This is not surprising in a consideration of education, and Foucault suggests in his conclusion to *Discipline and Punish* that the book will 'serve as a background for various studies of normalization and the power of knowledge in modern society'. *Discipline and Punish* traces the shift from the spectacle of punishment to disciplined institutional punishment via the constitution of apparatuses which function to define power relations in terms of everyday life; the school and the classroom are specifically mentioned as apparatuses of this sort. In the nineteenth century they emerged as particular organizations of space and persons experienced by virtually all people, at one and the same time totalizing the power of the state and producing and specifying particular individualities. This is Foucault's political 'double bind'.

But education works not only to render its students as subjects of power, it also constitutes them, or some of them, as powerful subjects. The effects of power are both negative and positive. Major examples of the latter are the historic shift in gender relations in the nineteenth century which made it possible for women to take advantage of the new practices of credentialing and meritocratic selection, and the appearance in the twentieth century of a new professional and managerial 'education-generated class' – Bernstein's 'new middle class'.

What is on offer here is an exploration of the application of Foucault's work within the field of education. And education, as the new role for intellectuals and knowledge experts after 1800, as the establishing of the credentialing society, as the primary institutional experience of virtually all young persons, is fundamental to a Foucauldian analysis of modern society. This book can be read as an illustration of facets of this new power of education. Its view is, via Foucault, to render the familiarity of mass education strange. The majority of the chapters are substantively focused on a particular area or issue but the Foucauldian perspective plays a slightly different role in each chapter. Thus while Dave Jones and Richard Jones maintain a fairly purist adherence to Foucault's techniques of historical analysis, Kenway and Smith *et al.* operate within a broader theoretical and analytical frame. Kenway draws in part on Gramsci, while Smith *et al.*

work within a more general post-structuralist, deconstructionist perspective. Dowbiggin and Goodson attempt to draw Foucault into relation to a more mainstream history of ideas and curriculum history perspectives.

Part I is more expository and exploratory. Marshall considers the question of the implementation of the Foucauldian perspective for the work of historians of education, although he notes Foucault's project is normally seen as anti-history. Foucault stresses discontinuity, complexity, and circumstance and shows little interest in causality. He writes against rather than within the canons of historical scholarships. Marshall also indicates Foucault's debt to Nietzsche. Hoskin's chapter goes in search of the elusive link between power and knowledge, the meaning of the hyphen that joins them. Following the clues in various Foucault texts, he finds the solution, the principle of coherence, in the examination, or more generally in that which is 'the educational' in different epochs.

In the historical chapters, Dave Jones, Richard Jones, and Dowbiggin and Goodson each contribute, in different ways, to what Foucault has called 'the history of the present'. They attempt to excavate and analyse some of the key concepts that provide the bedrock of contemporary educational practice. Thus Dave Jones offers a genealogy of the urban schoolteacher; Richard Jones explores the emergence of modern educational practices and modern scientific knowledge in post-revolutionary France; Dowbiggin and Goodson compare the rise of psychiatry in France and geography in England to illustrate the establishment of key disciplinary professions and their relation to the state.

The final section is concerned with some common aspects of the contemporary restructuring of education, particularly the deployment and effects of the 'radical/critical' discourses of the New Right in struggles over 'what is to count as education'. Smith *et al.* compare and deconstruct two competing texts which embody and advocate competing versions of 'multiculturalism' and 'education'. Kenway investigates the New Right political and media campaigns launched in defence of state funding for private schools in Australia and their effects upon the grounds of educational debate and the constitution of educational commonsense.

My own short chapter offers a critique of the development and application of management in education, and the ways in which management operates to control, classify, and contain teachers' work, towards the end of governmentality, in its 'best' and 'most economical' form. As Foucault explains:

> The art of government . . . is concerned with . . . how to introduce economy, that is the correct manner of managing

individuals, goods and wealth within the family ... [h]ow to introduce this meticulous attention of the father towards his family, into the management of the state.

(Rabinow 1986: 15)

Management provides a paradigm case of a disciplinary technology, a form of bio-power, which employs scientific categories and explicit calculations to objectify the body – the worker – and to render individuals docile and pliable. In this chapter and in several of the others, Foucault's view of the relationship between economic change – changes in the accumulation and mechanisms of power – provides a backdrop. Historical moments in the transformation of the state and the economy are taken to be mutually dependent, but with 'the growth and spread of disciplinary mechanisms of knowledge' preceding and providing preconditions for economic transformations.

The bulk of Foucault's analytical effect is weighted towards the subjection of individuals to the accumulation of power in the state by the use of technologies of discipline and confession. He gives little attention to the ways in which such domination might be resisted or subverted by those subject to it. And yet, as indicated by the interview extract quoted earlier, he does see his work as providing a mechanism of critique, or a tool of subversion. He is reticent about specifying an ideal society beyond that which is, but he is adamant that there 'are more secrets, more possible freedoms, and more inventions in our future than we can imagine in humanism as it is dogmatically prescribed on every side of the political rainbow' (Martin *et al.* 1988: 13). Thus for Foucault

the real political task in a society such as ours is to criticize the working of institutions which appear to be both neutral and independent; violence which has always exercised itself obscurely through them will be unmasked, so that we can fight fear.

(Foucault 1974: 171)

This is very much the spirit in which this book was conceived and is offered. It is to be hoped that the application of Foucauldian analysis to education will unmask the politics that underlie some of the apparent neutrality of educational reform. We leave the last word to Foucault, who commented in an interview, 'I'm proud that some people think that I'm a danger for the intellectual health of students' (Martin *et al.* 1988: 13).

REFERENCES

Bernstein, B. (1975) *Class, Codes and Control*, vol. 3, London: Routledge & Kegan Paul.

Dreyfus, H.L. and Rabinow, P. (eds) (1982) *Michel Foucault: Beyond Structuralism and Hermeneutics*, Brighton: Harvester Press.

Foucault, M. (1971) *L'ordre du discours*, Paris: Gallimard.

———(1974) *The Archaeology of Knowledge*, London: Tavistock.

———(1982) 'The subject and power', in H.L. Dreyfus and P. Rabinow (eds) *Michel Foucault: Beyond Structuralism, op. cit.*

Hargreaves, A. (1986) 'Record breakers?' in P. Broadfoot (ed.) *Profiles and Records of Achievement*, Eastbourne: Holt-Saunders.

Martin, L., Gutman, H., and Hutton, P. (eds) (1988) *Technologies of the Self*, London: Tavistock.

Rabinow, P. (1986) *The Foucault Reader*, London: Peregrine.

Sharp, R. and Green, A. (1975) *Education and Social Control*, London: Routledge & Kegan Paul.

Part I
Foucault and education

2 Foucault and educational research

James D. Marshall

INTRODUCTION

Michel Foucault is an enigma: an iconoclast and intellectual who appears to come from nowhere (Lemert and Gillen 1982) and to claim no intellectual lineage. Describing himself, he said (Foucault 1984b: 383f.):

> I think I have in fact been situated in most of the squares on the political checkerboard, one after another and sometimes simultaneously: as anarchist, leftist, ostentatious or disguised Marxist, nihilist, explicit or secret anti-Marxist, technocrat in the service of Gaullism, new liberal, etc. An American professor complained that a crypto-Marxist like me was invited to the USA, and I was denounced by the press in Eastern Europe for being an accomplice of the dissidents. None of these descriptions is important by itself; taken together, on the other hand, they mean something. And I must admit that I rather like what they mean.

Foucault should be taken for himself and not classified neatly into recognizable categories.

Academics, however, seem exasperated that Foucault does not fit into recognizable categories and does not employ recognizable methodologies. Some historians (e.g., Maxcy 1977) see him as a structuralist; others object that he plays fast and loose with historical data and time, appealing to concepts like rupture and discontinuity which, they claim, fail to explain (Megill 1979). Philosophers find him incoherent, or protest that his methodology wavers between the philosophical, the politically strategic, and a moral onslaught (Fraser 1985). Marxists believe that what appears as a radical position on the Left cuts across the central and basic tenets of Marxism, or perhaps transcends Marxism because it is a critique of these assumptions. In some cases, Foucault is seen as providing important insights into individualization and the operation of forms of power. One Marxist suggests, more

11

radically, that 'the classic discourse of socialism is rendered problematic' (Smart 1983, 1986).

But Foucault, like many French intellectuals, did not write just for an academic audience; for example, works such as *Discipline and Punish: the Birth of the Prison* (Foucault 1979a) were read by both criminologists and criminals alike. However, a burgeoning array of academic critiques attests to the interest that his work has aroused in academic and professional circles. In general, however, Foucault has been ignored by educationalists.

References are made to Foucault by educationalists interested in questions of social control and the exercise of power. With the exception of a chapter in a book by Madan Sarap (1982), these are generally passing references to his analysis of power. There are, however, some major exceptions. Henriques *et al.* (1984) explore the ways in which psychology is involved in constructions of the individual and society. In particular, Valerie Walkerdine (1984) examines the work of Jean Piaget in a section devoted to the effects of psychological practices in the social regulation of practices and the construction of notions of the individual. She adopts a Foucault-type approach to argue that the developmental psychology of Piaget, in so far as it has been adopted by a child-centred pedagogy, has not had any hoped-for liberating effect but, rather, has become part of a set of scientifically legitimated practices whose object is the developing child. She argues that such practices through surveillance, observation, and classification normalize children but do not seem to acknowledge or even understand the point that the developing child is an 'object' produced by those very same practices (see also Walkerdine 1986).

It should be noted that Walkerdine's interest is in the notion of the developing child and the ways in which psychology has produced this 'subject' as its object for scientific investigation and thereby prohibits other formulations of the individual–social dualism. Her approach is to concentrate upon Foucault as archaeologist looking for the set of socio-historical conditions that has permitted this 'subject' to become an object of scientific investigation. But Foucault is to shift his ground in his later work away from epistemes and archaeology *per se*, and towards bio-power and how this produces subjects of certain kinds. Though he was to concentrate on modern forms of sexuality, his concern was more with the ways in which these were produced by modern forms of power. The developing child was not his concern as such; neither was psychology *per se*. The subject of the developing child reveals a particular set of parameters along which individuals are normalized. Thus Walkerdine would be compatible with Foucault in that she has correctly seen that the notion of the developing child is not liberating. Yet her project, challenging the reduction of problems to formulations in terms of 'the child's acquisition of' and 'the development of' is seen by her as a pre-requisite to the reconstruction of a new 'liberating' psychological subject. Foucault was not interested in the truth of such matters within the human sciences.

An archaeological approach is adopted also by Jones and Williamson (1979) to determine the discursive conditions that made possible the emergence of types of statements on mass popular education and peda-gogic practices in the nineteenth century. As they freely admit, they concentrate upon 'writings of the nineteenth century' and the relations between these writings. Whilst their conclusion – that schooling cannot be reduced to notions of social control and socialization but should rather be seen in terms of the extension of forms of modern power or the securing of governance – is certainly very compatible with Foucault, their approach is perhaps rather narrow, concentrating as it does upon statements (which Foucault was to abandon). Foucault insisted also that the site for analysis must be the present. Jones and Williamson's 'present' is the nineteenth century.

Hoskin (1979) interprets examinations as essentially normalization procedures. The examination is an important part of school ritual and, for Foucault, an essential aspect of the exercise of power. Hoskin concentrates on the written statement, but Foucault's later comments on power relations direct attention to much wider notions of practices and methodology.

Arnold Davidson (1986) argues that for Foucault archaeology and genealogy are very different methodologies. The differences can be represented by these two succinct comments on 'truth':

> '[T]ruth' is to be understood as a system of ordered procedures for the production, regulation, distribution, circulation and operation of statements. . . .
> 'Truth' is linked in a circular relation with systems of power which produce and sustain it, and to effects of power which induces it and which extends it. A 'regime' of truth.

For example, in relation to sexuality, archaeology would identify changes in the rules for the production of discourse that first made it possible to speak about sexuality, and not merely sex, whereas genea-logy would indicate that sexuality was a positive product of power, incited by techniques of surveillance and examination. The former attempts to isolate the level of discursive practices and formulate the rules for the production and transformation of such practices, whereas the latter widens the scope of inquiry and concentrates on the forces and relations of power connected to discursive practices. Power–knowledge is necessary for genealogy but not for archaeology.

It is not clear, however, that the radical nature of Foucault's thinking

James D. Marshall

has been grasped by the majority of educationalists. Foucault does not just speak about such things as power, domination, and the construction of subjects in ways that can be tacked on, so to say, to resistance theory, reproduction theory, or whatever. Instead, his views radically undercut the ways in which such talk, as well as more traditional liberal talk of education, is even formulated.

While there is much that is problematic in his work (see Hoy 1986 for a collection of critical papers on Foucault), nevertheless what he says on the philosophy of the subject and the form in which power has come to be exercised in modern states is, as Walzer (1986) says, 'right enough to be disturbing'. Foucault's major concern is with what can be called loosely 'the philosophy of the subject', by which he means a problematic dominating modern way of thought, that privileges the subject as the foundation of all knowledge and of all signification. His philosophical project is to investigate the ways in which discourses and practices have transformed human beings into subjects of a particular kind. It is important to note that for him, 'subject' is systematically ambiguous; it means both being tied to someone else by control and dependence, and being tied to one's own identity by a conscience or self- knowledge.

These senses are not contradictory for Foucault. The subject is the basis upon which discourse is founded and, at the same time, the mode of objectification which transforms human beings into subjects. Such discourse serves all attempts at understanding, defining, and conceptualizing what it is to be human. In other words, 'subject' carries the twin meaning of an active knowing subject and of an object being acted upon – a product of discourse. In terms of discourse we can say that the subject both speaks and is spoken of; in epistemological terms we can say with Foucault (1970: 323) that 'man appears in his ambiguous position as an object of knowledge and as a subject that knows'.

Foucault can be understood as launching a strong critical attack upon liberal post-enlightenment notions that enlightenment is to be obtained by a form of maturity achieved through the use of reason. Foucault, whilst acknowledging the importance of Kant's attempt to preserve the normative role of reason in the face of the collapse of metaphysics, sees Kant's philosophy as a response to a particular historical situation (Foucault 1984a). What Foucault sees as important and distinctive in Kant's thought is that it arises from and in response to his own sociohistorical condition. According to Foucault's (1984a) account of Kant,

> the way out that characterises Enlightenment is a process that releases us from the status of 'immaturity'. And by 'immaturity', he means a certain state of our will that makes us accept someone else's authority to lead us where the use of reason is called for.

This sense of enlightenment is important to Foucault as it permits a point

14

of departure into what Foucault and others have termed an attitude of modernity, in which the notion of man as a rationally autonomous subject is a focus for critique.

Modern power has emerged in the name of governance. This latter notion is introduced by Foucault in his important paper 'Govern-mentality' (Foucault 1979b). In this paper he traces a shift in the relations between the sovereign and individuals from the time of Machiavelli to the modern state. Foucault notes a shift in thinking of obedience to a violent and imposed power where property was protected at any cost, towards a theme of governance of the self, children, family, and state. This notion of governance is identified initially in the notion of a family as model but modern notions of governance and power emerge when the family is seen no longer as a model but becomes instead the instrument of government. Here the emergence of economic theory was important because it permitted the identification of problems specific to populations and not reducible to the dimension of the family.

Population and its welfare then become the central theme of governance, according to Foucault. The control of populations to ensure political obedience and a docile and useful workforce for the demands of an emerging capitalism become the central concerns in this art of governance.

Rather than the violent exercise of power of the sovereign upon the body of the subject (see the harrowing account of the public execution of Damiens in the opening pages of Foucault's (1979a) *Discipline and Punish*), we see instead the emergence of lenience with offenders and other people classified as delinquent. From the violence of Damiens' public execution we move to a quiet, ordered, and private scenario in which peoples' abilities and knowledge about themselves are gently and quietly shaped in a gentle, 'caring' institution. There were many such institutions to emerge but Foucault notes in particular the prison, hospital, asylum, military, work place, and school. Within such insti-tutions knowledge has been developed about people, and their behav-iour, attitudes, and self-knowledge have been developed, refined, and used to shape individuals. These discourses and practices have not only been used to change us in various ways but are also used to legitimate such changes, as the knowledge gained is deemed to be 'true'.

Foucault identifies this knowledge, developed by the exercise of power and used in turn to legitimate further exercises of power, as power–knowledge (Foucault 1981). He refers to the institutions at which this power has been or is exercised as disciplinary institutions.

Disciplinary institutions organize physical space and time with activities that have been developed over time to change people's behaviour along a number of parameters. Here the examination plays a critical role, for it determines not only whether a person is governable –

that is, likely to lead a docile, useful, and practical life – but also because it identifies to the individual the 'true' self, whereby (s)he becomes classified as an object in various ways for others and is tied to the 'true' self as a subjected or politically dominated being.

This true self is a person with certain beliefs about him/herself. These descriptions in part permit the individual to be dominated through these classifications as hyperactive, homosexual, autonomous rational being, and so on. But in Foucault's thought these true selves are but fictions or constructions as there is no real *man*. In particular, autonomous man is a construction of post-enlightenment and humanist thought.

Foucault inverts our normal beliefs about autonomous man by adopting a particular methodology – genealogy.

FOUCAULT AS GENEALOGIST

One may consider Foucault's work (given that he does use historical data and in as much as this makes some historians shudder) as writing a new kind of history. Given the present splintering of history and historical methodology, there may be something to be said for this interpretation. In what ways then, if at all, is Foucault presenting us with a 'new' history?

At one time history could have been conceived as narrative writing within the humanities, concerned with great events, great people, and the emergence of our constitution and institutions. However, this comfortable arena has now been invaded by what can loosely be called 'social history'. Social history introduced not just a different set of topics such as the family, women, and classes, but also brought with it from other social science disciplines a bewildering number of methodologies. These include economics, class analysis from sociology, and 'thick' interpretation from anthropology. Methodology in history had always been disputed historically, at a meta-level by philosophers, but this was a new conflict at the level of *doing* history.

The basic impact of Foucault's work is historical (with strong implications for philosophy) and its differences from other social history force consideration of these general questions. Whilst his work is read across a wide variety of disciplines, his work is often seen by historians as *anti-history* in the sense that he is not at all interested in pursuing these questions and revitalizing an historiographic tradition once seen as sound. His work can be said to be anti-history in the following general ways.

1. He writes no complete history of the past. *Discipline and Punish* opens with the execution of Damiens and ends with an analysis of the carceral, but is not treated as a development or emergence of one form

of punishment rather than another. Historical data are suddenly injected into his 'story' with no apparent theory of selection. It is not perhaps the best account of the past of the prison, as it really was (see, e.g., Rusche and Kircheimer 1939). What annoys historians is that Foucault fully agrees on this point, claiming that he was not trying to present a conventional history. But if not, what was he trying to do? In what ways is his work historical?

2. He does not advance historical causes. For example, in the same work he notes the sudden incarceration of people in the early nineteenth century but gives no explanation, even though the fact of incarceration is critical for his account of the human sciences. At best, he identifies spaces in which possibilities were created and whereby certain events were 'outcomes'. But these were not causal outcomes. It might be thought that various moves in law, demography, and the rise of capitalism, say, might indicate a space out of which incarceration was a possible causal outcome. That is, we understand it because it makes sense against our general knowledge and understanding of human affairs. But the problem with Foucault is that he presents us with new relationships, and ones that present a new landscape. Given past understandings, there is not even a possible causal relationship.

3. Foucault employs a bewildering amount of data drawn from widely different sources. Details of the construction of military instal- lations are juxtaposed in *Discipline and Punish* with details of the con- struction of hospitals, schools, and prisons. These at first sight are different kinds of structures, meeting different kinds of needs. Yet the analytic grid of power–knowledge which Foucault employs shows a new relationship between these constructions. Foucault has returned to the analysis of space, claiming that since Kant, western thought has been dominated by philosophical considerations of time. But why these spaces? Why not the home as in, for example, Philippe Aries (1962)? Why select these spaces rather than the home? Foucault does not tell us. The analytic grid of power–knowledge is not much help either as the home might well be selected as an appropriate locus for an analysis of power relations at the micro-level favoured by Foucault. If there is a theory for the selection of this data then it is not articulated or immediately obvious.

4. Foucault provides us with no teleological unfolding of reason in general, or the reasoning of particular thinkers or of great men. Indeed, in so far as he turns to reason, it is often to the house of unreason – the madhouse. There is no notion of a future for mankind, or of history preventing us from reliving our mistakes. Yet reason is, in Foucault's history, a product of socio-historical circumstances. Nevertheless, there is no account of history that provides hope or suggests ways to avoid a return to the abyss. At best, Foucault says that he is writing the history

17

of the present, of the conditions that make us think now that we are people of a certain kind. History will not then offer us liberation from forms of domination.

5. Neither is Foucault writing a history of ideas, though this was the title of the chair which he held at the prestigious College de France. History of ideas tends to be written as though there is a development or emergence of an object in a more or less continuous or rational fashion. Against this view Foucault believes that there is no one object such as madness which can be tracked through time. There are ruptures that not only cut across the emergence or development of themes but which also make the notion of the continuous existence of an object called 'madness' problematic. Objects are constituted in particular epistemes and these have to be first understood.

6. Foucault can be seen as following Nietzsche's views on history (Foucault 1977a). There is little doubt that Nietzsche was adapted for Foucault's ends. Megill (1979) refers to it as a 'presentist' view of history.

But in so far as Foucault uses Nietzsche, he may not be fully responsible for the Nietzsche revival in France. According to Lash (1984) this responsibility should be attributed to Gilles Deleuze. Lash claims further that Foucault was heavily influenced by 'Deleuze's infectious interpretations of the May–June days'. While there can be no doubt that the events of May–June 1968 did affect Foucault (he states this himself on several occasions) nevertheless, it must be noted that Foucault was very well acquainted with Nietzsche as he had, after all, taught courses on him.

In the paper 'Nietzsche, history, genealogy' (Foucault 1977a) Nietzschean themes on the nature and role of history are asserted. Instead of reaching outwards towards an objective truth, history turns inwards for Foucault, becoming story, plot, myth, and fabrication. It is something that is to be used in the present and for the future; it is not something that captures 'reality', and certainly not a reality of the past. In this sense then we can begin to see why Foucault is alleged to write anti-history.

He develops two Nietzschean concepts in this paper: the concepts of *herkunft* (descent), and *enstehung* (emergence). These are contrasted in the article against the notion of origin. On the differences, he says (Foucault 1977a: 144):

> A genealogy of values, morality, asceticism and knowledge will never confuse itself with a quest for their 'origins', will never neglect as inaccessible the vicissitudes of history. On the contrary, it will cultivate the details and the accidents that accompany every beginning; it will be scrupulously attentive to their petty malice; it

will await their emergence, once unmasked as the face of the other.

Genealogy as descent is not a continuous and uninterrupted notion. There is a multiplicity of factors that must be unravelled from lowly sources and subjugated knowledges that will play havoc with notions of continuity. There are errors and accidents to be discovered which will disturb notions of order. The search for descent is not a search for firm foundations; on the contrary, it discovers moving sands, fragmented and incoherent events with faults, errors, omissions, faulty appraisals, and pious claims and aspirations. The move is in general to show that 'historical truths' rest upon complex, contingent, and fragile ground.

The concept of emergence sees the present not in any final way, as a result of historical development, but rather as a stage in the warlike confrontation between opposing forces in the quest for control and domination. Historical developments are conceptualized then as manifestations of stable mechanisms of governance, as exercises of power to restore stability, or as out-and-out contests or struggles. Emergence concentrates on domination–subjection relationships as exemplifying the underlying balances of political forces. We are to look at historical 'developments' then not as culminations of historical processes, intentions of great actors, or hidden political designs, but instead, as manifestations of the balances of power over people, though no one person or collective may have exercised that power or ultimately be held responsible.

In brief then, genealogy disrupts historical form by concentrating on historical objects not usually considered the province of historical enquiry – even in contemporary approaches under the rubric of social history. The body, for example, occupies a central theoretical position for both Foucault and Nietzsche, though their accounts differ (Lash 1984). The madhouse becomes a site for genealogical analysis of reason; the gaze or surveillance, a critical element in the development of modern power; and so on (for detailed analyses of these sites, see Cousins and Hussain 1984).

But, it might properly be objected, enough of this general account of genealogical method. What would one do if one did genealogy? What does Foucault do? How does genealogy work in practice? It is difficult to answer this short of reading or providing a total analysis, say, of *Discipline and Punish*. Nevertheless, an attempt will be made to look at the book's structure, presentation, and argument, in so far as these reflect genealogical method.

First, the book is divided into four sections, covering the 'history' of punishment from brutality to what might be called 'the gentle way'. The third section on discipline is concerned with generalizing the notion of discipline into wider contexts, or with seeing how discipline is diffused into many institutional settings. The fourth section is an analysis of the function of nineteenth-century prisons. The third section on discipline is the major section of the book and structurally represents a rupture or discontinuity with the earlier two sections. Similarly, the fourth section, returning as it does to an analysis of the functioning of the prison, represents a rupture with section three, which had been concerned with the infiltration of discipline throughout the social body. These structural breaks in presentation are important because the book is itself representative in its structure of the methodology that it purports to employ. There are important reasons for this, found in Foucault's total critique of modern culture, and especially in his views as to what was involved in being an author and thinking differently and creatively (Foucault 1977b).

Donnelly (1982) argues that these four sections employ different methodologies: the first two sections involve a genealogy of the birth of the prison, the third an evolutionary account of the general diffusion of discipline, and the fourth section a functionalist account of the later prison. I am not sure that Donnelly is correct, but in the first instance we will look at the first two sections which Donnelly seems happy to characterize as genealogical.

First, though the first two sections might be treated as a general history of the prison, this would be mistaken. It would be mistaken because Foucault is not primarily concerned with the prison – he is not writing a history of the prison – but is instead concerned with the present. The story that is told of the prison is an interpretation meant to help us understand modern power. Second, his concern is with the exercise of power so that the story of the 'emergence' of the prison is based on this aspect for the selection of data. Third, he detaches his 'history' of the prison from its traditional home in the juridical-legal framework – essentially the spheres of law and criminology (including early jurist versions of social contract theory). In asking the questions of how power is exercised in general and how people are punished in particular, Foucault shifts enquiry from the 'what' and 'why' of punishment, and gives new insight to those who are interested, as philosophers, criminologists, and sociologists, in punishment or its effects.

This is clearly a Nietzschean turn. Foucault's concern is not with writing on the emergence of the prison or as seeing this as an evolution towards more humane treatment of offenders, or as the rational outcome of post-enlightenment knowledge of man. In the very selection of his data he is a Nietzschean and far from neutral observer, concerned to reconstruct facts as they really were. He is not so much concerned with facts as events. These are best exemplified, perhaps, by the complexity of *I, Pierre Rivière, Having Slaughtered my Mother, my Sister and my Brother* (Foucault 1975). In this co-authored book a whole arena of competing discourses are brought together as an event – the trial of a peasant boy for murdering three members of his family. The cacophony caused in the space where these discourses intersect shows us the complexity of any event; on the evidence, his 'guilt' is most difficult to decide, especially when his own lucid story is added to the space.

If the early sections of *Discipline and Punish* were seen as mere narrative, the 'story' would go like this. First, the old style of punishment is analysed and shown to be rational, though incredibly brutal by modern sensibilities. Second, programmes for penal reform from the judiciary, ideologues, and reformers are introduced, with none granted the distinction of being a causal move towards new forms of punishment. Third, contemporary practices of discipline and their concern with the pathology of the person rather than with acts against the law, are introduced. Finally, in these sections we are introduced to the notion that the prison becomes the main form of punishment. But in this story there is no sense of a continuous development, no causal arguments, and no sense of the origins of the prison in some preceding 'facts'.

Rather, we are presented right at the outset with a very violent landscape – the public execution of the regicide Damiens. This can be contrasted very sharply with the later description of the activities in prison of young offenders. On the one hand we have the violent, horrible details of Damiens' execution as he died one thousand deaths; on the other hand, and only 80 years later, we have what appears to be an account of an institution in which the care, training, and rehabilitation of young offenders is of paramount concern, and which appears to be a forebear of a more modern, caring society. The contrast is not to shock (though it is certainly to defamiliarize) but rather to contrast two ways of exercising power. Indeed, he goes on to argue that what we find horrible and irrational in the case of Damiens is, given certain socio-historical conditions, quite rational. On this issue Charles Taylor (1986) says, 'I find Foucault quite convincing'. But how can something be meaningful which, from our twentieth-century perspective in which the individual seems so important, seems to be only irrational barbarism? Here Foucault's point is that maybe this twentieth-century perspective is not as rational or as 'evolved' as we think, but merely different. This then opens up the possibility of viewing the changes in punishment as changes in the technologies of power and, viewed from this perspective, in the modern prison we are exercising power just as the king did on the body of Damiens. It is a different kind of power, but power nevertheless.

Foucault has shown us in the present that (modern) power permeates our society by tracking the disappearance of one form of punishment and its replacement by another. By asking the question of how punishment is exercised, he is able to show us how modern power is exercised. The body, which was also important for Nietzsche, remains the locus of the application of power, but it is a power not meant to destroy but to save; it is no longer so much a power over life but a power to make life. It is not a power exercised in public space with pomp and splendour, but power exercised in private concealed spaces. Space is an important concept in this analysis and it is developed and discussed fully in section three. So, in answer to Donnelly (1982), the method of genealogy continues into section three with the contrasts between public space and cosmic order, and private space and normalcy.

In the public space of section one where order is manifested, individuals are made aware of their place in the grand cosmic order as it is restored by public executions on the scaffold. Spaces in the new form of power operate differently. It is important therefore for the genealogical method to continue into section three.

We are presented with changes in judicial practices, changes in patterns of offences, the development of disciplinary practices, and the control of populations through the control of bodies and souls – or 'bio-power', as it is called. But these changes are not familiar changes, and they are presented as changes, or differences, without underlying explanations. For example, incarceration becomes very popular although it had existed in the *ancien régime*, albeit not as a form of punishment. Suddenly, and within a very short space of time, everyone is incarcerated; change, yes but explained, no, according to Foucault.

The violent landscape with which Foucault presents us depends then upon the denial of more traditional approaches to historical data. Punishment is not merely repressive and cannot be seen merely within the juridical–legal framework. It should be considered within the wider disciplinary roles of the human sciences.

IMPLICATIONS FOR EDUCATIONAL RESEARCH

Clearly, a genealogical approach to educational research would involve considerable shifts in methodology and outcomes. Where and how might a Foucault approach proceed in education? Where should or might such research proceed and what general procedures would be followed?

First, whilst several general points on genealogy have been made, and Foucault's approach in *Discipline and Punish* outlined, it must be stated that Foucault does not offer a systematic theory of genealogy – he was opposed to any such systematization. Second, what he says he does and what he does in fact do are sometimes different; for example, section four of *Discipline and Punish* is not genealogical. But in general it can be said that he offers educational research a new framework – not for studying the past, but for assessing the present. The general framework is constituted by an analytic grid of power–knowledge, the method of genealogy, and new notions of time, especially of rupture and discontinuity.

Genealogy, however, takes each issue separately, exploring it in minute detail and reconstructing events so as to take account of subjugated and neglected knowledges. However, Foucault's failure to articulate this theory makes its application problematic. Rather than theorize about its limits of application, it may be better to see what can be done in practice.

The analytic grid is power–knowledge. The methodological imperative then is to examine processes of modern power in modern schools. In *Discipline and Punish* Foucault questions how punishment has been exercised in modern times and in the *ancien régime*. In answering this question the school surfaces on many occasions as a disciplinary block. Yet it must be emphasized that Foucault, even if he is writing a 'history' of the prison, is certainly not writing a history of the school. Schools enter as exemplifications of the exercise of power and the emergence of modern power. Yet they are not merely exemplifications of modern power because the school was an important site in which techniques and strategies of power were developed and refined. Perhaps what is needed is a study entitled 'Discipline and punish: the birth of the school', which would provide a unique analysis of the use and refinement of power–knowledge in the modern school in the cause of governance.

Important as the work of Walkerdine is, its concerns seem to be with the way in which the object – the developing child – has been constructed within developmental psychology and child-centred education. Foucault is of course intensely interested in the constitution of various types of subject like the developing child, but his major concern might be said to be the way in which forms of modern power constitute the subject – the developing child. Walkerdine of course realizes that the notion of the developing child is not one that permits a genuine liberation and that it is such versions of the subject, framed as they are within versions of a post-enlightenment humanist, or liberal framework, that are major concerns for Foucault. However, her concerns and approach are more with the conditions that have permitted a scientifically based and legitimated pedagogy based upon this notion of the subject to have emerged. In other words, her interests seem to be more in archaeological matters and epistemes than with how modern power per se permeates the modern school.

In an interview very soon before his untimely death, this point was reiterated by Foucault (1988):

My problem has always been . . .the problem of the relationship between subject and truth. How does the subject enter into a certain game of truth? . . . So it was that I was led to pose the problem power–knowledge, which is not for me the fundamental problem but an instrument allowing the analysis – in a way that seems to me to be the most exact – of the problem of the relationships between subject and games of truth.

This form of power also produces other games of truth and other notions of subjectivity within the school. More recently, in response to moral and social pressures we have seen the emergence of the hyperactive child and we may be about to witness the arrival of the unemployable child and the 'at-risk' child. If Foucault's thesis is correct these also must depend upon how modern power permeates the school and how a variety of other conflicting notions of the dichotomy of the individual and society can produce such subjects. That is, their production does not seem to depend upon quite the same notion of individual/social and requires wider data than that used by Walkerdine in her discussion of the developing child.

What is required then is a general question about the nature of modern power in the contemporary school. This should be an account that shows the general possibility of the developing child and the at-risk child, as well as other forms of subjectivity. In one of his last comments on power Foucault outlines a general grid for the analysis of power relations.

In general he says that an analysis of power relations should be conducted under five main headings (Foucault 1983a):

1. The systems of differentiations established by law, traditions, economic conditions, and so on which give some *prima facie* position for power relationships to be brought into play. For example, the legal, traditional, and pedagogic status of the teacher provides conditions for bringing power into play.
2. The types of objectives pursued intentionally by those who act upon the actions of others when power relations are brought into existence. For example, the teacher may be pursuing pedagogical objectives yet bringing modern power into play through normalization procedures.
3. The means of bringing power relations into play, by force, compliance, consent, surveillance, economic reward, and so on.
4. Forms of institutionalization. These may be a mixture of legal, traditional, hierarchical structures such as the family, the military, or the school.
5. The degree of rationalization that, depending upon the situation, endows, elaborates, and legitimates processes for the exercise of power.

Much of the early talk in the philosophy of education of teachers being *in* authority and *an* authority might be conceived in this light.

Clearly, Foucault provides us with no ready-made formula for analysing power in education. Nevertheless, there is a programme here which, combined with a genealogical approach that tends to show that the present and its discourse/practice is not as rational, humane, or developed as we might think, can throw genuine insight into what we are doing with children in the name of education. But this programme needs yet to be undertaken in education.

Finally, Foucault's analysis of power has disturbing implications for us as educationalists and educational researchers.

1. In suspending the normative notions of legitimacy and illegitimacy, Foucault directs our attention with his concept of power to a host of shaping processes – learning to speak, read, and write, for example – which the liberal framework would not normally identify as acting contrary to the interests of the child. In recent liberal discussions of power in education, power is considered to be exercised only when it is contrary to the interests of the child (White 1983; Burbules 1986). But, to draw upon the developing child example, the notion of development is already heavily value-laden, depending upon the ways of identifying the subject – the developing child – and thus what is in the child's interests, for example, acquiring the concept X, is far from clear.

2. He directs our attention here because in pursuing such educational objectives we are bringing into play modern power which is directed towards governmentality and a form of political domination. There is a fragile element even in classical liberal theory. In the case of Hobbes, as Pasquino (1986) reminds us, there is the need for discipline to ensure obedience to the contract. In *De Cive* (vol.1), Hobbes says that 'men can only become political subjects *ex disciplina*'. And in *Leviathan* there is considerable discussion of how this is to be achieved through education (Marshall 1981). Much of the talk of liberal education ignores what Hobbes, and Rousseau, were very well aware of, namely discipline. It is somewhat ironic to find at the very basis of classical liberal theory the recognition both of the necessity to ensure obedience to the contract and the realization that this is to be achieved through education. If we marry this to the traditional view of the educational pursuit of the rationally autonomous person then it would appear that such persons would be governable and not 'free'.

3. Whilst modern power permeates all of modern society, according to Foucault, it was developed and refined essentially in the disciplines and still has important bases and sources of legitimation in the disciplines and associated human sciences.

4. In the disciplines there are found certain views of man as a moral agent, sexual being, learner, or whatever. In the normalizing procedures of examination and 'confession' people are classified as objects and the truth about them is 'revealed' to themselves. In constituting the subject in these ways, modern power produces governable individuals.

Foucault seems extremely pessimistic about the possibilities of resistance and deinstitutionalizing knowledge because we seem so enmeshed in power processes that we are hardly conscious of and therefore may not understand. It is not therefore a question of the redistribution of education, its reorganization, or its cleansing of ideological content – familiar enough demands from the left and those concerned about equality and education. Education, because of modern power, must take on a new form in which freedom is not the traditional freedom which is meant to be achieved under the guise of rational autonomy.

Clearly, Foucault (1988) is arguing for a form of freedom but it is not one that he was ever to articulate fully.

5. As professionals we must take note of Foucault's violent landscapes. He claims that he is not trying to ridicule, supplant, or falsify other approaches to power, but rather that he is trying to offer us another aspect, or another mask, that reality 'wears'. In his view, we don't have to have a total world view to resist and oppose forms of political subjection and domination; we can do it at any point in time, as the various resistance groups in the western world are showing us. But the problem is to recognize when modern power is being exercised and whether resistance is the appropriate response. Foucault denies that he holds any explicit normative position, but without one, it is most difficult to see how to proceed. On these matters, some of his critics see him as incoherent (Rorty 1984, Taylor 1984).

There are then two broad parameters for educational research to pursue: first, in the area of the analysis of power relations in the contemporary school in accordance with the grid outlined above and Foucault's later (1983a) definitions of power and other concomitant relationships. Second, within the particular human sciences associated with education there is a need for more work like that of Walkerdine's in the search for practices that do not produce liberated children when such forms of 'liberation' are presupposed in the very formulation and practices of the production process.

REFERENCES

Aries, P. (1962) *Centuries of Childhood*, New York: Vintage.
Bernauer, J. and Rasmussen, D. (eds) (1988) *The Final Foucault*, Cambridge, Mass.: MIT Press.

Bouchard, D. F. (ed.) (1977) *Language, Counter-Memory, Practice: Selected Essays and Interviews*, Ithaca: Cornell University Press.

Burbules, N. (1986) 'A theory of power in education', *Educational Theory* 36(2): 95–114.

Cousins, M. and Hussain, A. (1984) *Michel Foucault*, London: Macmillan.

Davidson, A. (1986) 'Archaeology, genealogy, ethics', in D. C. Hoy (ed.) *Foucault: A Critical Reader*, Oxford: Blackwell, pp. 221–34.

Donnelly, M. (1982) 'Foucault's genealogy of the human sciences', *Economy and Society*, 11 (4): 363–79.

Dreyfus, H. and Rabinow, P. (1983) *Michel Foucault: Beyond Structuralism and Hermeneutics*, Chicago: University of Chicago Press.

Foucault, M. (1970) *The Order of Things*, New York: Random House.

————(1971) 'The discourse on language', in Foucault (1972) *op. cit.*, pp. 215–38.

————(1972) *The Archaeology of Knowledge*, London: Tavistock.

————(1975) *I, Pierre Rivière, Having Slaughtered my Mother, my Sister, my Brother*, New York: Random House.

————(1977a) 'Nietzsche, genealogy, history', in Bouchard, *op. cit.*, pp. 139–64.

————(1977b) 'What is an author?', in Bouchard, *op. cit.*, pp. 113–38.

————(1979a) *Discipline and Punish: the Birth of the Prison*, New York: Vintage.

————(1979b) 'Governmentality', *Ideology and Consciousness* 6: 1–21.

————(1980) *The History of Sexuality*, vol. 1, New York: Vintage.

————(1981) *Power/Knowledge: Selected Interviews and Other Writings*, edited by C. Gordon, New York: Pantheon.

————(1983a) 'Afterword: the subject and power', in Dreyfus and Rabinow, *op. cit.*, pp. 208–28.

————(1983b) 'On the genealogy of ethics', in Dreyfus and Rabinow, *op. cit.*, pp. 229–53.

————(1984a) 'What is enlightenment?' in P. Rabinow (ed.) *Foucault Reader*, New York: Pantheon, pp. 32–50.

————(1984b) 'Polemics, politics and problematisations', in Rabinow, *op. cit.*, pp. 381–93.

————(1988) 'The ethic of care for the self as a practice of freedom', in Bernauer and Rasmussen, *op. cit.*, pp. 1–20.

Fraser, N. (1985) 'Michel Foucault: a young conservative', *Ethics* 96: 165–84.

Henriques, J. *et al.* (1984) *Changing the Subject*, London: Methuen.

Hoskin, K. (1979) 'The examination, disciplinary power and rational schooling', *History of Education* 8 (2): 135–46.

Hoy, D. C. (1986) *Foucault: A Critical Reader*, Oxford: Blackwell.

Jones, K. and Williamson, K. (1979) 'The birth of the schoolroom', *Ideology and Consciousness* 5–6: 58–110.

Lash, S. (1984) 'Genealogy and the body: Foucault/Deleuze/Nietzsche', *Theory, Culture and Society* 2 (2): 1–17.

Lemert, C. C. and Gillen, G. (1982) *Michel Foucault: Social Theory as Transgression*, New York: Colombia University Press.

Marshall, J. D. (1981) 'Thomas Hobbes: education and obligation in the commonwealth', *Journal of Philosophy of Education* 14 (2): 322–31.

Maxcy, S. J. (1977) 'A structuralist view of American education',
     Paedogogica Historica 17 (2): 333–46.
Megill, A. (1979) 'Foucault, structuralism and the ends of history', *Journal of Modern History* 51: 451–503.
Pasquino, P. (1986) 'Michel Foucault (1926–84): the will to knowledge',
     Economy and Society 15 (1): 97–109.
Rabinow, P. (ed.) (1984) *Foucault Reader*, New York: Pantheon.
Rorty, R. (1986) 'Foucault and epistemology', in Hoy, *op. cit.*, pp. 41–50.
Rusche, G. and Kircheimer, O. (1939) *Punishment and Social Structures*,
     Ithaca: Cornell University Press.
Sarap, M. (1982) *Education, State and Crisis: A Marxist Perspective*, London:
     Routledge & Kegan Paul.
Smart, B. (1983) *Foucault, Marxism and Critique*, London: Routledge &
     Kegan Paul.
———(1986) 'The politics of truth and the problem of hegemony', in Hoy,
     op. cit., pp. 157–74.
Taylor, C. (1986) 'Foucault on freedom and truth', in Hoy, *op. cit.*, pp.
     69–102.
Walkerdine, V. (1984) 'Developmental psychology and the child centred
     pedagogy', in Henriques, *op. cit.*, pp. 153–202.
———(1986) 'Post-structuralist theory and everyday social practices: the
     family and the school', in S. Wilkinson (ed.) *Feminist Social Psychology:
     Developing Theory and Practice*, Milton Keynes: Open University Press,
     pp. 57–76.
Walzer, M. (1986) 'The politics of Michel Foucault', in Hoy, *op. cit.*, pp.
     51–68.
White, P. (1983) *Beyond Domination*, London: Routledge & Kegan Paul.

3 Foucault under examination

The crypto-educationalist unmasked

Keith Hoskin

THE MYSTERIOUS CASE OF DISCIPLINE

Foucault was always one for rendering the familiar strange. He was also one to engage in a relentless pursuit of understanding the strangeness that he discovered behind the mask of familiarity. Now that his life's work has passed the definitive full-stop of death is perhaps the time to render that work, which has been rendered familiar by the large and flourishing Foucault industry, strange to itself. To do so is to investigate nothing other than 'the mysterious case of discipline', with all of its subplots: power–knowledge, the self, bio-power, the clinical gaze, and so on. But perhaps such an investigation, like all good detective stories, is really very simple, and it is just that we do not realize it until we reach the end. Let me at least suggest as much: Foucault really discovered something very simple (but highly unfamiliar nevertheless) – the centrality of education in the construction of modernity. Thus the mysterious case of discipline is solved by investigating it as an essentially educational mystery.

I intend here to put Foucault himself under examination: to question what he meant by 'power–knowledge', to ask why he would have such strange digressions at the heart of certain texts (apparently obsessed with examining himself), and thus to answer a further question. Where does examining him and his work leave us? The conclusion will be transparent long before we reach the end. What he was doing all the time was an educational analysis, whether he thought he was talking about power or knowledge. Thus an early work, from his so-called 'archaeological' period, like *The Order of Things* (1966), is about nothing other than the nature of certain fields of knowledge – general grammar, natural history, and the analysis of wealth – and their transformation into other fields – philology, biology, and political economy – fields which, far from being logical consequents, were bizarre dislocations of their antecedents. But it is not about knowledge disembodied. It concerns the writing of one mode of knowing, the 'representational', in the seventeenth and eighteenth centuries, and its rewriting as another mode as we move into the nineteenth. What we confront here is, of course, a problem in educational history. How did one series of generations who wrote and constructed modes of knowing in one fashion (Foucault's representational episteme) give way to another series of generations who wrote quite different modes? By learning to write in a new register, obviously. But how did the young ones learn this? By learning under the tutelage of the old generation. So Foucault has bequeathed us an educational history mystery. Nowhere in his work does he allow the easy solution that tempts the easy-going historian: either to attribute the change to socio-political or economic (i.e., external) reasons like the French or Industrial Revolutions, or to resort to internal, individualist explanation (change as the result of towering geniuses having new insights). He leaves us with a conundrum: somehow, even as the young one were being taught in the old register, under the old episteme, they must have been learning how to learn in a new one. And how interesting – what they produced, out of an old, mostly forgotten set of knowledges, was something recognizably like the modern knowledge 'disciplines'.

Coincidence? There, not for the first or last time, is the word which is so intimately woven into the Foucault project, particularly when one begins to investigate the construct he named *pouvoir–savoir*, or power–knowledge. For 'discipline' is such a marvellously supple term. It turns the ambiguous trick of serving both sides of his power–knowledge equation. Yet what is discipline, and whence does it come?

The answer to that little mystery is easily given. It comes from the Latin *disciplina*, and in the Latin it has the same double meanings that it retains today, referring both to the ancient knowledge arts such as philosophy, music, and rhetoric, and to the problems of power, as for instance in *disciplina militaris* (military discipline). Etymologically, the term is a collapsed form of *discipulina*, which is concerned with getting 'learning' (the *disci-* half) into the 'child' (*puer/puella* represented in the *pu*-syllable in *-pulina*). Thus in its very etymological beginning the term is an educational one, and even there it manifests the two sides of a power–knowledge equation. For it concerns *ab initio* the dual process: the discipline that is presenting a certain knowledge to the learner, and the discipline of keeping the learner present before the knowledge. It concerns those technologies of control whose extreme form then was the *disciplina militaris*: yet it never ceases to concern the process of teaching and the objects of instruction.

Thus we have a promising clue. Discipline derives from an educational beginning, as *disciplina*, and appears intimately implicated in what Foucault would ultimately name as power–knowledge from its beginning. However, promising clues have a habit of turning out to be red herrings, and we must not put all our trust in etymology. Perhaps it is just coincidence, and Foucault had no educational object or discourse in view when he spoke of discipline, disciplinary power, and power–knowledge. We must proceed – *mais naturellement* – to the scene of the crime, the textual edifice he has left behind, and see what clues may be lurking in wait for us there. But as we go we should recall the lesson of every detective story: however hard people try to conceal and dissimulate the truth, that truth always reveals itself as their *modus operandi* discloses a hitherto unremarked pattern. But it reveals itself only to the true detective who knows how to examine and read what is, in retrospect, under the noses of everyone all the time. (Texts, of course, are always under one's nose as one reads them.)

FOUCAULT UNDER EXAMINATION

There is one particular text in which, with no argument, Foucault has recourse to an educational discourse at the very heart of the text, and offers us some well-made and thought-provoking ideas on the dynamics of educational practice. The text is *Discipline and Punish*, perhaps the most widely cited of his works in the Anglo-Saxon world over the past decade. The central section of the book is entitled 'The means of correct training'. It contends, in brief, that discipline as exercised upon the person, so as to produce 'docile bodies' (the term 'docile', interestingly, has its own educational connotation, being from the Latin *docilis*, or teachable), derives from little practices, or 'micro-technologies'. These micro-technologies bring together the exercise of power and the constitution of knowledge, in the organization of space and time along ordered lines, so as to facilitate constant forms of surveillance and the operation of evaluation and judgment. This is, be it noted, in a book directly inspired by and focused upon the problematic of the prison within the modern world, and the power of what Foucault called 'the carceral'. Its enduring metaphor – so often cited since Foucault recovered it from long oblivion – is of the panopticon, the 'all-seeing eye' of a surveillance which is also a judgment, which does not even have to be looking to make one feel watched. Yet this metaphor is only the crowning evocation of the book, not its heart. At that heart the concern with the carceral recedes, subordinated to a deeper problematic: that of discipline in general. Behind the Panopticon we find a particular and special micro-technology, identified as that which 'combines the deployment of force and the establishment of truth': the examination (Foucault 1977: 184).

Here is our obvious and non-controversial educational connection. The examination is, of all technologies, the most obviously educational, more so even than discipline, which tends over-easily to be misread as a technique solely of power and control. Both should be read as power–knowledge technologies, but as Foucault himself says, 'the superimposition of the power relations and the knowledge relations assumes in the examination all its visible brilliance' (1977: 185). (Of course this is not to deny that examinations are with much frequency and justification attacked as anti-educational. We are simply talking of the power of a technology whose genesis is educational; that examination, in all its varying forms, has maintained and extended its power to date is undeniable.) As Foucault puts it so well, examination spreads across the human sciences 'from psychiatry to pedagogy, from the diagnosis of diseases to the hiring of labour', functioning as 'a constant exchanger of knowledge' from the powerful (teacher, doctor, employer) to the powerless (pupil, patient, worker) but also in the other direction, as the subjects must make themselves known in answering the questions put in the examination (Foucault 1977). Thus 'in this slender technique are to be found a whole domain of knowledge, a whole type of power'.

But of course this clue is too obvious. Any commentator-detective can come along, examine the *corpus delicti*, and choose one plausible extract to build a case upon. This is what the Inspector Plodders in the detective story have done since Conan Doyle's Inspector Lestrade and, before him, Edgar Allan Poe's Parisian Prefect of Police, Monsieur G—. The true detective sees further and deeper, suspending judgment. Rightly so, when Foucault nowhere else digresses into an explicit *hommage* to the power of education; indeed, when even in this passage, he identifies the power of examination as lying outside the educational arena. It lies, in his discussion, in the medical arena, in 'the organization of the hospital as an "examining" apparatus' (Foucault 1977: 185), as much as in the school (Foucault 1977: 186) as it becomes an 'apparatus of uninterrupted examination [duplicating] along its entire length the operation of teaching'. It lies also in the military and bureaucratic fields, as examination yields (*ibid.*, p. 189) 'a whole meticulous archive constituted in terms of bodies and days' so that 'a "power of writing" was constituted'. But most of all it lies in the field of individuality, in the 'formation of a whole series of codes of disciplinary individuality', in which (a) 'the examination, surrounded by all its documentary techniques, makes each individual a "case"' (*ibid.*, p. 191) but only (b) by distributing and classifying the whole range of individual cases, with all (*ibid.*, p. 192) 'the features, the measurements, the gaps, the "marks"' that make them all, taken together, a population of cases, with norms and quantifiable deviations from the norm. This, in Foucault's account, is the real locus, or axis, of examinatorial power. It lies in the reversal of what it is to be an individual. Historically, the only individuals written about were the hero-figures of society, the 'memorable man' (*ibid.*, p. 193). Now under the new power of writing and examination, ordinary 'normal' people (and, of course, their newly invented opposite, the 'abnormal') no longer lie 'below the threshold of description'. We invent a new kind of individuality: 'the individuality. . . of the calculable man'. This is not so much an education change as a knowledge change, in Foucault's conclusion: 'All the sciences, analyses or practices employing the root "psycho-" have their origin in this historical reversal of the procedures of individualization.' Thus the education connection can be ruled out as anything more than a chance contingency. Inspector Plodder can eliminate it from his enquiries.

Those familiar with Peter Shaffer's *Sleuth* will know that Inspector Plodder has a near-anagrammatic double and *doppelganger*, Inspector Doppler, who appreciates double bluff and all the other shifts of duplicity. He, inevitably, is more in tune with the truth for our times – double truth – and the double truth of detection is that one must examine the obvious carefully in two opposite ways. First, one must examine in detail, for where better to hide a crucial tiny clue than within an obvious and therefore discounted one? Second, one must examine in the large: Poe formulated this principle of concealment in *The Purloined Letter*. In a game in which one party requires others to find a word upon 'the motley and perplexed surface' of a map, the novice chooses 'the most minutely lettered names; but the adept selects such words as stretch, in large characters, from one end of the chart to the other'. So there are two questions from Inspector Doppler: first, the easily overlooked detail. Whence come the 'marks', the numbers by which human qualities can be assigned a quantitative value? This is the precision tool that makes possible the science of the individual, as it makes possible the generation of popular statistics, norms, and deviations. Does it come from the medical, military, bureaucratic or 'psycho-' arenas? Or does it come from the educational? This question of the genesis of disciplinary power will certainly merit further enquiry. Second, the larger picture. The good Inspector, sensitive to the danger of overlooking the excessively obvious, will certainly want to know why there should be this digression into an educational, or quasi-educational, topic at the heart of a text ostensibly dealing with prisons and 'the carceral'. This apparent fascination with examination will have to be put under examination in its turn. Is it really only an isolated incident, or is it part of a larger pattern?

It is no doubt past time to leave the literary-sleuth ploy aside. However, there is a real double mystery here: first, of the fascination and examination to be found at the heart of Foucauldian texts (and of why it has been overlooked); and second, what is Foucault's power–knowledge really about, and how are we to understand it? The point of the ploy is to heighten the requisite sense of strangeness, which is necessary in putting Foucault under examination in this way.

Keith Hoskin

IN SEARCH OF EXAMINATION'S MARK

There is a particular passage, often quoted, in which Foucault reflected upon what power–knowledge relations might be about. It comes from an interview in the mid-1970s, when he was engaged on the *Discipline and Punish* project, and he was in a position to look back over his earlier major works, *Madness and Civilization*, *The Birth of the Clinic*, and *The Order of Things*, with a new vision. In a sense, as I have already intimated, that work had as its primary object knowledge and its discourses: the knowledge necessary to construct the category 'madness', the knowledge of the body and disease necessary to constitute the 'medical subject' (or 'subject of medicine'?), and the knowledge involved in establishing and disestablishing epistemes. None of these texts was just about knowledge or the history of ideas, as suggested by the still-unsolved mystery of what made the transition in epistemes happen. Foucault's own reflection on them says as much (Gordon 1980: 115):

> I ask myself what I could have been talking about. . . if not power? Yet I am perfectly aware that I practically never used the word and did not have that field of analysis at my disposal.

Foucault was talking at the point that power–knowledge was the new idea taking shape in his work, most notably in *Discipline and Punish*. (This is often seen as the first of his major 'genealogical' works, in which the concern was primarily with the practices and technologies of power, in contrast to the earlier 'archaeological' works in which in retrospect the emphasis was more on knowledge and the discourses that construct it.) But, as Foucault himself is saying here, the archaeological/genealogical distinction should not be taken as an absolute distinction. First, he was a man of too many parts to be conveniently divided into two; second, we would be ignoring how, in all the multiplicity, there was only one project. Even in all that early concentration on knowledge discourses, what could he have been talking about, 'if not power'?

But how, specifically?

At the heart of *The Birth of the Clinic*, that text on the genesis of modern medicine and the epistemological basis for the modern concerns with health, disease, life and death, there is a digression. At the same central point that *Discipline and Punish* develops the anomalous section on 'The means of correct training', *The Birth of the Clinic* has as its Chapter 5 'The lesson of the hospitals'. It too is anomalous. It abandons the epistemological concern with the invention of the modern 'medical gaze' and directs itself to the more mundane question of the reform of medical teaching, a reform which in a very short time. . . was to assume a much wider significance; it was recognized that it could reorganize the whole of medical knowledge and establish, in the knowledge of disease itself. . . more fundamental, more decisive forms of experience.

(Foucault 1973: 64)

The details of the chapter do not need rehearsing at great length here. All that needs emphasizing is that Foucault devotes the chapter to describing how a new, professional, and rigorous mode of learning to do medicine and become a doctor was constituted: that 'how' turned out to be a new rigorous mode of examination.

He documents the cut-and-thrust of debate over the structure of medical training during the post-Revolutionary period between two groups who can loosely be called 'republicans' and 'professionalizers'. The former were committed to the maximum open dissemination of expert knowledge and training (their emblematic organization being the *Société de Santé*, which was designed as a 'free, neutral organ of information'). The latter were not against dissemination necessarily, but they were for control first and openness only as a distant second. For the former one might become a doctor 'without having attended a school' so long as there were 'proof of capacity'. For the latter, only proper training in properly constituted institutions, duly examined, would do. The outcome of the debate is important. The professionalizers carried the day for their principle of prescribed and supervised institutional training and systematic, rigorous examination. A new professional regime of training and licensing doctors came into operation. This followed the general outline of a report submitted in 1797 by Calès (proof of the old maxim that 'he who draws up the first draft writes the final outcome'). Calès suggested that there should be five medical schools spread around France which all physicians, surgeons, and apothecaries would attend and in which 'studies would be checked by six examinations'. Thus all doctors would be qualified 'by a system of standardized studies and examinations' (Foucault 1973: 75–6). The final system adopted in 1803 with the full support of the Paris School of Medicine, simply improved on the draft. Where Calès had a simple unitary system of training, there was now a two-tier one. Six full medical schools examined and licensed doctors, while a network of teaching clinics in 20 civil hospitals provided a more basic course of instruction that would license a second category of 'health professional', the 'officers of health' whose remit was to treat the 'industrious and active poor'. The key difference between the groups was the scale of examination. The doctors did a four-year course involving four examinations and a final test in clinical medicine, 'internal or external, according to whether they wished to become physicians or surgeons'.

The officers of health did only a three-year course, and then 'would be examined by a department jury' (*ibid.*, p. 80).

Foucault, indeed, does not use the word 'power'. But he describes the moment when education discovers a new positive power to construct both a new kind of social-institutional force, the modern medical profession, and a new kind of 'knowing subject', the trained and licensed professional expert. These students were suddenly required to learn (and thus to learn how to learn) in a new way, particularly for the test in clinical medicine. They had to actively engage in the diagnosis and treatment of patients, and then be examined on their performance, in contrast to the traditional pedagogic regime which seldom demanded active engagement of this kind, depending instead upon lecture and demonstration by the professor or teacher. Foucault himself remarks upon the change by saying (Foucault 1973: 64) 'education was given a positive value as enlightenment', and expresses a sense of the historic shift in the mode of learning how to learn: 'a way of teaching and *saying* became a way of learning and *seeing*' (emphasis in the original). (One needs, perhaps, to stress how far this was an educational rather than a political-legal change. Foucault himself points out earlier (*ibid.*, p. 45) that a political-legislative precedent had been set under the Marly decrees of 1707. These stipulated that medicine should be taught in all French universities, that all students should follow compulsory courses in anatomy, pharmacy, and the use of plant remedies, and that examinations should be passed for each succeeding grade of qualification – *bachelier*, *licencié*, and *docteur*. In addition, Article 26 prohibited anyone below the degree of *licencié* from practising medicine or prescribing remedies. But students did not have to engage in active clinical learning, and the examination system was easily evaded. Those who chose to 'bought their examinations and got needy doctors to write their theses for them'. No modern profession of trained knowledgeable subjects ensued then. It ensued only as students learned in a new active way under, and for, examination, where they were graded, ranked, passed and, where the results objectively showed as much, failed.)

When we re-read *The Birth of the Clinic* in the light of *Discipline and Punish* we can see how specifically Foucault was already talking about power and dealing with the question of power–knowledge relations. The *modus operandi* is the same in both: a digression at, or into, the heart of the text, where examination lies in wait. Now, as Ian Fleming once said in similar circumstances, once may be an accident, twice coincidence, but if it happens three times something serious is going on, no mistake.

Foucault's last series of works, volumes two and three of the *History of Sexuality* project, *L'Usage des Plaisirs* (The Use of Pleasures) and *Le Souci de Soi* (The Care of the Self), have since his death been seen by some commentators (e.g., Cook 1987) as representing a third turn in his thinking, one towards subjectivity and the formation of the self. For Gilles Deleuze, Foucault proves to have worked with three 'ontologies': power, knowledge, and the self. For Cook (1987: 222), 'it is clear that Foucault himself claimed for subjectivity its own region in counter-distinction to the regions of power and knowledge'. Now it is certain that Foucault had not stood still, and that his concern with how humans construct a 'rapport with the self' (*rapport à soi*) did mark a new direction, in the same sense that it was 'neither a simple afterthought nor a subordinate move' (Cook 1987: 216). But how different is that direction? He was still talking about an aspect of the power–knowledge problematic, for he was concerned to describe the varying and historically changing ways that human beings have formed themselves, known themselves, and acted upon themselves in our western, Greco-Roman-derived, past. He was still – in fact more so – talking about the educational and pedagogic arena. From early in *L'Usage de Plaisirs* it is apparent that the rapports which the self is to discover for itself have a pedagogic connection. In the classical Greek period Foucault singles out a (homosexual) 'morality of men' (*morale d'hommes*) which depends upon self-knowledge (a variation on the Socratic theme 'know thyself') as shared among the powerful elite. How is this developed? As 'a morality thought, written and taught by men and addressed to men who were manifestly free' (Foucault 1984a: 29), and then as a set of practices (in the ancient Greek, *askesis*), which will ensure 'mastery' (*maîtrise*) over the appetites so long as the requisite effort is devoted to 'developing, perfecting and teaching them' (*ibid.*, p. 38).

What are we to make, then, of the following? At the heart of the last published volume, *Le Souci de Soi* (Foucault 1984b), the key practices involved during the high Roman era of the Greco-Roman past in the making of the *rapport à soi* are discussed. These practices are analysed at some length in Chapter 2, 'The culture of the self' (*La Culture du Soi*). They prove to be a life-long pedagogic practice practised on the self wherein one learns to internalize the pedagogic voice, which recommends the proper art of good living, within oneself until it becomes oneself. (One develops a teacher-learner duality, in which the pedagogic voice is, in a pattern still familiar today, taken inside and made so familiar a double to one's ignorance and incompetence that, like the cuckoo in the nest, it completely dominates. Unlike the cuckoo, though, it keeps the other self, to have it to kick around.) But what, specifically, do these practices boil down to?

Well, they require adults to turn themselves into 'over-age school-boys' (*écoliers vieillis*), and to follow 'various formulas' (*formules diverses*). These include 'morning or evening, keeping a few moments for recollection, for examining what one has to do, for memorising certain useful principles, for examining the day just past'. Foucault sees this as a Stoic continuation of 'the morning and evening examination of the Pythagoreans' (1984b: 64–5). There may also be exercises – 'care for the body, regimes of health, physical exercises but not to excess' – and not bodily ones alone: for instance, 'meditations, lectures, notes taken on books or extended conversations which one will re-read subsequently, the recalling to mind of truths already known but which must be internalised still better'. As Foucault (p. 66) observes: 'S'occuper de soi n'est pas une sinecure' (to busy oneself with oneself is no sinecure).

There can be no doubting the centrality of educational discourse to this analysis of practices. Around the 'care of the self, a whole activity of speaking and writing developed'. It was not a solitary practice but 'a veritable social practice', frequently grounded in 'more or less institutionalized structures' (p. 67). 'Epictetus for his part taught in a cohort which resembled nothing so much as a school [with] various categories of pupils' (*ibid.*). And when we finally reach the point that the central, focal practices involved in caring for the self are detailed (pp. 74–81), are we any more surprised to learn that Foucault names them as 'formes specifiées d'examen et des exercices codifiées' (specified forms of examination and of codified exercises)?

Three times is no coincidence. However, this is not to say that Foucault is here talking about 'examination' in the modern sense. He lays out, on the contrary, an exemplary clarification of the ways in which this particular Greco-Roman practice is neither the older Greek nor the newer modern rapport with the self. It was a particular kind of tripartite set of 'procedures of testing' (*procedures d'épreuve*): involving (a) exercises of self-denial such as sleeping on boards and wearing harsh clothing; (b) 'the examination of conscience' (*l'examen de conscience*), undertaken in the morning for the day ahead and the evening for the day just done; and (c) a constant 'work of thought upon itself' having the form of a 'continual filtering of one's mental pictures' (which seems to me the best rendering of *un filtrage permanent des representations*) so as 'to examine, control and test them' (Foucault 1984b: 75–9). This diverged, he maintains (*ibid.*, p. 80), from the old Socratic maxim, 'The unexamined life (*anexetastos bios* in the Greek, *une vie sans examen* in the French) is not worth living'. The Socratic way was to test both self and others 'before the bar of ignorance, understanding, and non-understanding of one's ignorance'. The new Greco-Roman way was 'an examination bearing upon the mental pictures and looking to test and discriminate one from another, thus transcending what one accepts "at first sight"'. It was thus a critical kind of reading of what was totally interior to the self with no rapport to those others that the Socratic way implicated. But it was not to be confused (*ibid.*, p. 81) with the later in-depth reading of the self to be found 'in Christian spirituality', which is a self-questioning 'on the deep-lying origin of the idea that surfaces. . . a deciphering of the meaning hidden beneath the surface representation'. This kind of interior self-reading sought purely to discriminate those mental pictures that were properly one's own from those that were not, and to reject the latter before they could become a threat to one's self-mastery.

Foucault, then, clearly establishes how far this practice of examination stands from any immediate modern connotations. And yet it is transparent that the terminology (*examen, épreuve*) is littered throughout his analysis here, which leads me to suggest that there can only be one conclusion. Foucault was a crypto-educationalist. Why else is there this thematic obsession with examination to be found consistently at the heart of some of his greatest works for over two decades – a theme that can only be described as welling up, despite the surface disparateness of the topics discussed, from hospitals to prisons to constructions of the self? The mark of examination was upon him, and so it would leave its trace each time he came close to the hidden heart of his life's project – a trace which every true detective will now recognize as the vital pattern of clues.

But there is no 'smoking gun', and since Watergate nothing less will do. So let us make one final examination, and move back just a few pages in this last passage of this last work (Foucault 1984b), to the very heart of its heart, between pages 77 and 79. Let us examine what Foucault has to say about the central technology of the self, the *examen de conscience*. In the space of these two pages Foucault, in citing the account of this technology given in the *de Ira* of the Roman neo-Stoic Seneca, uses the term *examen* some ten times. There is examination morning and evening: examination as a kind of 'little judicial scene', in which Seneca 'makes an examination' of his whole day; or rather, less a judicial 'examination' of the self accused before a judge, than an inspection or appraisal, striking out the errors as from an account-book and weighing up words and deeds. In such an examination one must be an inspector (*speculator*) whose concern is not to punish infractions but to correct errors and reinforce good practice. The 'ball-game' (*l'enjeu*) is about getting one's 'rational equipment' in shape. The examination is, in the current educationalist terminology, formative, designed to lead to future 'wise conduct'. But surely, one may object, the point is made; it does not need labouring. Why get obsessive about Foucault's apparent obsession with examination?

Precisely because it is an obsession, and an uncompromising proof of the mark that examination had placed upon Foucault (and *a fortiori* upon us, who have generally overlooked this hidden obsession in his work). For the strange, arresting truth of the matter is that one cannot attribute any influence or agency to Seneca for any one of these ten instances of the word *examen*; the simple reason being that Seneca never once uses the term *examinatio* or any cognate form in this passage. He uses (*de Ira* III: 36) *rationem reddere* (to render an account), *interrogare* (to question); he speaks of being the *speculator sui censorque secretus* (the inspector and secret censor of self); he writes *apud me causam dico* (I state my case at the bar of myself), and *totem diem scrutor* (I scrutinize my whole day), and *factaque... dicta mea remetior* (I measure over my deeds and words). But the one thing he does not ever do is examine. Only Foucault, the successful child born of the modern examinatorial world – graduate of the Sorbonne, man of two *Licences*, one *Diplôme*, a *Doctorat d'Etat*, and finally *Professeur* in the College de France – finds it natural and inevitable to call upon examination each time he discusses, as here, the intimately internalized practices of power and knowledge. He is, however unwittingly, the grand master of pedagogic power.

POWER–KNOWLEDGE IN EDUCATIONAL PERSPECTIVE

Let me sum up to this point. We have so far solved the minor mystery of the etymological provenance of 'discipline', and found it to be, from its beginnings, an educational term. We have discovered the hidden principle of coherence that runs like a thread through the whole textual corpus of Foucault's work and named it as examination, thereby unmasking him as a crypto-educationalist. But again, so what? Do we now pull that thread and watch as a kind of Derridean deconstruction takes place, as if this is the hidden point of contradiction in the textual weave which, once snagged, unravels the whole? On the contrary: we are now in a position to unsnag the Foucauldian text from the horns of a dilemma which has begun to become apparent, and perhaps to repair what would otherwise turn into a gaping hole in any continuance of his project.

The dilemma concerns the term that lies behind the mark, the examination, and discipline, to name but three obviously educational terms: power–knowledge. The dilemma is that power–knowledge as Foucault left it was a curiously unfinished and unresolved idea, and the problem with being unfinished is that people are quick to conclude that you are unresolvable. This is particularly true since the temptation is to grasp only one, and not both, horns of the dilemma before coming to one's conclusion.

The horns of the dilemma that is power–knowledge are (a) historical and (b) theoretical. And the problem with the construct is that it is unfinished in both respects. But perhaps it had to be. For things to have been otherwise Foucault would have had to be other than a *crypto*-educationalist. That at least is the conclusion to which this whole detective story has led. For each of the horns (and thus the whole dilemma too) can only be resolved by pursuing the educational conundrum explicitly until all its implications are laid bare, and this Foucault never did. He could not, in the last analysis, turn the power of examination inside out and resolve the theoretical horn. He did not, in fact, answer the rhetorical question that he posed at the heart of *Discipline and Punish*:

> But who will write the more general, more fluid, but also more determinant history of the 'examination' – its rituals, its methods, its characters and their roles, its play of questions and answers, its systems of marking and classification? (p. 185).

And so the historical project that kept bursting through remained unresolved as well. It is perhaps time to answer the rhetorical question, and thus put power–knowledge under examination from the educational perspective. In this way it is possible to resolve both horns of the dilemma in one move, simply by writing the general, fluid, and determinant history of the examination – that examination which we now can see marking the various stages of his life's work.

Writing such a history is not an easy task: as with many Foucault-inspired projects, one is investigating the kind of overlooked ignoble practices that nobody at the time treated particularly seriously. (For instance, finding an old examination answer-paper from before 1850 is a frustrating business: question-papers may be preserved, being the work of those who count – the teachers – but seldom the humble pupil-work.) But it remains an important task: if it is not done, the great, long-term project that Foucault initiated may, all too quickly, go by default.

NEW HISTORY? NEW THEORY?

Interestingly, there were only two major historical assaults on his work that Foucault took time out to respond to. The first was that launched by the then-young pretender, Derrida, in his 1963 lecture, later published as 'Cogito and the history of madness' (Derrida 1978). The second was the 1982 attack in the *New York Review of Books* by the aged socio- logical historian, Lawrence Stone. The first is usually seen as more of a theoretical critique, the second as the first shot in a still-flourishing Anglo-Saxon counter-revolution. Each found its crucial point of leverage – the point that drove Foucault to respond – in the historical arena. Derrida's was the more significant critique, at least for Foucault's own work. He argued that the kind of enterprise Foucault had begun – at that time with *Madness and Civilization* – could not be restricted to the limited, though important, time-span of relative modernity (i.e., from the seventeenth century, Foucault's 'classical age', on). He had, despite himself, begun on a history of the *logos*, that way of reason and reflection that has been the precondition of our (western) thinking and knowing since the (alphabetic) era of ancient Greece. In his words:

> The reason and madness of the classical age had a common root.
> But this common root, which is a *logos*... is much more ancient
> than the medieval period. ... Whatever the momentary break...
> of the Middle Ages with the Greek tradition, this break and
> alteration are late and secondary developments as concerns the
> fundamental permanence of the logico-philosophical heritage. ...
> *In all cases* a doctrine of *tradition*, of the tradition of *logos* (is
> there any other?) seems to be the prerequisite implied by
> Foucault's enterprise.
>
> (Derrida 1978: 39–41)

Foucault and Derrida, of course, never reconciled the theoretical differences between them, which were first marked out in this lecture. For Foucault, Derrida was – somewhat ironically (or was it prescience?) – the *petit pedagogue*, the little pedagogue. But the last series of his works are an acknowledgement that only a longer history, and a history of the culture of *logos*, no less, would do. Buried in the lengthy theoretical arguments was a central historical commonality. (This is not to say that Derrida did, or has done to date, much better than Foucault at following his own advice. His *Of Grammatology* set a pattern for his writing: of appreciating the ancient beginnings of the *logos* problem, particularly as represented by Plato and Aristotle, but then moving swiftly on to the familiar world of the Enlightenment and after, Rousseau, Saussure, and others of their ilk. There has been all too little serious appreciation given to the medieval moment, no pause to dwell on the nature of the 'break and alteration' that manifestly then took place.)

This agenda, which both Derrida and Foucault came to share even while neither of them was fulfilling it with adequate historical caring, is the one now to be followed, particularly in the light of the Stone critique, whose main concern was to rubbish the Foucault project as history by indicating that it was bad empirical history. Such a critique has a strong rhetorical fascination. (The logical flaw is transparent: bad data does not necessarily invalidate a theory. The data employed may not prove the conclusion reached. It may be inadequate to do so, as most famously was the case with the data on which Copernicus thought he had proved his heliocentric theory. But that does not prove, as in Copernicus' case, that the theory should necessarily be rejected.) The critique continues to be made, and now re-made (perhaps because Stone was the first to put into purple print what a lot of Anglo-American historians wanted to be true). That being the case, the fatal response is to belittle the critique as mere rhetoric: the proper response is to answer by constructing a more careful empirical history which does not thereby become mere empiricism, so turning Foucault's apparent weakness into a strength.

It is such a twin goal that a true history of examination can aspire to: a proper respect for the empirical concern, combined with a longer view than was apparent in Foucault until the last texts. If it is not a new history, it is certainly a new look to that made familiar in Foucault's works.

For instance, the explanations proposed in *Discipline and Punish* for the emergence of disciplinary technologies frequently resort to some kind of Christian precedent. The organization of an enclosed space for control and surveillance is related to monastic rule. The principle of cellular division comes from a 'monastic model'; discipline 'encountered an old architectural and religious method: the monastic cell' (pp. 141–3). The timetable 'is an old inheritance: the strict model was no doubt suggested by the monastic communities' (p. 149). Similarly, the earliest educational example that he gives of a numerical system for grading individuals and, of course, simultaneously generating a distribution of such grades is the Christian Brothers' system of giving merits and demerits for conduct. La Salle, the founder of the system, wrote his *Conduct of the Schools* just after 1700, and thus produced a judgemental system based on 'normal' behaviour and measuring deviations from it. This is described (p. 181) as 'a transposition of the system of indulgences'.

We now must pose a double question to such an explanation. First, after Derrida, why should the Christian moment be given a special privilege? Do we not question whether this particular disciplinary organization of time and space comes out of some ancient *disciplina*? How far is this an other-than-educational history? What we find, of course, is that the discipline of inculcating learning demanded certain delimited educational spaces – institutions in which teaching (in Latin often rendered as *institutio*) might take place. It also required equally the delineation of teaching time, both in the form of a school calendar and of a more-or-less formalized timetable. Marrou's still-unequalled *History of Education in Antiquity* (1964) provides the empirical data (pp. 207–8), as it also does for such other Christian and disciplinary practices as catechism, which (pp. 232–3) was developed for the study and retention of the words of Homer long before it was adapted for the study of the word of God. Versions of a disciplinary organization of time, space, and learners are an integral part of ancient educational practice, as first developed in Greece and then copied and maintained throughout the Latin *and* Greek institutions of the Greco-Roman world. From these institutions as Marrou remarks (pp. 439–44), they progressed into the Christian versions of Greco-Roman education. In such works as the *Rule* of St. Basil and the *Institutes* of Cassian, control of conduct, organization of space, and regulation of time were combined

43

with provisions for the teaching of reading and writing, and for catechizing the future lifeblood of the monastery. These Greco-Roman practices passed definitively into the western monastic tradition via the *Rule* of St. Benedict (c. 525 AD), which devotes some six chapters to the education of young novices, as well as the punishment proper to them (corporal). Thus, on the one hand, the Christian precedent turns out to lead us back beyond Christianity to the Greek tradition.

On the other hand, do we not have to look forward, past the monastic moment, to the immediate and proximate models for the disciplinary technologies that crystallize into a new power–knowledge apparatus, as 'disciplinary power', around the end of the eighteenth century? Once freed from the obligation to look for a specifically Christian model, we find an obvious educational genesis which presents itself for consideration. This is the set of institutions and practices that both disseminates and transforms the old monastic way, a set whose power was first, memorably, analysed in a work that was to initiate an entire new field of history, Philippe Aries's *Centuries of Childhood* (1962). It is a work which bears reading alongside *Discipline and Punish* as a companion piece, for the whole central section, Part Two, 'Scholastic life', demonstrates that our construct of 'childhood' is produced via the delineation of educational arrangements and practices that took up but went beyond older pedagogic traditions. The educational world he analyses is that of that medieval invention, the university, and all its offshoots. Within the university is developed, during the fourteenth century, the college as a safe space for student residence and controlled instruction. Within the college is developed the class, during the sixteenth century, as an instructional (and later architectural) subdivision. Once there are colleges and classes (as in the Jesuit system set down in the *Ratio Studiorum* just before 1600) there are timetables, attendance lists, codes of conduct, punishment books, rewards, and incentives. The 'child' is the object and product of this power–knowledge apparatus, where a power of writing implements a constant surveillance and judgment throughout the institutional space. At every prescribed moment, in every prescribed place, somebody should be doing and learning something. The schools of the Christian Brothers were an eighteenth century distillation of this set of pedagogic prescriptions, and demand to be understood as such.

The problem, the point of divergence, in reading Aries and Foucault together as companion pieces is that they focus on different time periods. Aries is looking at changes that take place for the most part before 1600; Foucault at ones that really only obtain some two centuries later. But here, finally, comes the beginning of a *denouement*. We can solve this apparent paradox and begin to resolve the dilemma of power–knowledge by doing the general but empirically careful and always educational history of the examination.

For what transpires immediately and beyond any equivocation is that Foucault got his history of the examination wrong. It appears in certain small but important ways, most importantly where he suggests that La Salle had, by around 1700, introduced a merit-demerit system. Inspection of the *Conduct* reveals that there is no such 'penal accountancy' integrating and measuring good and bad acts on a unilinear scale of so many 'plus points' for good acts and so many 'minuses' for bad ones. There was one system of punishments, including reprimands, penances, beatings, and expulsion, and a quite separate system of rewards, including praise and prizes. Merit-demerit systems of penal accountancy will be developed, but the evidence at present suggests that it is about a century later. The error is small but important, because behind it lies a much more significant one. Foucault, in suggesting that examination was an *invention* of the eighteenth century, perpetrated a fundamental and critical confusion. Examination as an educational practice within the culture of the *logos* was an invention of the twelfth century. Its invention is intimately bound up with the invention of the institution whose history Aries spends so much of his book investigating – the university. Examination in this medieval world is from its genesis a complex practice. It is both a certain mode of reading and rewriting textual authorities – the critical reading that looks beneath surface contradiction towards inner truth and that then writes its commentary upon the authorities so as to bring that truth to light. This reading, named by Abelard in his *Sic et Non* (c. 1120 AD) as *inquisitio*, or critical enquiry, is an essentially silent reading (Saenger 1982). The rewriting, as developed by the scholars of the twelfth century, is an essentially visually-oriented system of information technology (Rouse and Rouse 1979), involving the invention of visual lay-out devices from paragraphs, punctuation marks, and chapter division to alphabetical ordering, footnotes, and indexes. This close examination of texts cannot be dissociated from the emergent new stress on the examination, first informal and then formal, of learners. In the schools at Paris and Bologna, as best we can see, somewhere between 1150 and 1200 examination of learners by their teachers became formalized, as a final proof of pedagogic and disciplinary competence before admission into the guild of professors. This latter was a way of doing to people what was already being done to texts: subject them to scrutiny, look beneath the surface, and discover their inner truth. But it also proved to be the discovery of a new kind of power. This came about as the knowledgeable professors began, on the basis of examination, to discriminate worthy from unworthy apprentices. There was a prior right, vested in bishops, Cathedral chancellors, and the like, to grant a 'licence to teach', or *licentia docendi*, in a given geographical area. This was now challenged on the basis that licensing should be the prerogative of the knowledge experts, deciding on the basis of the new formal examination. It all erupted into a major quarrel at Paris between the professors and the Chancellor of Notre Dame. In 1213 Pope Innocent III (himself a former student of Bologna) decided in favour of the professors, and thus was established the legal basis for a new professional power: the power of the experts who professed in a certain knowledge field to examine and then give a licence or qualification to practise in that field on the basis of that examination. Such a licence was something quite new. It respected not geographical boundaries but disciplinary ones. Not surprisingly, the institutions empowered to grant such licences proliferated. By the sixteenth century there were several hundred spread around Europe. They, and the learning how to learn that they activated – under examination, naturally – are the educational focus of *Centuries of Childhood*.

How did Foucault go so wrong? It has seemed to me (e.g., Hoskin 1979, 1986; Hoskin and Macve 1986, 1988) he erred by confusing the invention of formal academic examination with the invention of modern formal academic examination. The difference between them is that the former was an oral form of examination, primarily, and the assessment made was on a qualitative as opposed to a quantitative basis. Written examination and arithmetical marks appear to develop, and then to predominate, from around 1800. The change in format and technology is decisive. Only the modern modes of testing activate the full power of writing (where everyone is required to write in order to demonstrate the inner truth about themselves) while putting an objective numerical value upon and inside you.

The Jesuits, for example, had a highly developed form of qualitative assessment before 1600, using constant emulation: pupils were ranked in their classes according to performance, and would change ranks as others did better or worse than them, but there was no objective mark or grade put upon each piece of work, there was no objective self-validation for the perfect '10 out of 10' or '100%', and no big, fat zero to signify total failure. There was no discourse to put such value upon the self, in the way that since 1800 has become familiar, for instance, in the most notorious numerical offshoot of the examination mark – the intelligence quotient. The link between the invention of numerical grading and of IQ is not often made in such an explicit way. But it remains the case that no culture before our nineteenth century one ever had recourse to such a tactic of quantifying human qualities. Furthermore, it is worth recalling these words of Francis Galton's, who while not the inventor of the intelligence quotient as such is still the acknowledged progenitor of the field of intelligence studies. They were written at the beginning of the main body of his seminal 1869 text *Hereditary Genius*:

> I look upon social and professional life as a continuous examin-ation. . . . In ordinary scholastic examinations marks are allotted in stated proportions to various specified subjects – so many for Latin, so many for Greek, so many for English history, and the rest. The world, in the same way, but almost unconsciously, allots marks to men. It gives them for originality of conception, for enterprise, for activity and energy. . . and much besides of general value, as well as for more specially professional merits. . . . Those who have gained most of these tacit marks are ranked, by the common judgement of the leaders of opinion, as the fore-most men of their day (pp. 49–50).

Thus begins the first 'scientific enquiry' into the 'objective quanti-fication' of the inner truth of the self, the 'genius' that is henceforward presumed to underlie and guarantee brilliant examination performance. It is quite touching to see Galton prove this by reference to those tests of genius and merit whose 'fairness and thoroughness. . . have never had a breath of suspicion cast upon them' (p. 59), the Cambridge University mathematics examinations. He moves effortlessly from comparisons of performance as measured by these exams – the lowest man with honours has fewer than 300 marks, the lowest wrangler ('top honours' man) about 1,500, and one senior wrangler (the 'top of the top') more than 7,500: 'Consequently the lowest wrangler has more than five times the merit of the lowest junior optime, and less than one-fifth the merit of the senior wrangler' (p. 60) – to conclusions about underlying competence. In one year the senior wrangler (p. 61) 'obtained 9,422 marks' while the bottom man with honours had only 'one-thirtieth the number'. But, if anything, this observed difference underestimates the difference in 'mathematical power' because the best are slowed up by 'the mechan-ical labour of writing': 'in other words, the senior wranglers mentioned above had *more* than thirty or thirty-two times the ability of the last man on the lists of honours. They would be able to grapple with problems more than thirty-two times as difficult' (*ibid.*).

My point is only secondarily to poke fun at the fatuity of the Galtonian calculus of ability. Primarily, it is to signal the strangeness of it all: a world which a century earlier did not think of – perhaps would not have dreamed of – quantifying human qualities in this way could find it perfectly acceptable, and indeed 'natural', for remember, Galton was one of the cultural successes of 1869 and the book made him world famous. But then he was writing for a world in which written examination and numerical grading had become 'natural', a world that had learned how to learn under modern examination.

That transformation, which Foucault mistook for the invention of examination, is the secondary elaboration of examination's power. It marks the onset of the period in world history when education, the perennial handmaiden of power, power's supplement, has become its centre. It is the time of the credential society, suffering from the diploma disease, a society even deemed ripe by some for deschooling. Yet even deschooling suffers from the paradox that Foucault named as power–knowledge, since it is, first, an idea proposed by those most highly educated, and second, a proposal that founders constantly on the rock of examination – the now-universal need to attend institutions and obtain their various kinds of qualifications.

The point that I would stress about Foucault is that despite the egregious errors in his history, he had that ability, or knack, or nose even, for sensing the significant. Now it is our task – humbler but still important – to broaden and deepen the furrows he ploughed. For instance, in relation to Aries, once the error in his history is pointed out, the resolution between *Discipline and Punish* and *Centuries of Childhood* is straightforward. Aries traces one way in which power–knowledge operates to construct the human subject in the first epoch of examinatorial power. He demonstrates that as people come to learn how to learn under examination, in the institutions and internalizing the practices that proliferate around the university, there emerges a new object of this whole apparatus, the child. It is not yet the psychologized child, the differentiated child who is variously labelled from genius to defective (or gifted to 'special needs'). That child is the product of the second epoch of examinatorial power, Galton's work obviously being one strategic step along the path to its production. While we still await an adequate account of the transformation from the one to the other, we can at least grasp the way in which the two constructions, like the Aries and Foucault projects, are linked. Both are reflections of and upon stages in the progress of examinatorial power.

The same can be said in relation to other Foucault texts. Once viewed via a two-stage history of examination, *The Birth of the Clinic* becomes an account of the transformation in 'learning how to learn' to be a doctor. During the thirteenth century the universities developed three higher faculties, law, theology, and medicine, which licensed their graduates as doctors. Through examination these groups became the first (sometimes today called the 'old') professions. Down to 1800 law, the church and medicine remained the only real professions, with their university-sanctioned licenses and all the abuse of privilege that this entailed. Students continued to learn by observing dissections, hearing lectures, taking oral examinations, and being assessed qualitatively (one does 'brilliantly', 'fairly well', 'abysmally', etc.) – by 'teaching and saying', as Foucault puts it. This suddenly changes to 'learning and seeing', or rather to doing dissections, working in clinics, writing examinations, and being quantitatively marked on them. Here the profession begins to reconstruct itself in a more modern guise, with new abuses of privilege, naturally, but also finding itself in a field of expanding professionalization: not just doctors, surgeons, and officers of health, but dentists, pharmacists, nurses, health visitors, and even funeral directors (Hoskin 1986).

In such a re-reading we can begin to see how a text like this, supposedly 'archaeological', was in a very precise way about power–knowledge all the time, even though Foucault did not then employ the term. And we can see finally that Foucault's historical dilemma was that he was always, until the last works, writing only half a history, because we can begin to render explicit the other tacit, earlier, half. We do so by bringing the full power of examination out of concealment.

This brings me finally to the other horn of the Foucauldian dilemma, which, like the historical one, is a dilemma in itself: the theoretical problem of power–knowledge. Just as Foucault produced only half a history, he arguably produced only half a theory. In the light of his dictum that

> power and knowledge directly imply one another; that there is no power relation without the correlative constitution of a field of knowledge, nor any knowledge that does not presuppose and constitute at the same time power relations

we should have anticipated a form of double theory. There would have been the analysis, as in *Discipline and Punish*, of how power relations shape and direct modes of knowing and knowledge, but there would also have been its correlative, the analysis of how knowledge relations shape and direct modes of power. This is one well-made criticism in J. G. Merquior's *Foucault*, (1985): that the roles of 'hard science' and 'sustained cognitive growth' in the construction of modern power–knowledge relations were never properly addressed. As Merquior goes on 'no history of the present can ever be truly cogent that makes little or no room for an account of science, its nature and impact' (p. 150).

One does not have to rest content with Merquior's intemperate conclusion – 'to put it bluntly, the historian of the present bungled his project' – so discharging oneself from further thought on the matter. One can observe, for instance, that the omission derives in part from the fact that the work that had as its primary object knowledge and its discourses was the earlier archaeological work, when by his own admission Foucault was not thinking in terms of power. None the less, once he moved on to the genealogical approach, the criticism is valid:

he developed only half a theory, of power–knowledge but not of knowledge–power.

The resolution of the first half of the theoretical dilemma, so trenchantly put by Merquior, is simple (in conception, at least). It is necessary simply to apply a genealogical analysis to the problem of knowledge–power, which is precisely what Rick Jones, as he demonstrates in this volume, has set about doing. He has returned to analyse the emergence of a 'hard science', biology, discussed in archaeological terms by Foucault in *The Order of Things*, in terms of a rupture or discontinuity in the practices of knowing, that is, genealogically. And what do we appear to be confronted with? A transformation in the mode of 'learning how to learn': a new power of examination: the fact, as in *The Birth of the Clinic*, that a practice of learning and seeing was replacing one of teaching and saying for the very generation who appear to produce the key figures, such as Bichat, in the development of the new biological discourse.

The double question – is all of this, with its privileging of the 'educational', a 'new history' and a 'new theory' – is ultimately trivial. If, by plying an educational analysis, one can develop a fuller and deeper analysis of the ways in which power and knowledge have functioned to imply and promote each other, that is surely all that matters. Surely so, except that there is one theoretical problem that still awaits consideration. I have left it till last because, in the last analysis, the whole Foucault project and any future post- Foucauldian project stands or falls on the answer to it, and if it cannot be satisfactorily answered, any lasting worth in any such project falls with it. The problem is, just what is 'power–knowledge'? Is there any substance there? Or is it, in that famous last analysis, empty, vacuous, no more than a piece of almost Keatsian poetics: '"Knowledge is power, power knowledge" – that is all Ye know on earth, and all ye need to know.'

Michael Walzer (1983) has raised this possibility, when he says

> Sometimes Foucault seems to be committed to nothing more than an elaborate pun on the word 'discipline' – which means, on the one hand, a branch of knowledge and on the other, a system of correction and control. . . . Social life is discipline squared. Discipline makes discipline possible (the order of the two nouns can be reversed).

It is the most significant point of all. There is a certain plausibility in what Foucault writes. We can appreciate that there is something there, something we can recognize operating in the world and within us, not just knowing, but a *frisson* beyond the pure act of knowing; not just power but a power which feels beyond reproach because it is validated by expertise. But knowledge is also not power, and power not knowledge. How are we to – indeed, are we to – get beyond the easy option of the pun and get a purchase on power–knowledge that is substantial?

There can be only one way: by treating with all seriousness the doubleness in a word like 'discipline', which is from its Latin beginning about both power and knowledge, but only while paying attention to the provenance of the word. Power and knowledge do not in any simple way imply each other; they do so only in certain specific and specifiable respects, through the operation of a third term, which is not the same as, or reducible to, either one of them. Discipline is one candidate for such a third term, as is examination; examination after all was the term which for Foucault embodied 'the superimposition of the power relations and the knowledge relations'.

What we may well need to consider is how 'the educational' may in different epochs, in different ways, function as the hyphen in the power–knowledge relation. We may come to regard hitherto unregarded shifts in 'learning how to learn' as the principle by which we can interpret fundamental shifts both in social organization and in the construction of the individual human subject. Foucault himself named examination (which we can now see is a quintessentially educational practice) as the key that simultaneously turns the trick of power (discipline) and knowledge (the disciplines) in the modern epoch since around 1800. For the earlier medieval transition in power–knowledge relations – a transition that gave us among other things, such terms as the university, the college, the class, the nation, the profession, and the network of *disciplinae* (all of them terms which gain their modern positive connotations first in the arena of 'the educational' during this epoch) – the appropriate hyphenating term may well turn out to be *inquisitio*. Where Abelard saw purely 'critical inquiry' and a careful reading of texts, the next generation discovered the power of examination, and two generations later, when a whole new process of 'learning how to learn' under examination had become second nature, *inquisitio* took on a very different connotation, as a new mode of judicial examination. How interesting, in this connection, that the first practitioners of the new inquisitorial mode of justice should be principally drawn from the new mendicant orders, the Dominicans and the Franciscans. And how interesting that they should almost all be graduates of the new universities. Is it coincidence that the Inquisition, before 1300, invented the first correctional use of imprisonment? As the graduate-inquisitors discovered the inner truth that most of those whom they examined, being poorly educated non-graduates, were heretics, they discovered the need to construct prisons, known as the *murus longus* and *murus strictus* (solitary confinement) for them. But these prisons were not for unregenerate heretics; they were, in the happy phrase, 'relaxed to the secular arm', that is, burned by civil authorities, since the church did not take life. Prison was the place for those who confessed their heresy, and who were then held until they were deemed to be purified and safe to send out again into society. Here again, what Foucault took to be a constitutive feature of the modern epoch turns out to have a longer, double, history.

The identification of the third term which functions as the hyphen, or principle of coherence, between power and knowledge will doubtless differ for different epochs. For the Greco-Roman world of Seneca it cannot be examination, as we have seen. But then the relations between power and knowledge were not those that have obtained in the modern epoch, so we would not expect it to be (even though that does not rule out some level of affinity between power–knowledge then and now, that affinity which led Foucault to name 'examination' as the practice which Seneca executed upon himself). Perhaps it might be *disciplina*. Perhaps for the still-earlier and purely Greek epoch, it must be *paideia*, the term that came to connote the 'culture' of the educated man, but whose etymology reveals it as denoting the bringing up, and shaping up, of the *pais* – the child, but also, in the Greek, the slave.

Again, in the long term and the last analysis, it makes no difference. What Walzer's argument makes clear is that the operation of power–knowledge can be understood only through paying attention to the hyphen, and to identifying the third term which lies concealed there. The name of the term like the specific powers and knowledges implicated in power–knowledge is inevitably bound to change at certain moments of discontinuity. Foucault's legacy to us is the identification of this mysterious but potent reality, power–knowledge, and his further obsession with examination. He thereby provided us both with a new construct for comprehending the stubbornly different levels of explanation usually known as the 'sociological' and the 'psychological', and with a clue to the secret (which he never revealed in so many words) of its operation. Thanks to Walzer, we appreciate that the operation of power–knowledge demands a third term: it operates perhaps via examination, or *inquisitio*, or *disciplina*, or *paideia*. The intriguing question, and continuing mystery, is: can that third term properly be other than an educational term? Is there any conclusion except that Foucault was a crypto-educationalist?

REFERENCES

Aries, P. (1962) *Centuries of Childhood*, London: Cape. (Originally published Paris, 1960.)

Cook, D. (1987) 'The turn towards subjectivity: Michel Foucault's legacy', *Journal of the British Society of Phenomenology* 18 (3): 215–25.

Derrida, J. (1978) *Writing and Difference*, London: Routledge & Kegan Paul.

(Originally published Paris, 1967.)

Foucault, M. (1967) *Madness and Civilization*, London: Tavistock. (Originally published Paris, 1961.)

————(1973) *The Birth of the Clinic*, London: Tavistock. (Originally published Paris, 1963.)

————(1974) *The Order of Things*, London: Tavistock. (Originally published Paris, 1966.)

————(1977) *Discipline and Punish*, London: Allen Lane. (Originally published Paris, 1975.)

————(1984a) *Histoire de la Sexualité*, vol. 2, *L'Usage des Plaisirs*, Paris: Gallimard.

————(1984b) *Histoire de la Sexualité*, vol. 3, *Le Souci de Soi*, Paris: Gallimard.

Galton, F. (1869) *Hereditary Genius*, London: Macmillan.

Gordon, C. (ed.) (1980) *Power/Knowledge: Selected Interviews and Other Writings of Michel Foucault*, Brighton: Harvester.

Hoskin, K. (1979) 'The examination, disciplinary power and rational schooling', *History of Education* 8 (2): 135–46.

————(1982) 'Examinations and schooling of science', in R. McLeod (ed.) *Days of Judgement: Science, Examinations and the Organization of Knowledge in Late-Victorian England*, Driffield: Nafferton Books, pp. 213–36.

————(1986) 'The professional in educational history', in J. Wilkes (ed.) *The Professional Teacher: Proceedings of the 1985 Annual Conference of the History of Education Society of Great Britain*, London: History of Education Society.

Hoskin, K. and Macve, R. (1986) 'Accounting and the examination: a genealogy of disciplinary power', *Accounting, Organizations and Society* 11 (2): 105–36.

————(1988) 'The genesis of accountability: the West Point connections', *Accounting, Organizations and Society* 13 (1): 37–73.

Marrou, H. (1964) *History of Education in Antiquity*, New York: Mentor. (Originally published Paris, 1948.)

Merquior, J. (1985) *Foucault*, London: Fontana.

Rouse, R. and Rouse, M. (1979) *Preachers, Florilegia and Sermons: Studies on the Manipulus Florum of Thomas of Ireland*, Toronto: Institute of Pontifical Studies.

Saenger, P. (1982) 'Silent reading: its impact on late medieval script and society', *Viator* 12: 367–414.

Stone, L. (1982) 'Madness', *New York Review of Books* 16 December, p. 36.

Walzer, M. (1983) 'The politics of Michel Foucault', *Dissent* 30: 481–90.

Part II

History, power and knowledge

4 The genealogy of the urban schoolteacher

Dave Jones

> The children were her masters, she deferred to them. . . . She could
> not speak as she would to a child, because they were not individual
> children, they were a collective inhuman thing.
>
> (Lawrence 1981: 376–7)

It was no small matter to get a young woman to stand before a gallery of
55 ill-nourished and verminous children and drill them in a series of
mechanical exercises. The central concern of this chapter is a modest
one: how did a set of often distorted and contradictory images and
strategies come to regulate the figure of the urban school teacher? In
posing this question we shall not assume that the urban schoolteacher
fits easily into a general history of educational progress. This figure and
the conditions of its emergence did not necessarily arise unproblem-
atically to civilize the dangerous and perishing classes of the urban
slum. Rather, it will be argued that the genealogy of the teacher is
characterized by discontinuity. In Foucauldian terms, this genealogy
traces the line of an ethical transformation in a discursive complex that
seeks to manage the urban population in depth and detail, initially
through a disciplinary machinery of micro-penalty, and subsequently
through a bio-power of tutelary agencies (Foucault 1986).

THE IMAGE OF THE DESTITUTE TEACHER

The urban school appeared against the backdrop of nineteenth-century
anxiety about 'the new landscape of the social' (Deleuze in Donzelot
1979). From at least the beginning of that century, philanthropic
evangelists, the established church, utopian socialists, and utilitarian
radicals expressed from different perspectives a concern about the moral
and intellectual condition of the urban poor. All these perspectives
agreed that cheap education represented a solution to this problem. It is
this concern that mobilizes a strategy of schooling to regulate the
nomadic, dissolute, degenerate, and marginal population of the urban

57

slum. As nineteenth-century philanthropy identified the undifferentiated squalor of the city as an object of concern, it introduced a pedagogical machinery to normalize it.

This educational discourse formed in contrast to what philanthropists and later royal commissioners considered the unsystematic and possibly morally dangerous education already available in the urban slum. The private adventure, or dame school provided this irregular and nomadic education. We shall describe it briefly because it was by systematically opposing it that the official discourse of popular education took shape.

The dame school was isomorphic with the slum. Its teaching was notable for its informality (Gardner 1984: Chap. 2). It occurred in a wide variety of settings. Most commonly, the teacher's home served as a school. It had none of the features that came to characterize the urban school: no registers of attendance, no regular schoolday, no classroom and no timetable. Neither was there a fixed term of attendance. Moreover, the teacher required no formal qualifications. It was common practice for widows with no visible means of support or workers crippled by an industrial injury to establish a small dame school. It was, in the pejorative assessment of the Newcastle commission, 'a complete refuge for the destitute', practised by, amongst others, grocers, tobacconists, sailors, painters, housekeepers, and ladies maids (*Reports of the Assistant Commissioners* 1861: vol. 3 394).

It was against such informal and immoral instruction that a discourse of cheap but moral schooling evolved. It had traditionally been the duty of religious and charitable institutions to educate the poor 'to thrive and be useful' in their 'appropriate situation in life' At the end of the eighteenth century, however, the British and the National and Foreign societies invented a specific technology that could provide cheap instruction for the poor. Bell and Lancaster's monitorial schools constituted this new 'engine of instruction'. Its appeal lay in Lancaster's claim that one teacher, through a judicious use of monitors, might educate a thousand pupils in his Borough Road school.

The new technology also attracted the attention of utilitarian and philosophic radicals highly critical of the instruction offered to the poor both by traditional philanthropy and informal dame schools. In the *Wealth of Nations*, Adam Smith had argued that education was too important to be left to voluntary religious bodies (Smith 1910: 264). Bentham and the 'education-mad' party of the early nineteenth century viewed this monitorial school as the machinery through which government could scientifically inculcate habits of morality. The school as an engine of instruction could manufacture a disciplinary society.

In his *Chrestomathia* (1809) Bentham outlined a science of schooling that would inculcate habits of calculation in the population. This would be achieved by the application of a polyvalent panopticon technology mediated by a system of rewards and punishments. In Bentham's educational scheme, each pupil would be taught to calculate the pleasure and pain consequent upon any act through the operation of daily aggregate registers. These registers promoted or degraded pupils according to their mastery of short lessons. Every pupil would, moreover, be competing to 'capture the place' of whoever occupied a higher rank. It was through examination and degradation that the school inculcated a utilitarian morality.

In this pedagogic science, however, the role of the teacher was minimal. In Bentham's chrestomathic vision, it was the technology of examination and surveillance that inculcated the principle of utility and formed a useful population. Indeed, for Bentham a technology of surveillance and examination applied equally to the teacher and the taught. The school, Bentham contended, had to be regularly examined by an inspectorate. The utilitarians had little regard for teachers and considered that wherever possible, schools should employ monitors. The only motivation that an adult teacher could have in elementary instruction was a 'fear of losing the situation', for 'in it he can find neither instruction nor amusement, nor except that fear any other form of interest' (Bentham 1816: 9).

Although they agreed about little else, the voluntary societies shared Bentham's low opinion of the schoolteacher. The philanthropic *Society of the Poor* considered that any well-intentioned and religiously principled character could begin a school armed with the Society's tracts and a copy of Dr Bell's *Account of an Educational Experiment* (Bernard 1970: 1).

Thus by the 1830s a discourse about the urban population, its indigence and immorality, had occasioned the formation of a strategy for reforming the poor. This reformation would be achieved through an apparatus – the school and a technology of observation and examination. In this strategy, however, there was only a minimal role for the teacher of the urban poor. The urban schoolteacher, whether a destitute grocer in a dame school or an examiner in the chrestomathia, was at best an unqualified drill master and at worse a purveyor of corrupt values.

THE GOOD TEACHER

It is the failure of the monitorial school as an engine of instruction for the labouring classes that occasions a reevaluation of the teacher. Indeed, the fact that the monitorial school failed only incited further speculation about the benefit of school to the moral life of the urban poor.

In the course of the 1840s the recently formed privy council on education and the voluntary societies reversed their opinion of monitorial instruction. The new Benthamite inspectorate of government-aided schools expressed serious reservations about the monitorial method. It seemed neither very effective nor disciplined. As one HMI remarked caustically of 'bawling' lessons at Borough Road 'Mr Lancaster had a notion, if he could allow boys to make a noise they would never consider it a drudgery to be taught' (Hurt 1971: 89).

The Inspectorate's criticism, however, served as a basis for different educational strategies. The Privy Council and its inspectorate formed as a new object of concern the actual method of instruction. By a strategic shift in the discourse of the urban school, the teacher's function altered from that of a mechanical instructor to one of a moral exemplar. From the 1840s the Inspectorate and the voluntary societies displayed a growing concern with the character and training of the good teacher.

Central to this new concern was the creation of a space in which the teacher would transmit ethical values to the children of the labouring classes. From the outset, teacher training was primarily concerned with ethical techniques; considerations of curriculum content occupied a secondary role. The new strategy made the teacher into an irresistible ethical image whose magnetic attraction would transform the progeny of the labouring classes into ethical subjects responsive to a bio-power (Foucault 1986).

The formation of this new teacher was itself a work of ethical training. The pioneers of this regime, like the secretary to the Privy Council on Education, Sir James Kay-Shuttleworth, established specific training schools. It was on sites like the Normal School at Norwood (subsequently Battersea Training College) and at David Stow's Glasgow Academy that the theory programme of the urban schoolteacher took shape.

The extensive commentaries written on teacher training in the 1840s and 1850s manifest a growing preoccupation with the selection of pupil teachers, the specific course of instruction, teachers' conduct in the schoolroom, and the school apparatus that best suits this pedagogics. The discourse of urban schooling after 1840 then became increasingly preoccupied with the mode *d'assujettissement* of the teacher (Foucault 1986: 356). How, in other words did the 'truth' of the teacher become discursively established as both a subject and object of power– knowledge?

In his *Second Report for the Training of Parochial Schoolmasters at Battersea* (1843), Shuttleworth outlined the technologies of self-transformation that would produce the urban schoolmaster. Shuttleworth regretted that the schoolmasters came from 'the lower orders'. 'They are the sons of small tradesmen, of bailiffs, of servants, or of superior mechanics,' he wrote of training college entrants in the 1840s (Tholfsen 1974: 123). Regret about the humbleness of the teachers' backgrounds continues to be a significant discursive trace throughout the following century.

Regret has strategic effects: it establishes the need for rigour in teacher training. At both government-supported normal schools and the training colleges of the voluntary societies (like St Mark's Chelsea), novice teachers underwent a quasi-monastic discipline. They were subject in fact to a confessional technology adumbrated by the normative principle of examination to prepare them for a secular practice. The regime of the training college paid meticulous attention to the surveillance, correction, and confession of the aspirant teachers. In Shuttleworth's view, they not only had to be inured to the humility and isolation of their lot, but they also had to adjust, paradoxically, to the relative promotion of their intellectual capacities. The pupil-teacher had to be instructed in techniques of monitoring the quality of his ethical self-formation.

From the moment the teacher enters the portals of the training college, like a secular novice he is prepared 'for the modest respectability of his lot' (Tholfsen 1974: 127). From the outset the pupil-teacher had to be penetrated, in Shuttleworth's resonant phrase, by 'a religious principle' (*ibid.*, p. 126). This is the crux of the training: the teacher must be taught to desire humility. Teacher training manuals emphasize the pedagogic value of 'modesty' and the vital 'qualifications' of humility and gentleness. The appearance of regular statements about the teacher's ethical transformation through the technology of the training college does not seek to conceal the purpose of this training. Shuttleworth states clearly:

> Obscure and secluded schools need masters of a contented spirit, to whom the training of the children in their charge, has charms sufficient to concentrate their thoughts and exertions on the humble sphere in which they live notwithstanding the privations of a life, but little superior to the level of the surrounding peasantry.
>
> (Tholfsen 1974: 127).

This care and attention to the pupil-teacher represents a significant shift from the view that the only interest a teacher might have in a school is the fear of losing his situation. The teacher now had to be imbued with the ethic of service. Novitiate teachers at Battersea milked and cleaned the cows, tended the pigs, cultivated the gardens, and subsisted on a plain and frugal diet (*ibid.*, p. 129). 'This regulation of behaviour extended even to dress: the humble teacher should not display any 'external signs of self-indulgence and vanity' (*ibid.*, p. 130).

The new training college aroused and heightened self-awareness. In this training, the virtue of morality and humility were consistently opposed to the corrosive vices of intellect and arrogance. The principal of the training college constituted the student's guide and moral exemplar, and rooted out the corrupting vice of degeneracy. This perpetual vigilance extended even to the student's private conversations. 'Low buffoonery, profligate jests,' Shuttleworth contended led to 'clandestine habits and the secret practice of vice' (p. 134). The care to establish this ethical regime through a combination of discipline, surveillance, and the application of technologies of the self Shuttleworth considered inestimable.

The inculcation of techniques of self-regulation far outweighed the teacher's intellectual training. The over-educated teacher would be prey to the 'vices' of arrogance, vanity, and dissatisfaction. Such a view of teacher education can only be explained by the incommensurable value attached to the teacher's 'character' A regime that inculcated mere 'intellect' without attending to moral character would, Shuttleworth averred, promote immorality. The products of such a regime would not regenerate the urban poor. Instead, they would constitute 'active agents of degeneracy of manners by which the humbler ranks of the society would be infected' (Tholfsen 1974: 137).

The virtuous teacher required a meticulous preparation for a curious destiny. He was to occupy a 'humble and subordinate position, and though master of his school, to his scholars he is to be parent and to his superiors an intelligent servant and minister,' going about his business dressed without 'foppery' in 'fustian cord' (*ibid.*, p. 129). The nature of the task necessitated, Shuttleworth contended, a five-year training period. This alone represented a sufficiently 'prolonged trial of character and conduct' that afforded a 'warrant of reliance'. This concern with the nature and extent of the preparation of the urban schoolteacher permeated the writings of mid-century educationalists. Inspectors like Jellinger Symons believed the good teacher required, in fact, 'a clear head, a good heart, a firm and above all a kind disposition, a vigorous spirit, great mental energy, liveliness of character and perfect command of temper' (Symons 1971: 126). The alternative offered a prospect of education in the hands of those 'in the strict practice of low vices, of no faith, disloyal or corrupt' (Kay-Shuttleworth 1969: 49).

This intense preoccupation with the humble virtue of the schoolteacher had strategic effects, for the trained teacher alone constituted the force 'to counteract the fact that pupils are taught in the school and trained in the streets' (Stow 1971: 13). The training would enable the 'master' to be the 'best book'. He had to be what 'he wishes to make the children'. For in his discourse, 'the moral temperament of the school will depend as closely on that of the teacher as will its physical aspect' (Symons 1971: 126).

Nevertheless, the physical aspect did matter. The teacher required both a method and an architecture that amplified and projected the moral presence. It was a technological combination of the trained teacher, the machinery of the gallery and the gallery lesson that 'formed a new era in education'(Stow 1971: 9). This strategy would actively facilitate the efficient moral training of the population where the mere normalizing space of the monitorial school had failed. The moral training of the population required not only an exclusive space but also that space occupied by the authoritative voice and loving gaze of the teacher. In his *Moral Training and the Training System with Plans for Improving and Fitting up Training Schools*, David Stow outlined the technology that enabled the teacher to transmit a moral presence. It was through 'the physical force in the voice and manner alone [that the schoolteacher] can command and sustain without coercion the attention of a school of even sixty or eighty children' (Stow 1971: 24). This technique of the voice combined with a simplicity of instruction to constitute the 'simultaneous method'. This method of instruction in the school gallery might be amplified by the object lesson. In this lesson the teacher could combine comprehension of everyday objects with the arts of life. The combination of gallery and object lesson enabled the teacher both 'to pour knowledge broadside into' the pupil and to 'quicken' and mould the moral sense (*ibid.*, p. 26–7).

The moral presence of the teacher combined with this careful mode of instruction required a specific architecture to project the authority of the teacher. Both the school building and the playground required appropriate design. The rapidly evolving science of education drew attention to the most effective size of a gallery and the correct height of desks to facilitate instruction. Of equal importance to this discourse was the playground. This 'uncovered school' would 'form the platform for the development of the real dispositions and habits of the children' (*ibid.*, p. 4). The playground constituted a 'sphere of moral superintendence'. Together with the gallery and under the authoritative gaze of the teacher, it constituted a 'machinery of moral synthesis'.

This machinery signalled a strategic shift in both the character of the teacher and the construction of the lesson. The teacher occupies the place of a model and a focus. The simultaneous method extends the time of the lesson, and the classroom becomes a space of silence, not of 'bawling'. *The Memorandum of the Committee of Council on Education respecting the organization of schools in parallel groups of benches and desks* summarized it thus:

The main end to be attained is the concentration of the attention of the teacher upon his own separate class and of the class upon its teacher to the exclusion of distracting sounds and objects and without obstruction to the headmaster's power of superintending the whole of the classes and their teachers.

(Symons 1971: 54)

The preoccupation with the mode of instruction reflects too a reversal of the assumption that a basic instruction in reading, writing, and arithmetic was sufficient to educate the urban population. From the mid-nineteenth century, both the government inspectorate and educational reformers of various persuasions increasingly argued that instruction in the 'mechanical rudiments' uninformed by a moral principle actually created a population disposed to crime. Thus in her influential *Reformatory Schools*, Mary Carpenter contended that 'it is not sufficient to found schools to communicate knowledge or even to impart religious worldiness... without wisdom to direct and power to guide these wild beings' (Carpenter 1851: 120).

Hence the crucial importance of the trained teacher who could suffuse the classroom with a scientific morality and induce an ethical population. Consequently, the teacher's scientific induction of morality could never have recourse to corporal punishment. Fear 'hardened the spirit' and blocked the subtle transformation of the child into an ethical subject responsive to shame. Educational science rejected corporal punishment as early as the mid-century. It rejected it, moreover, not from a progressive humanitarian sensitivity to physical suffering, but because the feelings had to be educated to respond to rituals of humiliation.

It was the loving teacher through the machinery of the gallery that shaped this receptivity. It took infinite pains. The child had to be taught to love the teacher and the school and not the mean backstreets. Consequently, the teacher required both patience and the ability to turn every event in the school, 'every ebullition of temper, all deviations from truth and modesty' (Symons 1971: 125), into a moral account. Above all, however, the teacher had to make even 'the children he likes least' love him. Love in fact was the instrument of moral training. It could educate the higher sensibilities. The teacher would achieve this education by dismissing an erring scholar from the gallery. This spectacle of degradation would moreover be amplified by the observation of the onlooking class. This additional power of 'the sympathy of numbers' would, Jellinger Symons averred, punish 'a child most severely' (Symons 1971: 122). The object of the exercise was to create an ethical regime that stimulated morality from the shame of offending rather than a 'fear of the rod',

It was not difficult to move from the notion of the humble and virtuous teacher exercising a moral tutelage over the schoolroom, to a view of the teacher as a good parent. The formation of the teacher in a specific moral machinery broadens into the view of the teacher as a model parent. The trained teacher would in fact introduce the undifferentiated and nomadic urban population to the model of the normal family in 'its thrift and separation' (Donzelot 1979: ix). The moral teacher's loving gaze is imbricated in the formation of the normal home and a domestic economy. It is at this point that specific statements about the female teacher appear with increasing regularity.

David Stow stated that the urban school should reflect and enhance the 'natural' relationship of the mid-Victorian bourgeois family:

> After the family order of father and mother there ought to be a man at the head of every juvenile and infant training school; and when practicable, his wife or sister ought to be the assistant. This proposal to carry the family system into the school is not to supersede parental training at home but to assist and strengthen it.
> (Stow 1971: 19)

The school would offer a model of the family:

> The perfection of the training system would be sixty to eighty boys and girls in one gallery or playground all learning one thing and under one master and mistress carrying out the family training of home.
> (Stow 1971: 21)

The value of the school in projecting the image of the model family stimulated an interest in a specific curriculum for girls and its supervision by the schoolmistress. This gender-specific curriculum had a significant impact on the development of the elementary curriculum and the genealogy of the teacher.

The school constituted a technology for transforming 'wild beings' into ethical subjects. The success of this strategy would be measured by the transformation of the habits of the urban population from a nomadic mass into stable, sober, isolated family units in which the mother formed the focus of domestic management. Thus although the schoolmaster represented a paradigm for moral excellence and his scholars its reflection, the moral foundation received its exemplification in the habits of domestic management imbued by the good schoolmistress. The organization of a domestic economy in the labourer's home would be the outward and visible sign of the regeneration of the urban poor. This goal demanded that the schoolmistress take a specific responsibility for teaching girls the inestimable value of needlework, baking, and cooking in forming 'admirable housewives.'

Dave Jones

The reception of the good teacher

This discourse of the schoolteacher has so far addressed only the theory programme. What happened when the trained teacher tried to transmit this scientific morality on the voluntary school site? It is at this level, Foucault contends, that strategy attempts to instrumentalize the real are subject to tactical resistance that in turn offers an opportunity to further shifts in discourse (Foucault 1980: 37–55).

As the debate surrounding the Newcastle Commission's investigation into the state of popular education and the subsequent Revised Code (1860–61) illustrate, there existed both political and public dissatisfaction with the urban schoolteacher and teacher dissatisfaction with their status that belie the optimistic forecasts for a moral science outlined by the teacher-trainers.

Traditional histories of education (Tropp 1957; Lowndes 1968) attribute this failure of the urban school to the view promulgated in the 1860s by the teacher-trainers themselves, that 'too much was expected from' the urban schoolteacher. It is this telling phrase that comes to haunt the genealogy. The excessive expectation in fact masks a set of conflicting and ultimately irreconcilable problems that the trained teacher was intended to solve. The teacher had a multivalent responsibility for moralizing the urban slum. The teacher had to inculcate not only habits of thrift, industry, and responsibility, but even, according to some educationalists, to maintain national defence and prosperity.

At the same time, contemporary commentators expected schoolteachers to know their place in a society that they had been trained to transform. The teacher occupied an intensely ambivalent strategic position. A series of socio-economic codes that affected income, housing, behaviour, and dress reinforced feelings of insecurity. Thus practising schoolteachers in London in the 1860s recalled that social mechanisms reinforced the humility that had permeated their education at the training college. Miss Chester, a Soho voluntary schoolteacher, noted how 'very humble' she had to be:

> Her dress was most severely restricted. Great fears were felt lest she should dress above her station. Hats and trimmings were punishable offences, and a dress as near as possible to a parish livery was insisted upon.

> (Cardwell 1899: 26)

This constant surveillance represented a source of enduring bitterness. It became increasingly common during the 1860s for trained teachers to leave the calling of schoolmaster for less demanding and better remunerated employment as office workers or railway clerks.

Just as schoolteachers were unable to fulfil the model of humility in practice, so the urban slum failed to correspond to their moral example as the training outlined. It was difficult for the teacher to transmit a moral example when, as *The Schoolmaster* remarked, parents 'of children who attend our national school do not value the school or the teacher' (Tropp 1957: 34). The fact that neither parents nor their children responded positively to the moral paradigm had tactical implications for the teacher in practice. Most significantly, the schoolteacher imposed the moral training not scientifically through a model machinery, but through the institution of a regime of corporal punishment. Teacher survival in the more problematic urban areas depended increasingly upon the physical intimidation of the headmaster and his ability to impose discipline.

Apart from the critical reception of the new technology of morality, government inspectors particularly drew attention to the inadequate delivery of education. A majority of teachers in the national schools were not in fact trained, or certified. Popular schooling depended for its growth not upon trained but upon pupil-teachers (Tropp 1957: 87–95). Indeed, the mid-Victorian philanthropic approach to popular education failed to deliver trained teachers to that part of the population where discourse claimed they would be most useful. The national schools of the 1850s and 1860s catered for the sons and daughters of the industrious working classes who could afford the school pence. The payment of these weekly fees effectively excluded the dangerous and perishing classes from the voluntary schools. Yet it was with these outcast classes in mind that the moral model had been developed.

The failure of the voluntary school to reach the most deprived ghettos of the urban slum and the failure of the schoolteacher to conduct himself with due social circumspection formed a resource for further strategy. The failure of the voluntary schoolteacher created the conditions of possibility for further educational discourse and the displacement of the teacher into a new regime of concern.

Two concerns shape the genealogy of the teacher at the end of the nineteenth century. The first addresses the failure of the teacher to effect an urban reformation. This failure subsequently elides with a wider concern about national decline and the implications of the extension of franchise after 1868. Both concerns shaped a new discourse of efficiency.

In terms of the urban schoolteacher, this meant that the government could assess the effectiveness of the schoolteacher. The Revised Code signifies a further evaluation of the teacher. It also indicates the polyvalent manner in which discourse may mobilize earlier strategies. The Revised Code represents a partial abandonment of the programme of the teacher as moral exemplar by supplementing ethical transformation with regular examinations. Payment by results achieved in an annual examination realized the utilitarian dream of a regulating norm applied to both teachers and pupils. As J.S. Mill commented, 'The results of teaching can only be tested by examinations conducted by independent examiners' (quoted in Robson 1980: 210). A carefully formed moral example was not enough – an independent examination alone guaranteed efficient instruction.

The attention paid to efficient teaching forms part of an emergent strategy of power that might be described as bio-political. Foucault contends that a multiplicity of techniques formed in the nineteenth century 'whose task is to take charge of life', by applying a series of regulatory and corrective mechanisms (Foucault 1986: 144). This bio-politics deplored the inefficiency with which voluntarist and philan-thropic initiatives sought to regulate social problems. The power to manage life advocated a collectivist government intervention to create an efficient population.

One event marks the impact of this strategy of power in the genealogy of the teacher – the Education Act 1870. Prior to 1870, the extent of state intervention in popular schooling had been minimal. This position altered fundamentally after 1870. Between 1870 and 1902, successive governments passed legislation that enabled school boards (and after 1902, LEAs) to provide and ultimately to compel all children of the working classes to attend an elementary school.

The collectivist vision of efficient schooling involved the production of a responsible, moral, and useful population. Analogous statements already haunted the genealogy of the teacher. Collectivism, however, located them in a fresh context of concern about national decline and the need to educate the population for democratic responsibility.

These new objects of concern shift the emphasis of the teacher's moral mission to one of producing a sober, healthy, and competitive working population. The regularity of statements about the need to address directly the social problem classes also established the fact that a free-market, voluntarist approach to popular education had failed. Consequently, government agencies had to take direct responsibility for elementary schooling; otherwise national decline would be irreversible.

A variety of institutional and governmental sites elaborated this collectivist position. Both liberal collectivists and Fabian socialists emphasized the centrality of extending free education beyond the nascent elementary to a secondary stage. This discourse involved an oddly inconsistent set of statements about the effect of the teacher on the urban slum. Sidney Webb, for instance, in *London Education* (1904) held that education in the metropolis fell far short of 'decent efficiency'. Nevertheless he believed the London slum to have been regenerated. However, there remained an urgent need to extend education to make the population efficient. In the Fabian view, the population constituted a 'resource' that had to be mined efficiently like iron or coal. Teaching, Webb contended, had shifted from a matter of individual philanthropic enterprise to a 'matter of national concern' (Webb 1904: 9–10).

Analogous statements about the fitness and efficiency of the population circulate from a variety of sources in the late nineteenth century and form a discursive regularity. An intellectually fashionable social Darwinism, together with a nascent eugenicist psychology and the New Imperialism, all found fault with the condition of the urban population. The press mirrored this concern. Socially influential papers like the *Morning Chronicle* regularly ran features written by intrepid explorers of 'darkest London' (Keating 1976: 14–16). The concern with the population of the abyss had the educational implication that schooling could no longer be left to haphazard charitable intervention. Efficient teaching required efficient, that is, governmental, intervention. The official journal of the National Union of Teachers warned in 1899

> The more one studies the stupendous responsibilities of the British people, the more one is impressed with the virtual necessity to breed and train the best human material possible. The danger to the British Empire lies within the homeland. The wastrel, the ne'er-do-well, the rickety and the criminal, these and not the Krupp gun or continental jealousy are the real danger.
>
> (Hurt 1979: 104)

It was precisely this marginal population of the rookeries and tenements that the successive legislation of the late nineteenth century attempted to recruit for the elementary school. By so doing, it volatilized and exacerbated conflicting strategies already at work in the genealogy of the urban schoolteachers. The appearance in school board schools after 1870 of 'street arabs' and 'roughs' from the 'abyss' on the one hand, and the operation of a code of annual examination on the other, modified educational strategy and affected the tactics available to teachers on the school site.

Strategically, the insistent demand for more efficient education disguised a latent conflict between a utilitarian and a medical norm of assessment. The universal utilitarian principle of annual examination opposed the medical and psychological discovery of defective and imbecile populations that required segregation. The medical norm achieves efficiency by pathologizing and excluding the defective, thereby establishing the external limit of the normal. The latent conflict between a segregating medical and a universal utilitarian principle of efficiency appears clearly in the 'over-pressure' controversy of the 1880s and leads to a gradual relaxation of the examining regime of payment by results.

In the late Victorian schoolroom itself, the teacher encountered resistance in applying the image repertoire of the examiner and the moral exemplar to the 'rough' population of the late Victorian citadel school. Resistance that necessitated a polyvalency of tactics on the school site that informed new strategies about what the teacher should be.

It was from a mixture of fear, disgust, and anxiety, rather than love, that the late nineteenth-century board schoolteacher approached a class of 'scholars'. The accounts of late nineteenth-century teachers describe the school population brought in by legislative compulsion in tones of shocked disapproval. The new scholars are 'sly', 'vicious', 'wild', and 'barbaric'. A London board schoolteacher of the 1880s viewed his pupils thus:

> Some were hardy enough, some were very intelligent in appearance, some were cowed and sly but vicious, and some were dulled into semi-imbecility by hunger, disease and ill-usage. They had no conception of the meaning of an order and the teacher was obliged to drill them again and again in the simplest movements.
>
> (Lowndes 1968: 113)

Similar teacher assessments legitimated a stern machinic order imposed through fear. Teachers resorted to a tactic of corporal punishment. It was, ironically, only by this tactic that the image of a teacher as a moral exemplar and an efficient instructor could be sustained. Teacher training and the architecture of the classroom required the teacher to be the focus of both authority and instruction, yet in order to sustain the silent attention of a class of 60 verminous, diseased, and half-starved scholars, the teachers could envisage no alternative to the application of a chilling discipline.

However, this tactic of imposing moral authority through physical fear raised serious difficulties. Central to the discourse of moral and efficient training was the view that education would regenerate the urban slum dweller by example and examination, not by fear and intimidation. This strategy of transforming the masses through the ethos of the school and the example of the teacher, moreover, informed the school boards and, subsequently, local authorities that monitored and managed urban education. Indeed this strategy exercised a particular appeal to those progressive urban authorities most committed to compelling the street arabs to receive the benefits of efficient schooling. The tendency of some street arabs' parents to resent and, on occasion, to react aggressively to the corporal punishment of their children exacerbated the already difficult position of the urban schoolteacher (Gardner 1984; Lawrence 1981: 398–403). Such widely differing perspectives on the relationship between the teacher and the child in the urban slum were never satisfactorily resolved.

Notably, in late-Victorian London tension developed between the progressive London Board, which advocated the abolition of corporal punishment, and school board teachers whose classroom control required its frequent application. This conflict highlights once more the essentially ambiguous nature of schoolteaching. Placed in the social abyss of late-Victorian England as an agent of efficient education, the actual instrumentalization of that efficiency was denied by the monitoring agency that demanded it. To avoid the proscription of progressive managers and violent parents, teachers resorted to a tactic of duplicity. A pupil-teacher of the 1890s observed;

> Every assistant master had a cane, so had the pupil teachers, but pupil teachers were not allowed to have a crook so that if any question arose they were pointers.
>
> (Lowndes 1968: 13)

In many urban areas, efficient education meant that the schoolteacher assumed the role of dragooning and drilling the excluded and marginalized children of the rookeries. In spite of the intense collectivist agitation about the education of the residuum and an extensive urban school building programme, there was surprisingly little modification to the regime of the schoolroom. The received theory of teaching required the imposition upon the schoolroom of the teacher's commanding presence. The architecture of the school and the method of teaching fixed the teacher in a procrustean machinery intended to enhance this presence. In fact, the atmosphere created in the urban classroom was not ethical and transformative but tense and machinic. This tension was heightened further by the annual examination required by the Revised Code.

The discourse of efficiency thus placed onerous demands upon the schoolteacher at the end of the nineteenth century. At the same time, the schoolteacher's status in the landscape of the social remained ambivalent. The schoolteacher was almost as much of an object of discursive suspicion as the population she was intended to regenerate. There developed a growing disparity between the discourse of efficient schooling and the training of efficient teachers. The discourse insisted that only an adequately trained teaching force could possibly effect the transformation of the urban slum, yet throughout the late nineteenth century, trained teachers constituted only a minority of elementary schoolteachers. After 1870 the formation of the urban abyss as an object of concern whose solution required a more efficient delivery of teaching paradoxically made efficient teaching at the level of the school site more difficult. Despite the fact that elementary teaching was of national concern, the pressures were such that many trained teachers left for less demanding occupations. Increasingly, school boards turned to untrained, uncertified supplementary female teachers.

By 1895 women constituted 73 per cent of the elementary school teaching force (Tropp 1957: 114). The contrast between the widely expressed public concern about the vital importance of teaching and the actual strategic implications of this concern haunts the genealogy of the teacher. The teacher's ambivalent role in society serves as a convenient focus for discursive suspicion and eventually blame, when urban regeneration does not take place. D. H. Lawrence, who experienced the ambivalent demands of elementary schoolteaching at a board school in Croydon, considered the elementary schoolteacher 'the poorest devil on the face of the earth':

> Set up as a representative of an ideal that is all toffee, invested in an authority which has absolutely no base except in the teacher's isolate will. . . [the teacher is] a mongrel who is neither a wage earner nor a professional, neither a headworker or handworker, neither living by his brain or his physical toil but a bit of both and despised for both.
>
> (quoted in Williams, Raymond and Joy 1973: 122)

The bio-teacher

At the start of the twentieth century the teacher occupied an increasingly difficult social position. The received methodology of teaching, in conjunction with the architecture of the school and the nature of the classroom, constrained the teacher to project an image of moral authority. The Elementary Code of 1904 required that teachers endeavour:

> by example and influence, aided by the sense of discipline, which should pervade the school, to implant in the children habits of industry, self-control and perseverance in the face of difficulties; they can teach them to reverence what is noble, to be ready for self-sacrifice, and to strive their utmost after purity and truth.
>
> (Maclure 1986: 155)

The size of school classes and the condition of the scholars rendered this code unrealistic. Its effect in the real world reduced many teachers to a brutal and machinic discipline.

However, the discursive insistence upon regeneration also provided strategic resources. We have already shown that the late nineteenth century witnessed a growing interest in the regulation of the life of the population. This bio-power established itself alongside the disciplinary machinery of universal examination, but increasingly drew its authority from the new 'truths' of medicine and psychology. The opening of the urban population to these truths required a technology of advice or insurance rather than a penal discipline. The urban schoolteacher was to find yet another role in an emergent tutelary complex.

The norms of health and medicine offered the elementary teacher a space in a complex of social agencies that advised the working-class home. In place of the teacher's isolated secular mission to project an image of moral authority into the urban slum, the new technology of insurance offered a partnership between home and school. Such an approach offered the prospect of reducing the tense and machinic nature of teaching by placing the school in a less hostile relationship with the parents and children of the urban slum. The teacher could work in alliance with other tutelary agents like the clinic and the social services to advise nescient parents on the creation of a healthy and sanitized home.

In the tutelary discourse the teacher could care for her pupils and emphasize education through the imagination rather than mechanical obedience (Macmillan 1904). In terms of an actual elementary curriculum, the tutelary discourse developed subjects that had been outlined in the theory programmes of the 1850s like needlework, domestic economy, and health, but gave them a greater viability through their interplay with a wider insurantial discourse about the mental and physical health of the urban population. In the teacher-training courses inspected by the Board of Education after 1902, the syllabi in 'Principles of teaching' demonstrate a growing concern with the psychology of child development, hygiene, physical training, and housecraft. The teacher accordingly acted alongside the medical officer in 'detecting and dealing with physically and mentally defective children' and devising 'methods of teaching hygiene to children' (syllabus for the Boards 1905–14).

This new tutelary relationship, however, had strategic consequences for the elementary schoolteacher. It placed her in a new caring and advisory relationship with the home, but in a subsidiary position to the scientific authority of the medical officer and the child psychologist. There would be no order of teaching 'specialist' in the insurantial scheme of things. The teacher occupied a semi-professional position guided by the diagnostic expertise of the clinic.

This semi-dependent role in a tutelary complex also exposed the school to the permeation by all manner of campaigns to improve the health and efficiency of the population. School boards of a progressive character took up at different times in the late nineteenth century a public demand that teachers take a concern in school savings, the diet of their pupils, the Prussian system of learning by doing, or the Swedish system of drill. This intense speculation about the health and efficiency of the population also manifested itself in ways that did not bear directly upon the curriculum but did affect the relationship between school and the urban working-class family. Thus progressive educators like Margaret Macmillan campaigned for baths in elementary schools and the value of a new order of teacher that made health a by-product of teaching (Macmillan 1904: 200).

Isomorphic with this development of the school within a tutelary complex was the growing emphasis on a pedagogy that showed a greater appreciation of the child's consciousness. The influential pedagogy of Freubel and Montessori emphasized the nurturing role of the school-teacher. In the view of Margaret Macmillan, the teacher, as a good or good enough mother, together with the temporary 'home' of the school, would 'transform the child of the mean streets and the slum'. Conveniently, in view of the staffing arrangements of elementary schools before 1914, the pedagogy of the caring teacher found teaching 'much more natural to the woman's nature' (Steedman 1978: 158). The tutelary assessment constituted a strategic shift from the teacher as a paternal law for the urban child to a mother-made-conscious compensating for the defective child-rearing of the urban slum. It offered too a seductive image of female teachers

> who have the charm of great actresses. They move with wonderful grace. Their voices are low, penetrating, musical. . . . Their dress is beautiful, simple and nothing is so remarkable as their power except their gentleness.
>
> (Steedman 1978: 158)

This provocative imagery accommodated the need to advise and regularize the family life of the urban slum much more readily than that of a paternalist headmaster. It was flexible. The gaze of the caring mother metonymically elided with the examination of the medical officer and the case file of the psychologist and the social worker, in the endless endeavour to identify 'the limit that will define difference in relation to all other differences, the external frontier of the abnormal' (Foucault 1982: 180).

Once more, however, there is no smooth transformation of the schoolroom classroom from disciplinary machinery into a space of 'natural inner movement'. At the level of the school, the tutelary programme of the bio-teacher either conflicted or merged with the other available formations of the schoolteacher. Few schoolmistresses corresponded to Margaret Macmillan's ideal. Too many of these teachers continued to come from the 'skilled and semi-skilled working classes' and were harassed rather than charming. The caring teacher, moreover, experienced difficulty in effecting the reality of a salubrious and hygienic school as a contrasting model to the depravity of the urban slum. The desire to transform urban girls into efficient homemakers degenerated into a practice that took place in 'a slovenly classroom as often as not unswept, filled with the fumes of uncovered gas rings', with the pupils 'about the various desks... under their ordinary class teachers, interfering with each others efforts to make beef tea, rock cakes and pancakes or to recook cold meats cooked by the previous class' (Lowndes 1968: 26).

In the discourse of efficiency and tutelage at the end of the nineteenth century there is a clear interplay between a code of efficiency 'which rules ways of doing things' (Foucault 1981: 10) and a 'production of discourses' about the bio-teacher and regimes of health and hygiene 'which serve to justify, found and provide reasons and principles for these ways of doing things' (Foucault 1981: 10). These strategies encounter resistance and adaptation in their attempt to instrumentalize the real. Yet they do constitute ethical regimes through which both teacher and subsequently pupil 'govern themselves by the production of truth'. The truth of the caring teacher is linked to effects in the real that seek to transform the ethical life of the urban abyss.

Through a genealogy of the teacher, then, we can trace a curious line of transformation of 'moral technologies' (Foucault 1981: 4). The teacher is a suspicious figure that requires continual examination within an examining technology – the school – which attempts to establish a disciplinary utopia based on a felicific calculus. Subsequently, the teacher through a process of self-examination is transformed into a moral exemplar to project an ethical verity into the unknown of the Victorian city. This transformative morality pictures the teacher as an ideal father, a good and rational parent, and eventually, in an interesting reversal of gender, a good and nurturing mother. Always, however, this imagery is *in loco parentis* to remedy the inadequate parenting of the urban tenements. In this last image the teacher forms an element within a tutelary complex that exercises a bio-power to advise the urban family and examine the extent of its pathology.

This image repertoire congeals in the formation of the good teacher and plays consciously across the classrooms and staffrooms of the contemporary urban school. These images occupy a technology that orders and examines the phenomenon of urban growth. This technology, moreover, has always failed. The genealogy of the urban schoolteacher is the passage of a failure which, paradoxically, induces a more extensive examination of the need for urban schooling.

REFERENCES

Bentham, Jeremy (1816) *Chrestomathia* (2nd edn), London: Foss and R. Hunter.

Bernard, Thomas (1970) *Of the Education of the Poor. Being the First Part of a Digest* (Social History of Education Series), London: Woburn Press.

Cardwell, J.H. (1899) *The Story of a Charity School: the centuries of popular education in Soho 1699–1899*, London: Hansom and Comba.

Carpenter, Mary (1851) *Reformatory Schools for the Children of the Dangerous and Perishing Classes and for Juvenile Offenders*, London: G. Gilpin.

Donzelot, Jacques (1979) *The Policing of Families*, London: Hutchinson.

Foucault, Michel (1980) ed. Gordon, C. *Power/Knowledge*, New York: Pantheon.

——(1981) 'Questions of Method', *Ideology and Consciousness*, 6, 2, pp. 78–87.

——(1982) *Discipline and Punish*, London: Peregrine.

——(1984) *The History of Sexuality*, vol. 1, London: Penguin.

Gardner, Philip (1984) *The Lost Elementary Schools of Victorian England*, London: Croom Helm.

Hurt, J.S. (1971) *Education in Evolution: Church, State, Society and Popular Education 1800–70*, London: Hart Davies.

——(1979) *Elementary Schooling and the Working Classes 1860–1918*, London: Routledge & Kegan Paul.

Kay-Shuttleworth, J. (1843) *Second Report for the Training of Parochial Schoolmasters at Battersea*, Privy Council Committee on Education.

——(1969) *Memorandum on the Present State of Popular Education*, London: Woburn Press.

Keating, H.S. (1976) *Into Unknown England 1866–1913*, London: Fontana.

Lawrence, D.H. (1981) *The Rainbow*, London: Penguin.

Lowndes, G.A.N. (1968) *The Silent Social Revolution*, Cambridge: Cambridge University Press.

Maclure, Stuart (1986) *Educational Documents 1816 to the Present Day*, London: Methuen.

Macmillan, M. (1903) *Education Through the Imagination*, London: Lambert.

Rabinow, Paul (1986) *The Foucault Reader*, London: Penguin.

Regulations and Syllabus for Acting Teacher's Certificate Examination 1903–18, 1918 Board of Education, Whitehall.

Report of the Assistant Commissioners Appointed to Enquire into the State of Popular Education in England, vol. 3, (1861) London: Eyre and Spottiswoode.

Robson, J.M. (ed.) (1980) *The Collected Works of J.S. Mill*, vol. 21, London: Athlone Press.

Smith, Adam (1910) *The Wealth of Nations*, vol. 5, London: Seligman, Dent Everyman.

Steedman, Carolyn (1978) 'The mother made conscious: the historical development of primary school pedagogy', *History Workshop Journal*.

Stow, David (1971) *Moral Training and the Training System with Plans for Improving and Fitting up Training Schools*, Manchester: University Press.

Symons, Jellinger (1971) *School Economy: A Practical Book on the Best Mode of Establishing and Teaching Schools* (Social History of Education Series), London: Woburn Press.

Tholfsen, Trygve K. (1974) *Sir James Kay-Shuttleworth on Popular Education*, New York: Columbia University Press.

Tropp, Asher (1957) *The School Teachers: The Growth of the Teaching Profession in England and Wales from 1800 to the Present Day*, London: Heinemann.

Webb, Sidney (1904) *London Education*, London: Longmans.

Williams, Raymond and Joy, (1973) *D.H. Lawrence on Education*, London: Penguin.

5 Educational practices and scientific knowledge

A genealogical reinterpretation of the emergence of physiology in post-Revolutionary France

Richard Jones

INTRODUCTION

The importance of post-Revolutionary France has long been recognized by both historians of education and historians of science. As far as education is concerned, it was in France during this period that one of the first truly national education systems was planned and eventually established. It was also here that many of the educational practices which are central to modern education systems were first systematically applied. This leads H.C. Barnard to conclude that

> modern education, in its administration, its curriculum and its philosophical theory, dates in large measure from the France of the eighteenth century and receives its clearest and most complete exposition at the time of the Revolution.
>
> (Barnard 1969)

As far as science is concerned, there is, if anything, even greater reason for historians to study this period. According to C.C. Gillispie, during the half-century between 1780 and 1830 'the French community of science predominated in the world to a degree that no other national complex has since done or had ever done' (Gillispie 1980). For much of this period the College de France, the Ecole Polytechnique, and the Muséum d'Histoire Naturelle were the world's leading scientific institutions and savants like Antoine Lavoisier, Pierre-Simon Laplace, George Cuvier and Xavier Bichat were widely regarded as world authorities in their respective scientific fields. There were also important changes taking place, particularly in the training and career opportunities that were available to scientists. This prompts Gillispie to comment:

> [P]urists may argue that only in consequence of these changes in France and later abroad does it become appropriate to speak of

'scientists' and 'science' in the sense of fully professional persons
cultivating the modern disciplines, notably physics and biology,
with their modern array of specialities and problems.

(Gillispie 1980)

Moreover, it was in this intellectual environment that the conceptual
foundations of many of the modern scientific disciplines emerged (Merz
1965). With regard to the study of the living world, this process can be
characterized as a shift from eighteenth-century natural history – with its
emphasis on surface structure and classification – to nineteenth-century
biology, with its emphasis on internal organization and physiology.[1]

The near simultaneous emergence of modern educational practices
and modern scientific knowledge raises the following question. Are
these two events related in any way? Most historians would have little
hesitation in answering 'yes'. They are likely to point to the ways in
which the various institutions of higher education encouraged the
exchange and dissemination of scientific ideas.[2] They may also highlight the role that these institutions played in the gradual professionalization of science, via the provision of secure scientific posts, the
establishment of recognized scientific qualifications, the publication of
scientific journals, and so on.[3] In other words, they would claim that the
educational environment of post-Revolutionary France helped to bring
about an increase in the rate of scientific progress. What they are much
less likely to claim is that this environment played a significant part in
determining the nature of the knowledge that emerged during this period
of rapid change. This study will reinterpret the emergence of physiology
in post-Revolutionary France in the light of Michel Foucault's *Discipline and Punish* (1977). In doing so, I hope to indicate that the relationship between educational practices and scientific knowledge may be far
more intimate than previous historical studies have suggested.

There is no shortage of commentaries on Foucault's later genealogical work but there is a shortage of studies that actually apply this
work.[4] One of the main reasons for this state of affairs is the absence of
a comprehensive, programmatic statement of what the genealogical
approach involves. The latter must therefore be pieced together by
combining Foucault's scattered theoretical pronouncements with his
genealogical studies of the prison and sexuality.[5] Is this task worth the
effort? Yes, because it reveals an approach that challenges traditional
interpretations of modernity and, in doing so, provides the basis for a
radically different interpretation. As Charles Lemert and Garth Gillan
point out, it is an approach that casts a critical light on

those disciplines, born at the same time as the industrialization of
Europe, which functioned behind their enlightened, reformist

exteriors to control human behaviour: penology, psychology, clinical medicine, the sciences of life.

(Lemert 1982)

It is also an approach that calls into question the causal role which many historians ascribe to wider socio-economic developments or the conscious manipulations of the 'great men' of history. Instead, it shifts historians' attention to the specific discursive and non-discursive practices that had a direct impact on the lives of 'ordinary' individuals, practices like the disciplinary 'techniques' and 'instruments' that operated in prisons, schools, factories, and which – according to Foucault – provided the conditions of emergence and existence of both the disciplined subject and the wider disciplinary society.[6]

Foucault's main aim in *Discipline and Punish* was to reveal the way in which social control is brought about in modern western societies. He argued that since the end of the eighteenth century social order has been maintained not by overt sovereign or legal power, but by far more subtle forms of disciplinary power. This change was brought about by the deployment of four main disciplinary techniques: the division and distribution of bodies in space, the division of time – and therefore activity – into periods, the detailed control of activity, and the creation of tactical networks for the efficient deployment of bodies and activities. Hence his comment that

[t]he meticulousness of the regulations, the fussiness of the inspections, the supervision of the smallest fragment of life and of the body will soon provide, in the context of the school, the barracks, the hospital or the workshop, a laicized content, an economic or technical rationality for this mystical calculus of the infinitesimal and the infinite.

(Foucault 1977)[7]

Most of these techniques of disciplinary power emerged well before the appearance of modern disciplinary institutions – prisons, asylums, and schools – at the end of the eighteenth century. Many of them had been long-established practices in monasteries, armies, and workshops. In fact, Foucault argued that a necessary precondition for the appearance of modern disciplinary institutions was the gradual dissemination of disciplinary techniques from marginal institutions during the seventeenth and eighteenth centuries.

An important feature of *Discipline and Punish* is the way in which it helps to clarify Foucault's previous comments on the relationship between power and knowledge. He had always been highly critical of those epistemologies which presented knowledge – or at least certain branches of it – as the product of unbounded reason. He argued that such epistemologies help to ensure our continued domination because they create the illusion that knowledge exists separately from power. In contrast to this, Foucault maintained that an inextricable link exists between the two:

> [P]ower and knowledge directly imply one another... there is no power relation without the correlative constitution of a field of knowledge, nor any knowledge that does not presuppose and constitute at the same time power relations. These 'power-knowledge relations' are to be analyzed, therefore, not on the basis of a subject of knowledge who is or is not free in relation to the power system, but, on the contrary, the subject who knows, the objects to be known and the modalities of knowledge must be regarded as so many effects of these fundamental implications of power-knowledge and their historical transformations.
>
> (Foucault 1977)[8]

Foucault's reference to 'the subject who knows' raises another important feature of *Discipline and Punish*, that is, the status of the individual within modern western culture. Although individualism has been a characteristic feature of western culture since the time of the ancient Greeks, it is only in the last two centuries that it has come to dominate all aspects and all sections of that culture. The emergence of this modern emphasis on the individual is traditionally presented as a progressive development. It is taken to be a sign of the gradual liberation of the individual from communal practices and beliefs, a liberation that allowed individuals to be 'themselves'. But Foucault's genealogy of western culture calls this traditional 'liberal' interpretation into question. In the same way that Nietzsche attempted to demonstrate the 'ignoble' origins of modern western morality, so Foucault attempted to demonstrate the ignoble origins of the modern individual. Thus he presented the latter not as a sign of increasing autonomy, but as a sign that one form of social control had been transformed into another.

As indicated above, Foucault believed that these historical transformations were the result of the dissemination of certain discursive and non-discursive practices. In *Discipline and Punish* he concentrated on the role that the modern prison system played in the dissemination of modern disciplinary practices. This tends to give the impression that penal practices occupied a privileged position with regard to the emergence of the modern field of power-knowledge. But out of the multitude of practices that are associated with the emergence of modernity, educational practices surely deserve particular attention. They played a central role in the increasing professionalization and bureaucratization of western society and they eventually had a direct impact, via mass education, on all sections of society. There is therefore considerable scope for genealogies of educational practices, that is, historical studies that attempt to demonstrate that modern educational practices provided the conditions of emergence and existence for new forms of knowledge and new modes of power – a new field of power–knowledge.

In this chapter I will begin by discussing certain features of French education in the late eighteenth century. I will then turn my attention to physiology during this same period, particularly as presented in a recent study by John Pickstone. Having outlined various sociological interpretations of the emergence of physiology, I will attempt to show the potential for a genealogical interpretation, one that pivots around the role that new educational practices may have played in the emergence of physiological knowledge.

THE EDUCATIONAL CONTEXT

During the eighteenth century France probably had a greater range of educational institutions, ranging from 'little schools' to universities, than any other European country. But these institutions were badly distributed and lacked any central co-ordination. This led to considerable variation both in the educational provision available in different parts of the country and in the standard of instruction offered – and the level of attainment expected – in similar institutions. Given this situation, there were two key developments in French education during the late eighteenth century. The first was the gradual move towards a national education system. As early as 1763, Louis-René de Caradeuc de La Chalotais had published his influential *Essay on National Education*. Although this was largely a powerful critique of clerical control of French education, it also contained positive suggestions, many of which were to be repeated by later reformers. Thus in 1768 Rolland d'Erceville presented a report on education to the Parlement of Paris. This called for the setting up of a national education system based on educational districts, each of which was centred around a university. The universities would be responsible for assisting and inspecting the colleges within their respective district. The colleges, in their turn, would assist and inspect the elementary schools within their area. Many other examples could be given of pre-Revolutionary education reports that advocated the establishment of a national education system. As R.R. Palmer (1985) comments:

> Everything seemed to tend, whether coming from royal officials, parlements, the church, the universities, *philosophes*, Physiocrats, or individually inspired reformers, in the direction of a centralisation and indeed bureaucratisation of the education system.

The second key development was the increasing use of the examination. It is important to note that although this practice is central to the operation of modern education systems, it only achieved this position during the course of the nineteenth century. Throughout most of the history of western education, the examination was only of peripheral importance. From the late eighteenth century onwards, however, its role was gradually extended. According to Keith Hoskin (1982):

> The examination is transformed; from being the final proof of competence at the end of one's apprenticeship in knowledge, it becomes a constant observing presence in educational practice, a regular means of testing performance and keeping students 'up to the mark'.

Although this transformation was apparent in existing educational institutions, it was particularly striking in the new institutions which were established during the second half of the eighteenth century.

In the light of the developments outlined above it is worth noting three government initiatives which date from the pre-Revolutionary period. During the 1750s the government established the *Ecole Militaire*, together with 11 'feeder' *écoles militaires*, for boys between the ages of 11 and 15. In order to ensure uniformity between these colleges they were all required to use the same textbooks and set the same exams. The latter were used not only to rank the students – and hence determine which branch of the service each would be sent to – but also to assess the performance of the teachers. The second initiative was the establishment of the *agregation* at the Louis-le-Grand in 1766. The original purpose of this course was to train teachers. Places were filled by competitive examination and in 1767 it was decided that students must pass an examination at the end of their second year before being allowed to complete the course. According to R.R. Palmer, the *agregation* represented a highly significant step in both the nationalization of education and the professionalization of teachers (Palmer 1985). The third government initiative was the establishment of the *Ecole Polytechnique* in Paris in 1794. This was essentially a preparatory school for the newly reorganized *écoles d'application*. The latter then prepared students for the main branches of public service – the Bridges and Roads Service, Military Engineering, the Mining Service, and so on (Bradley 1975). Selection for the *Ecole Polytechnique* was based on competitive examinations and graduation depended on the outcome of a final examination. Its fame is based on the fact that it was the first educational institution to have purpose-built research laboratories and to teach science for its own sake, rather than as an adjunct to another subject. It is less well known that it was one of the first educational institutions to introduce a quantitative marking system for its examinations.

From the examples given above it is clear that the practice of the examination was beginning to occupy a central place in many key areas of secondary and higher education. But what about the medical faculties of the universities? It was here that the majority of those who went on to study physiology received their higher education. During most of the eighteenth century there were 22 faculties of medicine, the most important being those at Paris, Strasbourg, Montpellier, Reims, and Toulouse. The education offered within these faculties was far from rigorous; neither teachers nor students took the formal instruction or the final examination very seriously (Palmer 1985). Although regular examinations before, during, and after a course had been introduced into some Jesuit colleges during the late sixteenth century, it was only in the late eighteenth century that this practice became a standard feature of medical education. Up until that time medical students only had to demonstrate their knowledge when they presented themselves for a degree at the end of their course. Even this final examination was often regarded as a formality. Examiners usually limited their questions to topics which the candidate had previously specified. They also prompted candidates during orals and ignored the fact that theses had often been written – for a suitable fee – by the students' teachers. In fact it was not until 1760 that the authorities at Montpellier decided it might be a good idea to actually fail some of the medical candidates in order to maintain standards (Brockliss 1987). This move towards more rigorous assessment was reinforced immediately after the Revolution when the *cahiers* of 1789 complained about the state of medical education and called for the systematic use of rigorous examinations.

Between 1789 and 1791 approximately 60 plans for the reform of education were published, almost all of which assumed the need for a national, state-controlled system arranged in a hierarchy with three, four, or five levels. During this same period the Assembly was creating an administrative hierarchy consisting of communes, cantons, districts, and 83 departments, and was reorganizing all public bodies so that they fitted within the boundaries of these administrative units. It was against this background that Talleyrand delivered his famous report on education to the Constituent Assembly in September 1791. Before dealing with this report, however, it is important to note a key feature of post-Revolutionary thought. During the Enlightenment the human mind was widely regarded as a *tabula rasa* which was 'written on' by the environment in which the individual was raised. Hence everyone was born equal and any differences in intellect were due to the different circumstances into which individuals were born. According to Palmer, this 'pervasive environmentalism' led to considerable interest in education, 'in a general atmosphere of expectation for the improvement of society' (Palmer 1985). But, as Frank Manuel points out, one of the 'crucial developments' in modern western thought was the

> reversal from the eighteenth century view of men as more or less equal, or at least similar, in nature and hence in rights, to the early nineteenth century emphasis upon human uniqueness, diversity, dissimilarity, culminating in theories of inequality and organicism.
>
> (Manuel 1972)

This reversal was clearly apparent in Talleyrand's report on education, which was based in part on information submitted by Lavoisier, Laplace, and Condorcet. Here Talleyrand drew an analogy between a well-organized state and a 'vast workshop'. Implicit in this analogy was the view that different individuals were born with different faculties. Far from treating everyone as if they were born equal, the education system should encourage the development of these differences. The end result would be individuals with a variety of different talents who could then be allocated a suitable place within the national workshop. For it 'is not enough that all should work in it; each must be in his place'. Given this analysis it comes as no surprise that Talleyrand called for the establishment of a national education system and for the more widespread use of rigorous examinations. If the 'vast workshop' was to be provided with a suitable labour force, then a national education system was essential; if the place of each individual within this workshop was to be determined, then their innate faculties and nurtured talents had to be accurately assessed.

Talleyrand's report made fully explicit some of the main trends in eighteenth-century French education. In doing so, it is generally regarded as having set the agenda for the education system that emerged in France during the first half of the nineteenth century. From Talleyrand's report onwards it became increasingly clear that any intention of achieving equality via a national education system had been superseded by the need to train an educated elite. As Maurice Crosland comments, 'The Revolution had replaced an aristocracy of birth by an aristocracy of achievement' (Crosland 1975). It was surely no coincidence that an unprecedented reorganization and expansion of public administration took place during the period of the Directory government (1795–99), leading to the creation of a finely divided and highly specialized bureaucracy.[9] This growth of bureaucracy was closely associated with professionalization. The medical profession was a particularly good example, as doctors increasingly came to receive both their training and their certification within the state education system. These changes were carried even further under Napoleon. The national examination system which was established in 1808 gave the state a monopoly in awarding degrees and allowed it to control access to the professions. According to Robert Gilpin these examinations 'were a logical part of the Napoleonic education system, a system whose purpose was to train a relatively small and highly qualified elite to govern and manage France' (Gilpin 1968).

THE EMERGENCE OF PHYSIOLOGY

Physiology comes from the Greek word for nature (*physis*) and was traditionally taken to mean 'the study of nature'. It was only in the late eighteenth century that it took on its modern meaning of 'the study of the functioning of living things'. As John E. Lesch points out, it was developments taking place in France that largely brought about this change in definition:

> Between 1790 and 1821 physiology in France achieved self-definition as a science, a degree of autonomy from medicine, and an official recognition from the scientific world – and these to an extent that existed nowhere else.
>
> (Lesch 1984)

During this period those who studied and wrote about physiology were overwhelmingly physicians and surgeons. Their primary aim was to achieve a complete understanding of the organization of the human body, that is, the way in which it co-ordinates the activities of its differentiated parts. It is therefore important to note the high prestige of the medical profession throughout this post-Revolutionary period. According to John Pickstone, this prestige went well beyond the status routinely accorded to individuals with exceptional talents.

> The medical profession and education were very important not only for the government's programme of reform but for its legitimation. The basis of contemporary political and social theory was the naturalistic account of man which the 'ideologues' and especially the philosopher physician Cabanis were providing. This science of man incorporated experimental physiology and medicine on the one side, as it reached out to psychology and the social sciences on the other.
>
> (Pickstone 1981)

It was therefore no coincidence that within a few years of Talleyrand's report on the need for specialist education, a group of medical men who had risen to prominence under the Directorate announced two new areas of human inequality – physiological and psychological differences. Cabanis, in particular, emphasized differences in physiology and behaviour between one time of life and another, between individuals living in different climates, and between individuals with different temperaments. This did not constitute a decisive break with egalitarian ideals because Cabanis' ultimate aim was to bring about an elimination of these differences. He believed that developments in physiology would eventually lead to an all-embracing theory of man that would provide the basis for human perfection. None the less, an emphasis on the individual and individual differences soon came to dominate a wide spectrum of medical discourses.

The most important physiologist during the period of the Directory government was undoubtedly Xavier Bichat.[10] He began his short but highly productive career at the age of 22 when he became the favoured student of Pierre Dessault at the Hôtel-Dieu. Dessault was one of the leading surgeons of the period and was also responsible for a number of innovations in the teaching of surgery – including his use of oral examinations, every ten days, in order to test his students on the material taught in the preceding ten days (Lesch 1984). Although Bichat was influenced by others, he spent most of his time carrying out dissections, hence his comment: 'I went so fast because I read so little. Books are memorials of facts. Is there a need for them in a science where the materials are ever at hand? I used the living books, the sick and the dead' (quoted in Hall 1969). Two major assumptions guided Bichat's work on the relationship between structure and function in the human body. The first was his belief that life consists of an ensemble of functions that resist death. His second assumption was that the body could be analysed into individual elements – the tissues – which combine to form the organs. He referred to the study of these tissues as 'general anatomy' and argued that it was at this level that any attempt to account for both the vital properties of organs and the symptoms of disease should begin. For it was individual tissues that provided the basis for life, the functions that organs carried out depending on the combination of tissues they contained. Thus the functions that maintained life were dependent on a complex, hierarchical division of labour involving tissues, organs, and organ systems.

Bichat's work on the organization of the human body led him to divide humans into three physiological types, according to whether the motor, sensory, or intellectual function was dominant – it being extremely rare for one individual to develop all three faculties equally. Manuel argues that this had major implications for post-Revolutionary society:

Cabanis had still concentrated upon the flexibility and easy educability of any human trait through laws and medicine; Bichat's iron law of physiology dictated that only one of the major capacities should be trained. . . .Perfectibility lay not in an identical Spartan education for all men, but in the stimulation of uniqueness, in specialization. This led to the conception of an organic society based upon differentiated functions.

(Manuel 1972)

Pickstone goes further than Manuel and argues that even Bichat's basic work on general anatomy had a socio-political dimension. He claims that 'the physiology taught by Bichat reproduced many of the organizational principles manifest in the political theory and practice of post-Revolutionary France', that is, it 'represented a kind of bureaucratic corporatism' (Pickstone 1981). He goes on to draw direct parallels between Bichat's physiology and the socio-political organization of France under the Directory government. For example, both Bichat's physiology and Directory bureaucracy involved parallel functional systems that were hierarchically ordered and subject to some degree of central co-ordination. This arrangement led to the same ambiguity with regard to local autonomy, in both physiology and government 'local autonomy was really little more than the local representation of national executive systems' (*ibid.*).[11] Pickstone defends his thesis by pointing to the close relationship between professional and intellectual groups on the one hand and the Directory government on the other. These groups tended to see themselves as 'architects of a new order, in which their own concerns were paradigmatic for society as a whole' (*ibid.*).

Does the existence of this homology between Bichat's physiology and the organizational principles of post-Revolutionary France demonstrate that Bichat's work was ultimately the product of his socio-political context? Before attempting to answer this question, it is instructive to note that there was at least one contemporary of Bichat's who realized – in both senses of this word – the wider implications of his work. This was Saint-Simon, whose social theory was strongly influenced by both Cabanis and Bichat. In common with the philosophers of the Revolution, Saint-Simon believed that the ideal society should be based on natural man. But, as Manuel point out:

From a cursory reading of the physiologists. . . Saint-Simon came away with a different version of the natural: the natural was inequality. . . . Confirmed in the belief that physiology was the only sound foundation upon which to construct a social theory, after numerous experiments with variant schemata of social classification in the final phase of his thinking he devised a plan that was a direct adaptation of the Bichat typology.

(Manuel 1972)

The name that Saint-Simon gave to his social theory – 'social physiology' – renders this ancestry totally transparent. But even without such a name the influence of Bichat is obvious. Saint-Simon identified three social functions – economic, artistic, and rational – that were carried out by three social classes – industrial, artistic, and scientific. These three classes can be read off directly from Bichat's three physiological types – motor, sensory, and intellectual. In addition, Saint-Simon's ideal society consisted of a harmonious association of different individuals, all of whom co-operated to ensure the efficient functioning of the whole society. This meant that he placed little emphasis on individual autonomy and great emphasis on the special attributes of individuals and their role in the overall functioning of society. It is also highly significant that the term *organisation* played a key role in Saint-Simon's social theory. In fact, it is around this time – from the second decade of the nineteenth century onwards – that this term began to shift from biological to common usage (Haines 1978).

The fact that Saint-Simon's social theory is 'in line' with the post-Revolutionary ideal of a rational bureaucracy gives Pickstone cause to doubt the existence of a simple causal link between Bichat and Saint-Simon:

> Commentators who see Bichat simply as a source for Saint-Simon will perhaps not need to reflect on the possibility of a political source for Bichat.... But if we take seriously what the history of biology seems to proclaim... then we must be prepared to recognize reflection of the cultural situations of the observers in the accounts they produced of the animal body.... Saint-Simon would not have used Bichat had he not found there a description of functional systems that corresponded to the pre-existent outlines of his own politics. It is more reasonable to view the suitability of Bichat for Saint-Simon as arising from their common background than to see it as fortuitous; the resemblances are too extensive to be explained by chance.
>
> (Pickstone 1981)

This raises once again the question of the relationship between post-Revolutionary physiology and its wider socio-political context.

ATTEMPTS AT A SOCIOLOGICAL INTERPRETATION

It seems clear that a homology – or, perhaps more correctly, a series of homologies – existed between French physiology and post-Revolutionary society. Although this suggests that certain links existed between biological knowledge and its socio-political context, it does not in itself indicate the nature of these links. Was it simply a case of physiology influencing the ideas of social theorists and statesmen? Did the socio-political ideas that prevailed at the time influence the work of physiologists? Were the discourses of physiologists, social theorists, and statesmen determined by a more fundamental influence which was common to them all?

What explanations do contemporary historical studies advance when faced with homologies between scientific knowledge and its wider socio-political context? The first point to note is that many of these studies make no attempt to offer an explanation. This leads Stephen Shapin to admit that social histories of science are 'often thought to be completed when it can be concluded that science is not autonomous, or that science is an integral part of culture' (Shapin 1982). But there are an increasing number of studies which do attempt to go beyond such broad generalizations, studies that present various sociological interpretations of the emergence of scientific knowledge. There are, for example, several accounts of nineteenth-century biology that are written from a neo-Marxist perspective. Of particular relevance to the present study is Roger Cooter's paper on the popularization of physiology in early nineteenth-century Britain (Cooter 1979). Here Cooter argues that the dissemination of physiological knowledge played an important role in 'naturalizing' the emerging industrial order:

> While urbanism and industrial capitalism were fragmenting an older social unity (or impression of unity) and replacing it with the more independent alienated structures of modern society, physiology was presenting holistic images of cohesive parts in dynamic interaction. . . . Regularity yet change, order yet progress; this was the service of the organismic metaphor.

Cooter claims that artisans – the main group to be influenced by this physiological rhetoric – failed to perceive the 'ideological power that Reason had assumed'. Thus, guided by the 'true light of biology', they came to 'evaluate life not in terms of their mutual exploitation and social exclusion, but in terms of their individual adjustment to inherently bourgeois values' (*ibid.*). He also claims that those individuals who were responsible for popularising physiology – most of whom had a medical background – were also unaware of the ideological role of the organismic metaphor.

One of the most common approaches that contemporary social historians advance to account for homologies between science and the wider society concentrates on the scientist's perceptions of his/her wider social interests. This 'anthropological' approach is based on the assumption that the scientist is, in Shapin's words, 'an active, calculating actor whose intellectual products are crafted to further the variety of his interests'. Such an approach is clearly apparent in L.S. Jacyna's study of the 'cultural relations' of French physiology during the early nineteenth century. Here Jacyna argues that 'physiologists' had a vested interest in the extension of physiology into the sphere of ethics and social policy

(Jacyna 1987). For if physiology had this comprehensive importance, then 'its practitioners were qualified to form a new priesthood in society' with 'wide-ranging powers in the fields of the regulation of personal conduct and public policy'. This leads Jacyna to conclude that 'physiology *qua* science of man' was 'an ideology that answered the interests of a professional group' (*ibid.*). Although this conclusion suggests considerable overlap between Jacyna's and Cooter's interpretations, the differences between the two are, in fact, considerable. In particular, where Jacyna emphasizes the importance of the conscious perceptions of individual scientists – albeit members of a larger scientific community – Cooter emphasizes the subconscious influence of large-scale socio-economic developments.

What interpretation does Pickstone provide in his study of post-Revolutionary French physiology? In the main body of his paper, he places considerable emphasis on developments in education and suggests that the Paris School of Medicine acted as an important link between physiology and its socio-political context. He argues that the knowledge that was formulated within the Paris School of Medicine – particularly Bichat's physiology – played a major role in legitimating the emerging bureaucratic order while, at the same time, the formulation of this knowledge was itself influenced by the prevailing socio-political conditions.

> Bichat's physiology was created and was popular within a highly structured, bureaucratic medical school, itself part of the new executive apparatus of the Directory. In this sunset of the Enlightenment, scientific rationalism finally attained political influence, and was embodied in a series of parallel administrative, educational and military systems, extending and rationalizing the bureaucracy of the *ancien régime*. Bichat's physiology was linked to this context both through the formal organization of medical teaching and through the contemporary 'science of man' in which 'ideology' was said to be a branch of zoology, and politics a division of medicine.
>
> (Pickstone 1981)

Pickstone goes on to point out that the post-Revolutionary period was an 'exciting time to be a medical man in Paris' because for the first time for nearly 300 years, Paris could claim to be one of the main centres in Europe for medical education. The School of Medicine – founded as the *Ecole de Santé* in 1794 – supported a large and enthusiastic medical community whose primary concern was 'how medical education ought to be structured' (*ibid.*). Bichat was one of the leading figures within this medical community, as a founder member of the *Société Médicale*

91

d'Emulation which was specifically concerned with educational reform.[12]

There was also a national dimension to developments in medical education. During the course of the eighteenth century, increasing concern had been expressed about poor training and standards in medicine. As Pickstone points out, this led to a radical change in French medical training during the period of the Directory government.

> The state educational system would train doctors and grant them diplomas. Pupils would enter, interns would be promoted, and staff would be appointed by means of competitive examinations; some pupils at least, would receive scholarships, and the staff would receive salaries – all very familiar to us now, but unknown in early nineteenth century Britain and novel in France.

But this reform was only part of a total reorganization of the French education system. As a result of this reorganization:

> The syllabus had to be planned, books had to be produced, the various levels of teaching had to be co-ordinated, the teachers had to be taught. While not without precedents in the royal machinery of the *ancien régime*, the design and production of such massive cultural and political equipment gave emphasis to the novel and fashionable notion of *organisation*. In such conditions a professional ideology was inevitable. Expertise was required and popular sentiment could not be relied upon; the system required central direction, a bureaucratic form and highly qualified personnel.

The education system therefore displayed the same emphasis on specialization and bureaucratic organization that Pickstone identifies within other areas of Directory administration and within Bichat's physiology. This leads Pickstone to claim that government, education, and physiology shared a common dependence on certain late eighteenth-century 'linguistic forms and organizing principles'.

TOWARDS A GENEALOGICAL REINTERPRETATION

Recent social histories provide ample evidence of the existence of links between post-Revolutionary physiology and its socio-political context – albeit with considerable disagreement concerning the exact nature of these links. In doing so, they suggest that there is plenty of scope for a genealogy of physiology. But would such a study constitute an original contribution to the history of physiology? Would it yield an interpretation that differed from the sociological interpretations that are currently available? It is fairly clear that genealogy has little in common with the anthropological approach that Jacyna adopts. Foucault would surely have rejected the epistemological primacy which the latter accords the knowing subject – Shapin's 'active, calculating actor'. Although Foucault did not regard individuals as mere pawns of power, he did not believe that they were aware of the broader consequences of their actions. As he commented to Dreyfus, 'People know what they do; they frequently know why they do what they do; but what they don't know is what what they do does' (quoted in Dreyfus 1982). In other words, the tactics involved in the operation of power may involve the conscious subject but the overall strategy of a particular field of power–knowledge relations is ultimately non-subjective.

What about the neo-Marxist approach? A superficial analysis of Foucault's conception of power–knowledge could give the impression that it provides support for a neo-Marxist interpretation of the relations between physiology and the wider society. Viewed from this perspective the emergence of an emphasis on the individual, individual differences, the division of labour, hierarchical control, co-ordination, and so on – together with the associated rise to prominence of certain forms of knowledge such as physiology – take on the appearance of an anonymous political strategy that aimed to naturalize the new industrial order. There are also certain more specific similarities between genealogy and neo-Marxism. For example, they both emphasize the way in which power has increasingly come to operate on the individual and the way in which social control has increasingly become synonymous with self-control. But a number of major problems confront any attempt to equate genealogical and neo-Marxist interpretations. The most significant is Foucault's total rejection of the notion of ideology.

> The notion of ideology appears to me to be difficult to use for three reasons. The first is that, whether one wants it to be or not, it is always in virtual opposition to something like the truth. . . . The second inconvenience is that it refers, necessarily I believe, to something like a subject. Thirdly, ideology is in secondary position in relation to something which must function as the infrastructure or economic or material determinate for it.
>
> (Foucault 1980)

Foucault's first and second objections require no further elaboration, given his long-standing attacks on the notions of 'the truth' and 'the subject'. His third objection concerns the epistemological privilege that Marxists traditionally grant to the power relations established within the prevailing mode of production. When viewed from a genealogical perspective, power cannot be accorded a privileged position in relation to knowledge. Power and knowledge are inextricably linked and neither can be regarded as being in a 'secondary position' in relation to the other. Moreover, Foucault was critical of any approach to history that ascribed a causal role to wider socio-economic developments and that presented specific discursive and non-discursive practices as mere products of these wider developments. He did not deny that this wider dimension existed, but he did deny that it provided the main basis for historical explanation. Thus in *Discipline and Punish* he frequently referred to political, economic, and demographic developments. But his primary concern throughout this work was to identify the specific practices that provided the conditions of emergence and existence of the wider disciplinary society.

If genealogy is incompatible with the belief that knowledge is either the anonymous product of wider socio-economic developments, or the conscious product of the knowing subject, what alternative interpretation can the genealogical approach provide? More specifically, what would a genealogy of physiology involve? It would obviously attempt to identify the complex configuration of discursive and non-discursive practices that provided the conditions of emergence and existence of the post-Revolutionary emphasis on organization. Given the potentially infinite number of practices that existed at this time, where should a genealogy of physiology begin? A possible starting point is provided by Pickstone's analysis of the developments that took place in French education during the post-Revolutionary period. Here Pickstone points out that government, education, and physiology shared a common dependence on certain late eighteenth-century 'linguistic forms and organising principles'. But he also provides grounds for believing that the education system played a major role in the dissemination of these linguistic forms and organizing principles. This is a suggestion that can usefully be developed in terms of Foucault's genealogical approach. For when viewed from a genealogical perspective, Pickstone's study raises the following question. Were the new educational practices dependent on new linguistic forms and organizing principles, or did the new educational practices – particularly the systematic use of the examination – constitute an important part of the conditions of emergence and existence of these new linguistic forms and organizing principles? In other words, were the new educational practices associated with the precipitation of a new field of power– knowledge – whose most characteristic expression can be represented by the term *organisation* and whose most characteristic effects were an increasing emphasis on the individual, individual differences, the division of labour, hierarchical control, co-ordination, and so on? If this was the case, it would help to explain the near-simultaneous emergence of this emphasis in government administration and in physiology. For both administrators and physiologists were increasingly receiving their training under the new educational regime. It would also help to explain why this emphasis emerged in other western countries during the course of the nineteenth century. For although France was one of the first countries to introduce a modern, highly centralized education system, complete with the systematic use of written examinations and quantitative marking, similar systems appeared in most western countries during the course of the nineteenth century.

What evidence is there in Foucault's genealogical work to suggest that educational practices can be associated with the simultaneous precipitation of new knowledges and new powers? It is in *Discipline and Punish* that Foucault made his most explicit references to education. Here he made a number of direct comparisons between the practices that were introduced into various disciplinary institutions during the course of the late eighteenth and early nineteenth centuries. His most detailed references to the effects of educational practices come in his discussion of the three 'instruments' of disciplinary power: hierarchical observation, normalizing judgment, and the examination. Foucault began by pointing out that it was probably the 'humble' nature of these instruments that ensured that disciplinary power was able to invade gradually the traditional procedures of sovereign power. Although he concentrated on the emergence of the prison, he devoted a considerable amount of space in this section to the operation of these instruments within schools. With regard to hierarchical observation he highlighted the architecture of the *Ecole Militaire*, which combined 'sealed compartments between individuals' with 'apertures for continuous surveillance' by officers. He also described some of the systems of supervision that were established during the reorganization of elementary teaching. These involved finely divided divisions of labour, such as that devised by Batencour: 'In order to help the teacher, Batencour selected from among the best pupils a whole series of "officers" – intendants, observers, monitors, tutors, reciters of prayers, writing officers, receivers of ink, almoners and visitors.' Foucault's analysis of these developments led him to the following conclusion.

Hierarchized, continuous and functional surveillance may not be one of the great technical 'inventions' of the eighteenth century, but its insidious extension owed its importance to the mechanisms of power that it brought with it. By means of such surveillance, disciplinary power became an 'integrated' system, linked from the inside to the economy and to the aims of the mechanism in which it was practised.

(Foucault 1977)

95

Hierarchial observation therefore ensured that a system which depended on individuals could be integrated into an efficient, functional whole.

In his discussion of normalizing judgment, Foucault emphasized the role of 'micro-penalities' which cover areas of human behaviour not covered by the legal system.

> The workshop, the school, the army were subject to a whole micro-penality of time (lateness, absences, interruptions of tasks), of activity (inattention, negligence, lack of zeal), of behaviour (impoliteness, disobedience), of speech (idle chatter, insolence), of the body ('incorrect' attitudes, irregular gestures, lack of cleanliness), of sexuality (impurity, indecency).
>
> (*ibid.*)

The basis for such judgment was the 'norm', a notion that made its first overt appearance in early nineteenth-century medical physiology. This notion was central to the introduction of a standardized education system, the organization of a 'national medical profession capable of operating general norms of health', and the 'standardization of industrial processes and products'. By making the slightest deviation from 'normal' behaviour subject to a scale of punishment, the individual was 'caught in a punishable, punishing universality'. In addition to punishments for 'bad' behaviour, there were also rewards for 'good' behaviour. This demonstrates that the ultimate aim of disciplinary power was normalization – not repression. Thus the Christian Schools 'organized a whole micro-economy of privileges and impositions', and in doing so, operated 'a differentiation that is not one of acts, but of individuals themselves, of their nature, their potentialities, their level or their value'. Foucault pointed out that:

> In a sense, the power of normalization imposes homogeneity; but it individualizes by making it possible to measure gaps, to determine levels, to fix specialities and to render the differences useful by fitting them one to another. It is easy to understand how the power of the norm functions within a system of formal equality, since within a homogeneity that is the rule, the norm introduces, as a useful imperative and as a result of measurement, all the shading of individual differences.
>
> (*ibid.*)

This raises the question of how such differences are to be measured. It is here that the third and final instrument of disciplinary power makes its appearance.

Foucault regarded the examination as the most important instrument of disciplinary power because it combines hierarchical observation with normalizing judgment: 'It is a normalizing gaze, a surveillance that makes it possible to qualify, to classify and to punish.' Foucault pointed to the increasing 'organization of the hospital as an "examining" apparatus' and argued that this played a central role in the creation of the 'well-disciplined' hospital – 'the physical counterpart of the medical "discipline"'. He also pointed to the emergence of the school exam-ination, which constituted 'a perpetual comparison of each and all that made it possible both to measure and to judge'. Because of these effects Foucault regarded the examination as the main individualizing technique within the disciplinary mode of power.[13] Of particular significance is the way in which it 'introduces individuality into the field of documentation':

> Thanks to the whole apparatus of writing that accompanied it, the examination opened up two correlative possibilities: firstly, the constitution of the individual as a describable, analysable object . . .and, secondly, the constitution of a comparative system that made possible. . . the calculation of the gaps between individuals, their distribution in a given 'population'.
>
> (*ibid.*)

The examination, with 'all its documentary techniques', turned each individual into a 'case', that is, an individual 'who has to be trained or corrected, classified, normalized, excluded, etc.' This led Foucault to conclude that

> the examination is at the centre of the procedures that constitute the individual as effect and object of power, as effect and object of knowledge. It is the examination which. . . assures the great disciplinary functions of distribution and classification, maximum extraction of forces and time, continuous genetic accumulation, optimum combination of aptitudes and, thereby, the fabrication of cellular, organic, genetic and combinatory individuality. With it are ritualized those disciplines that may be characterized in a word by saying that they are a modality of power for which individual difference is relevant.
>
> (*ibid.*)

Thus Foucault returned once again to individual differences – and to the use of biological terminology to described such differences.

Foucault's descriptions of hierarchical surveillance, normalizing judgment, and the examination make it clear that they provided the conditions of emergence of new modes of power. There are also striking similarities between Foucault's account of the effects of these disciplinary instruments and the descriptions that Manuel and Pickstone provide of the socio-political organization of post-Revolutionary France. In particular, all three point to the increasing emphasis, from the late eighteenth century onwards, on the individual and on various forms of social organization which depended on the classification of the individual. But if these disciplinary instruments constituted the conditions of emergence of new modes of power, what arguments did Foucault present to suggest that they constituted the conditions of emergence of forms of knowledge? Although he provided frequent hints that knowledge is intimately associated with the operation of disciplinary power (for example, when he referred to notions like the truth and the norm), it was when dealing with the 'whole apparatus of writing' which accompanied the examination that this issue came to the fore. Here he pointed to the existence of a 'small historical problem' concerning the entry, towards the end of the eighteenth century, of 'the individual (and no longer the species) into the field of knowledge'. He went on to argue that:

> To this simple question of fact, one must no doubt give an answer lacking in 'nobility': one should look into these procedures of writing and registration, one should look into the mechanisms of discipline, and of a new type of power over bodies.
>
> (Foucault 1977)

In other words, the new 'procedures of writing and registration', many of which were closely associated with the new practice of the examination, played a key role in the emergence of the individual as both subject of knowledge and object of power. This documentation of the lives of 'ordinary' people was in marked contrast to the situation prior to the eighteenth century when only the lives of the noble and celebrated were chronicled. But, according to Foucault, the 'carefully collated life' of mental patients, delinquents, and schoolchildren 'belongs, as did the chronicles of kings or the adventures of the great popular bandits, to a certain political function of writing; but in a quite different technique of power' (*ibid.*). This led him to pose the following question:

> Is this the birth of the sciences of man? It is probably to be found in these 'ignoble' archives, where the modern play of coercion over bodies, gestures and behaviour has its beginnings.
>
> (*ibid.*)

Thus the human sciences – particularly clinical medicine, psychiatry, psychology, criminology, and penology – were inextricably linked to a new form of writing whose prime purpose was the detailed documentation of the lives of ordinary individuals. But why did Foucault regard this form of documentation as 'ignoble'? He argued that it allowed the human sciences to replace traditional legal principles with principles of physical, psychological, and moral normality. This ensured that the population could be divided into distinct categories – a process that was central to the effective deployment of other disciplinary techniques. The human sciences therefore played an important part in the creation of disciplined subjects, that is, individuals who conformed to certain standards of sanity, health, docility, competence, and so on.

It was in his discussion of the human sciences, outlined above, that Foucault's analysis of the relationship between power and knowledge became most explicit. But although his genealogical studies contain frequent references to the human sciences, his references to the natural sciences are few and far between. Does this indicate that the latter occupy an epistemological 'space' which is independent of power–knowledge relationships? Nowhere in Foucault's theoretical pronouncements does he indicate that this is the case; neither does he hasten to deny it. Why, then, did Foucault neglect the natural sciences in his later work? In an interview he gave the following answer:

> If we pose to a science like theoretical physics or organic chemistry the problem of its relations with political and economic structures of the society, haven't we posed a question which is too difficult?... If, on the other hand, we take a science like psychiatry, wouldn't the possibility of answering the question of its relation to society be much easier to pose?... Isn't it the case that in as dubious a science as psychiatry one could seize with more certainty the intertwining of the effects of knowledge and power?
>
> (Foucault 1980)

There is a suspension of judgment here that none the less leaves a major gap in his genealogical work. It also raises the possibility that it may be in the nature of genealogical analysis that it is unable to confront the natural sciences. If this is the case, Foucault's genealogy of western culture faces a major problem. If the natural sciences cannot be shown to function as power–knowledge practices – and not just as knowledge practices – then his conception of power–knowledge will be seriously weakened. Having said this, the present study would seem to suggest otherwise. It provides ample evidence that the emergence of physiology – one of the key areas of modern biology – was inextricably linked to its wider socio-political context. It also raises the following question. If disciplinary practices were so all-pervasive in their effects, and if they were able to provide the conditions of emergence and existence of the human sciences, could they not also have provided the conditions of emergence and existence of new discourses within the natural sciences – particularly within biology, which has such close links with the human sciences? Far more work is necessary before a definitive answer can be given, but the present study indicates that educational practices may provide a rewarding point of departure. What comes into view is a way of seeing the emergence of new discourses in the natural sciences not as transformations in pure knowledge relations, but as transformations in power–knowledge relations.

CONCLUSION

In summary, Foucault's conception of power–knowledge implies that all forms of knowledge have a political dimension which cannot be adequately conceptualized by privileging either wider socio-economic developments or the conscious intentions of the knowing subject. Instead, the historian must concentrate on the specific practices that provided the conditions for the simultaneous emergence of new forms of knowledge and new modes of power – new fields of power– knowledge. With regard to the history of biology, there would seem to be considerable scope for a genealogical analysis of the emergence of the nineteenth-century emphasis on internal organization and physiology. Such an analysis would concentrate on the specific practices that constituted the conditions of emergence and existence of this new biological discourse and it would have to demonstrate that these practices also provided the conditions of emergence and existence of new modes of power. There is considerable evidence to suggest that the new educational practices that emerged towards the end of the eighteenth century could provide a useful point of departure for this genealogy of physiology. Here it is interesting to note a comparison which Hoskin makes in a paper on 'Examinations and the schooling of science':

> In the same way that Karl Figlio has suggested that certain areas of scientific discourse in the early nineteenth century pivot round the metaphor of organization, I would suggest that nineteenth-century discourse on science education pivots round the concept of the examination.

> (Hoskin 1982)

Within the present context there would appear to be more to this comparison than meets the eye. For there is considerable scope for a genealogical analysis of the relations between 'the metaphor of organization' and the practice of the examination – an analysis that may reveal the existence of unexpected links between educational practices and scientific knowledge.

NOTES

1   See, for example, the entry on 'Life' in the *Dictionary of the History of Science* (1981) which states:

Although the nature of living things has concerned natural philosophers since Antiquity, "life" as a general concept emerged in the 1800s. Its emergence coincided with the introduction of biology as a new scientific field and with the growing conviction that the essential nature of animals and plants was the same, lying in their organization rather than in their visible structure (Bynum 1981).

It is interesting to note that this entry may well have been influenced, albeit indirectly, by Foucault's account of the emergence of biology in *The Order of Things* (1970). After all, no historian prior to 1966 – the publication date of the original French edition – presented this conceptual change in quite such explicit terms. Unfortunately, Foucault failed to 'return' to the natural sciences in his later work. This has left a serious gap in his genealogy of modern western culture, a gap which the present study attempts to address.

2   See, for example, L.W.B. Brockliss' study of *French Higher Education in the Seventeenth and Eighteenth Centuries* (1987). Here he states that 'the impressive record of French mathematics, physics, and medicine in the Revolutionary epoch would have been quite impossible without the educational facilities that the colleges and faculties offered the aspiring scientist in the last decades of the *ancien régime*.'

3   See, for example, Maurice Crosland's study of 'The development of a professional career in science in France', in Crosland (1975).

4   Major commentaries on Foucault include Mark Cousins and Athar Hussain's *Michel Foucault* (1984) (a book-by-book critical commentary); Hubert L. Dreyfus and Paul Rabinow's, *Michel Foucault: Beyond Structuralism and Hermeneutics* (1982) (particularly good for locating Foucault's philosophical position); Charles D. Lemert and Garth Gillan's *Michel Foucault: Social Theory and Transgression* (1982) (one of the few commentaries to deal in detail with Foucault's historiographical 'space'); Pamela Major-Poetzl's *Michel Foucault's Archaeology of Western Culture* (1983) (concentrates on Foucault's early work, but has an excellent collection of references); J.G. Merquior's *Foucault* (1985) (sets out to do a 'hatchet-job' on Foucault); Mark Poster's *Foucault, Marxism and History* (1984) (a neo-Marxist commentary that contains a number of interesting insights); Alan Sheridan's *Michel Foucault: The Will To Truth* (1980) (very readable, but rather uncritical for a major study); and Barry Smart's *Foucault* (1985) (useful on Foucault's relevance to social sciences).

5   Despite the difficulties that Foucault's work poses for those who want to use it, it continues to be cited in a wide range of disciplines. In fact, by the late 1970s Foucault was one of the 25 most cited twentieth-century arts and humanities authors – more frequently cited than well-known figures like Carl Jung, Jean Piaget, Bertrand Russell, and Max Weber (Megill 1987).

6   This emphasis on specific practices has been highlighted by several commentators. Thus Dreyfus and Rabinow conclude that: 'We have no recourse to objective laws, no recourse to pure subjectivity, no recourse to totalizations of theory. We have only the cultural practices which have made us what we are' (Dreyfus and Rabinow 1982).

7   Foucault's analysis of the association between reason and domination has been linked by some commentators to Weber's work on 'instrumental

rationality'. See, for example, John O'Neill's study of 'The disciplinary society: from Weber to Foucault' (1986). For some brief comments by Foucault on the significance of Weber and the Frankfurt School, see 'Structuralism and post-structuralism: an interview with Michel Foucault' (Foucault 1983).

8 Hence Foucault's claim that 'Truth is a thing of this world: it is produced only by virtue of multiple forms of constraint. And it induces regular effects of power' (Foucault 1980).

9 The Directory (1795–99) was the first regime to be established after the execution of Robespierre and it was eventually replaced by Napoleon's Consulate. It gets its name from the five Directors, each of whom had his own bureaucratic domain. For further details see Martyn Lyon's study of *France under the Directory* (1975).

10 No book-length studies of Bichat are available, but he is dealt with in some detail in W.R. Albury's 'Experiment and explanation in the physiology of Bichat and Magendie' (1977); John V. Pickstone's 'Bureaucracy, liberalism and the body in post-Revolutionary France: Bichat's physiology and the Paris School of Medicine' (1981); and John E. Lesch's *Science and Medicine in France: The Emergence of Experimental Physiology, 1970–1855* (1984). For Bichat's significance for the history of medicine, see Foucault's *The Birth of the Clinic* (1973).

11 For a much more detailed presentation of these parallels, see Pickstone's study (Pickstone 1981).

12 Another individual who played a major role in introducing the notion of organization into the study of living things – George Cuvier – was even more closely associated with educational reform than Bichat. Cuvier was the leading naturalist of the period and, in *The Order of Things* (1970), Foucault credits him with a key role in the emergence of biology. It is therefore interesting to note that he was appointed an inspector-general of education by Napoleon and was given the task of establishing the *lycées*, or higher schools, in the chief cities of the south of France. In 1809 and 1810 he organized the educational system of the Italian provinces and went on to become a leading member of the Council of State, (Gillispie 1960).

13 In the introduction to the section on the examination, Foucault wrote:

It is yet another innovation of the classical age that the historians of science have left unexplored. People write the history of experiments on those born blind, on wolf children or under hypnosis. But who will write the more general, more fluid, but also more determinant history of the 'examination' – its rituals, its methods, its characters and their roles, its play of questions and answers, its system of marking and classification? For in this slender technique are to be found a whole domain of knowledge, a whole type of power.

(Foucault 1977)

In fact, Keith Hoskin has begun to analyse the new fields of power–knowledge associated with the emergence of the school examination (e.g., Hoskin 1982 and 1986). He highlights a major shift, beginning in the late eighteenth century, from oral to written examinations, placing particular emphasis on the associated emergence of quantitative marking systems.

REFERENCES

Albury, W.R. (1977) 'Experiment and explanation in the physiology of Bichat and Magendie', in W. Coleman (ed.) *Studies in the History of Biology 1*, Baltimore: Johns Hopkins University Press, pp. 47–131.

Barnard, H.C. (1969) *Education and the French Revolution*, Cambridge: Cambridge University Press.

Bradley, Margaret (1975) 'Scientific education versus military training: the influence of Napoleon Bonaparte on the *Ecole Polytechnique*', *Annals of Science* 32: 415–49.

Brockliss, L.W.B. (1987) *French Higher Education in the Seventeenth and Eighteenth Centuries*, Oxford: Clarendon Press.

Bynum, W.F. (1981) *Dictionary of the History of Science*, London: Macmillan.

Cooter, Roger (1979) 'The power of the body: the early nineteenth century', in Barry Barnes (ed.) *Natural Order: Historical Studies of Scientific Culture*, Beverley Hills/London: Sage Publications.

Cousins, Mark and Hussain, A. (1984) *Michel Foucault*, London: Macmillan.

Crosland, Maurice (1975) 'The development of a professional career in science in France', in M. Crosland (ed.) *The Emergence of Science in Western Europe*, London: Macmillan.

Dreyfus, Hubert L. and Rabinow, P. (1982) *Michel Foucault: Beyond Structuralism and Hermeneutics*, Brighton: Harvester.

Foucault, Michel (1970) *The Order of Things*, London: Tavistock.

———(1973) *The Birth of the Clinic*, London: Tavistock.

———(1977) *Discipline and Punish*, London: Allen Lane.

———(1980) 'Truth and power', in Colin Gordon (ed.) *Power/Knowledge: Selected Interviews and Other Writings 1972–1977 by Michel Foucault*, Brighton: Harvester.

———(1983) 'Structuralism and post-structuralism: an interview with Michel Foucault', *Telos* 55: 195–211.

Gillispie, C.C. (1960) *The Edge of Objectivity: An Essay in the History of Scientific Ideas*, Princeton: Princeton University Press.

——— (1980) *Science and Polity in France at the End of the Old Regime*, Princeton: Princeton University Press.

Gilpin, Robert (1968) *France in the Age of the Scientific State*, Princeton: Princeton University Press.

Haines, Barbara (1978) 'The inter-relations between social, biological and medical thought, 1750–1850: Saint-Simon and Comte', *The British Journal for the History of Science* 11: 19–35.

Hall, T.S. (1969) *Ideas of Life and Matter*, vols. 1–2, Chicago: University of Chicago Press.

Hoskin, Keith (1982) 'Examinations and the schooling of science', in Roy MacLeod (ed.) *Days of Judgement*, Driffield: Nafferton Books.

———(1986) 'Accounting and the examination: a genealogy of disciplinary power', *Accounting, Organizations and Society* 11: 105–36.

Jacyna, L.S. (1987) 'Medical science and moral science: the cultural relations of physiology in Restoration France', *History of Science* 25: 111–46.

Lemert, Charles C. and Gillan, G. (1982) *Michel Foucault: Social Theory and Transgression*, New York: Columbia University Press.

Lesch, John E. (1984) *Science and Medicine in France: The Emergence of Experimental Physiology, 1790–1855*, Cambridge, Mass.: Harvard University Press.

Lyons, Martyn (1975) *France under the Directory*, Cambridge: Cambridge University Press.

Major-Poetzl, Pamela (1983) *Michel Foucault's Archaeology of Western Culture: Towards a New Science of History*, Brighton: Harvester.

Manuel, Frank (1972) 'From equality to organicism', in F. Manuel (ed.) *Freedom from History*, London: University of London Press.

Megill, Allan (1987) 'The reception of Foucault by historians', *Journal of the History of Ideas* 48 (1).

Merquior, J.G. (1985) *Foucault*, London: Fontana.

Merz, John (1965) *A History of European Thought in the Nineteenth Century*, New York: Dover.

O'Neill, John (1986) 'The disciplinary society: from Weber to Foucault', *The British Journal of Sociology* 37: 42–60.

Palmer, R.R. (1985) *The Improvement of Humanity: Education and the French Revolution*, Princeton: Princeton University Press.

Pickstone, John V. (1981) 'Bureaucracy, liberalism and the body in post-revolutionary France: Bichat's physiology and the Paris school of medicine', *History of Science* 19: 115–42.

Poster, Mark (1984) *Foucault, Marxism and History: Mode of Production versus Mode of Information*, Oxford: Polity Press.

Shapin, Steven (1980) 'Social uses of science', in G.S. Rousseau (ed.) *The Ferment of Knowledge: Studies in the Historiography of Eighteenth Century Science*, Cambridge: Cambridge University Press.

———(1982) 'History of science and its sociological reconstruction', *History of Science* 20: 157–211.

Sheridan, Alan (1980) *Michel Foucault: The Will to Truth*, London/New York: Tavistock.

Smart, Barry (1985) *Michel Foucault*, London: Tavistock.

6 Docile bodies

Commonalities in the history of psychiatry and schooling

Ivor Goodson and Ian Dowbiggin

INTRODUCTION

In this chapter, we shall argue that there are important similarities between the ways in which French psychiatrists in the nineteenth century constructed their knowledge-systems and the ways in which educators shape the form of their subjects within the secondary-school curriculum. In making the connection between psychiatric knowledge and school subject knowledge we do not wish to obscure the many differences between the two. School teaching is of course unlike the activities of psychiatrists in several fundamental ways. But psychiatry and the teaching of school subjects might be viewed as sharing the same context of professionalization of knowledge into rigidly defined 'disciplines'.

As Young *et al.* (1971) have argued, those in positions of power are responsible for the assumptions that underlie the selection and organization of knowledge in society. The task for the historian of curriculum, as for the historian of psychiatry, is to recover the complex patterns of structuralization and distributions of power that influence the way in which a society selects, classifies, transmits, and evaluates the knowledge it considers to be public.[1] This involves reconstructing the relationship between profession and state and the struggle among constituencies and agencies with interests in the social consequences of professional practice. By so doing, the historian reveals what forms of knowledge are legitimized and sanctioned within an institutionalized structure, that is, what kinds of knowledge are authorized through patterns of resource allocation, status distribution, and career prospects. The historian also seeks to shed light on the way in which socially approved structures of knowledge legitimize the relations of power between professional and client at specific times in the past, for nineteenth-century asylums and public schools shared the institutional task of creating, transforming, and disciplining forms of behaviour and character in order to produce mechanisms for what Foucault has called 'constant policing'. In other words, out of the power relations between state and profession emerge both a 'discipline' and a mode of disciplining self, body, emotions, intellect, and behaviour. 'Power produces knowledge', as Foucault (1979) has written in *Discipline and Punish* and knowledge in the service of the modern nation state with its various interest groups and power brokers produces fields or 'disciplines' whose authorities exercise an increasingly thorough and meticulous control over the body. To quote Foucault again, 'the disciplines' become 'general forms of domination' which create 'subjected and practised bodies, "docile" bodies'.

We maintain that this process is particularly visible through the historical study of subjects in the secondary curriculum and the construction of knowledge-systems in organized psychiatry. We are left then with the full force of Foucault's warning in *Discipline and Punish*:

> Perhaps we should abandon a whole tradition that allows us to imagine that knowledge can exist only where the power relations are suspended and that knowledge can develop only outside its injunctions, its demands and its interests. Perhaps we should abandon the belief that power makes mad and that, by the same token, the renunciation of power is one of the conditions of knowledge. We should admit rather that power produces knowledge (and not simply by encouraging it because it serves power or by applying it because it is useful); that power and knowledge directly imply one another; that there is no power relation without the correlative constitution of a field of knowledge, nor any knowledge that does not presuppose and constitute at the same time power relations. These 'power–knowledge relations' are to be analysed, therefore, not on the basis of a subject of knowledge who is or is not free in relation to the power system, but, on the contrary, the subject who knows, the objects to be known and the modalities of knowledge must be regarded as so many effects of these fundamental implications of power–knowledge and their historical transformations. In short, it is not the activity of the subject of knowledge that produces a corpus of knowledge, useful or resistant to power, but power–knowledge, the processes and struggles that traverse it and of which it is made up, that determines the forms and possible domains of knowledge.
>
> (Foucault 1979: 27–8)

However, our analysis shows that Foucault's interpretation of the influence of professional knowledge is one-dimensional and fails to take into consideration the distinctive ways in which secondary schools and asylums practise domination and enforce docility. Indeed, we make a distinction between the 'docile bodies' of professionals and the 'docile bodies' of students and psychiatric patients. Docile bodies of knowledge 'discipline' not only the subjectivities of the clientele whose interests and needs are presumed to be served; they also discipline the professions with which they are associated by encouraging their members to pursue agendas concerned chiefly with career structures. In that sense they are highly effective in undermining the common interests of professional and client and postponing the emancipatory possibilities of this relationship. Similarly, while the disciplinary bodies of knowledge characteristic of professionalization are intended to enforce docility, their target groups or classes are never as pliant and docile as it might be hoped they will be. As recent accounts of psychiatry and schooling have shown, the human objects of domination demonstrate resistance and display oppositional behaviour in the face of social reproductionist mechanisms. This is not to say, as Henry Giroux (1983) has astutely observed, that all oppositional behaviour is emancipatory. However, it does point to the need for continued study of the way in which 'domination', in Giroux's words, 'reaches into the structure of personality itself' and engenders compliance as well as forms of resistance that both have radical significance and ultimately lead to the negation of dissent.

PSYCHIATRY IN NINETEENTH-CENTURY FRANCE

From roughly the beginning of the nineteenth century to the First World War, French psychiatry changed from a new medical specialty with an uncertain future to an accredited branch of organized medicine with academic and professional status. Yet this was not a painless or uncontested process. Throughout the nineteenth century French psychiatrists – or 'alienists' as they called themselves – had to confront and surmount many obstacles. The most serious obstacle was the psychiatric failure to demonstrate in pathoanatomical terms what precise organic conditions corresponded to the varieties of psychological symptoms a typical asylum physician encountered. This failure made it extremely difficult for psychiatrists to maintain that they were legitimate physicians, for their medical credentials rested on the supposition that they cured the mind thanks to their understanding of the somatic conditions which caused madness. Without these medical credentials, they could not plausibly justify their efforts to oust the clerical orders of the Catholic Church from public asylums, arguably the most important professional task for nineteenth-century French psychiatrists. Nineteenth-century psychiatrists, then, longed to be recognized as bona fide physicians, and in pursuit of this goal they followed a strategy calculated to win the profession a foothold in the expanding university system of the 1870s and 1880s. Like school subject teachers, asylum doctors believed that the key to securing augmented resources and expanded career opportunities for their occupational practice lay in the establishment of their medical specialty as a distinctly academic discipline with university chairs, able students, examinations, and fully accredited clinical courses.

In the status passage from 'alienists' to psychiatrists, the construction of particular kinds of knowledge played a vital role. As we shall argue, medical claims to expert knowledge of madness in the second half of the nineteenth century were valuable to psychiatrists interested in professionalization because they conveyed the impression that asylum alienists were something more than 'moral entrepreneurs' to use Eliot Freidson's (1970) terms. They aspired to lay claim, in Freidson's words, 'to knowledge of an especially esoteric, scientific, or abstract character that is markedly superior' to the claims to knowledge of 'amateurs' such as the clerical orders of the Catholic Church. The evolution of psychiatric knowledge enabled alienists to forge 'a political settlement' with the French state that guaranteed their status, material interests, and social authority in the face of persistent public criticism. As we shall see was the case with the teachers of school subjects and the associated bodies of school knowledge, so with psychiatrists and psychiatric knowledge a number of stages can be discerned in the evolutionary profile.

Psychiatry began by justifying its status as a medical specialty and as a socially useful profession with appeals to its utilitarian role in curing the disease of insanity. But for a variety of reasons that we shall outline below, these appeals had become outmoded or irrelevant by mid-century. In order to enhance their prestige and power to command the material resources of the state Ministry of the Interior, psychiatrists in the second half of the nineteenth century gradually developed a body of abstract biomedical knowledge and empirical data regarding the pauper classes. When deployed by psychiatrists this body of knowledge enabled the struggling profession to gain the status and state support it coveted. As psychiatric knowledge became more academic and specialized, it assumed a positivist form which complied with the trend towards experimental medical science in the medical faculties of the state university system. This tendency in late nineteenth-century psychiatric knowledge symbolized a desertion of the medical responsibility to cure the mentally ill. Yet the trade-off was not disadvantageous for the psychiatric profession. Thanks to the remarkable capacity of psychiatric knowledge to reproduce in abstract form the class relationships, division of labour, and cultural hegemony of late nineteenth-century France, psychiatry by 1914 had emerged as a bona fide profession with scholarly and institutional ties to the state university system, and had played a pivotal role in the process of state formation begun in the 1840s (Pinkney 1986; Corrigan and Curtis 1985; Curtis 1983).[2]

To understand the similarities between nineteenth-century French psychiatry and curriculum history, it is necessary to first discuss the main professional, social, and intellectual features of psychiatric life from 1800 to 1914. Psychiatry took root around the turn of the nineteenth century. The Revolution had swept away most of the royalist, clerical, and aristocratic corporations of the old regime, and in the process organized medicine had undergone its own revolution. No longer an elite corps of practitioners who wrote in Latin and served the upper classes, medicine after 1789 became a middle-class profession based on the hospital system created by the revolutionary leaders in the 1790s and consolidated under Napoleon I in the early years of the century. Thus from its revolutionary inception psychiatry was a hospital specialty which, after the example of the renowned Philippe Pinel, committed itself to curing the patient population housed in institutions such as Salpêtrière and Bicêtre.

For the first third of the nineteenth century psychiatrists embraced an attitude of therapeutic optimism. They believed that they could cure a substantial number of institutionalized patients with 'moral treatment'. 'Moral treatment' was the name given by Pinel and his follower Etienne Esquirol to a psychodynamic approach to therapy which featured reasoning, intimidation, persuasion, and education. Moral treatment was also consistent with a diagnostic classifications system organized according to mental symptoms rather than organic lesions. In other words, psychiatrists developed a discourse of professional knowledge that endorsed an optimistic approach to therapy based on the disposition, character, and emotional needs of the individual patient. It reflected the great hopes many early psychiatrists felt about the possibility of curing madness in asylums.

During the middle third of the nineteenth century, therapeutic optimism in psychiatry began to wane. In a development similar to that which took place in nineteenth-century America and described by David Rothman (1971) in his *Discovery of the Asylum*, the mental hospitals of France, crowded even at the best of times, became seriously congested with patients suffering from incurable physical illnesses, mental retardation, or senile dementia. More and more psychiatrists confessed their doubts that the bulk of their patients could be cured with either individualized moral treatment or standard physicalist remedies. Instead, they argued that the asylum psychiatrist's duty was to manage the hospitalized population by organizing the lives of the inmates down to the smallest detail. Psychiatrists began to advocate a collectively-oriented moral treatment that stressed surveillance and conformity to moral norms rather than activist therapy. They did so not because it offered the best hope for curing patients, but principally because it enabled the psychiatrist to control them.[3]

This form of therapeutic pessimism, which satisfied itself with making patients docile and pliable, spread as the century progressed. But as the institutional possibilities for actively reducing the incidence of madness declined, other issues attracted psychiatric interests around mid-century. In 1838 the French government passed a law that established the guidelines governing admission to and release from asylums. It also authorized the departmental Prefects of France to build new public asylums, thereby improving the chances of employment for the growing number of physicians drawn to the study and treatment of mental illness. The problem was that the construction of new asylums was notoriously slow. In addition, the relative decentralization of the French political structure led to conflict between psychiatrists and Prefects over the administration of mental hospitals. Psychiatrists reacted by making overtures to the Minister of the Interior, urging him to centralize the entire administration of the asylum system. They believed that the centralization of the asylum system would serve their material interests as a profession by establishing uniform standards for pay, promotion, pensions, and working conditions.[4] It was clear, then, that by the 1850s a host of issues had arisen to divert psychiatric attention from their original aims. As psychiatric commitment to the mental health of their patients became increasingly difficult to sustain, psychiatrists grew more aware of the need to enhance their professional status and their relations with the sources of political power and patronage in France in order to ensure that the allocation of material resources for the asylum system did not diminish with the fading of public enthusiasm for mental institutions.

An important part of the psychiatric campaign to improve the status and legitimacy of mental medicine in the middle third of the century was the successful attempt to form a psychiatric learned society that presumably would represent the profession's interests. Founded in 1852 with its own journal, the *Annales médico-psychologiques*, the *Société médico-psychologique* acted much in the same way as have subject associations in the history of curriculum: it increasingly served to unify the subgroups into a coalition promoting enhanced status and prerogatives. The timing of the *Société*'s founding is crucial: it came at a time of much psychiatric in-fighting and conflict. In the 1840s and 1850s tensions had developed between one group which essentially urged a return to the moral treatment of Pinel and a group that wanted psychiatry to become more 'biological' – in other words, more closely associated with trends in academic medicine and science. The eventual triumph of the 'organicists' is evident in the pages of the *Annales médico-psychologiques* and the history of the *Société médico-psychologique* in the second half of the nineteenth century. Thus the centripetal tendency of the *Société* contributed to the transition in psychiatry from a loose amalgamation of subgroups or idiosyncratic individuals into a more or less unified profession dedicated to pursuing its own interests in terms of material resources and career opportunities (Dowbiggin 1985; Ritti 1914).

During the 1860s psychiatry pursued its professional interests by expressing its willingness to serve the French state in a variety of capacities. For example, psychiatrists eagerly performed 'medical police' functions for the imperial government of Louis Napoleon when an epidemic of hysteria broke out in the Alpine village of Morzine in 1862 (Goldstein 1984). Yet for the most part, psychiatrists remained wedded to their asylums as the prime locus of their professional activity. Their principal concern was to serve the state as salaried employees within the asylum system. To ensure that public disfavour did not tempt the state to revoke psychiatric powers or restrict funding of the asylum system, psychiatrists committed themselves to convincing the state of their political good faith.

Psychiatric efforts to ally themselves more closely with the French state and the dominant social classes began in the 1860s and continued until the First World War as psychiatrists increasingly cited and contributed to the formulation of degeneracy theory.[5] In the process, they constructed a biomedically and culturally resonant body of knowledge which enabled them to appear medical and scholarly. The emergence of degeneracy theory among psychiatrists in the final third of the nineteenth century supplied a rationale and a rhetoric for mental medicine that justified the psychiatric abandonment of its patients without, in any serious way, blaming asylum physicians for doing so. Degeneracy theory bolstered psychiatrists in their growing belief that their task lay less in ministering to the insane than in the institutional classification and subordination of patients. It also reinforced the image of psychiatrists as a corps of specialist and expert professionals who were dealing with a grave problem that threatened social peace and stability. Finally, it justified the place of psychiatrists in mental hospitals and the status of psychiatry as a genuine branch of medical science. In effect, psychiatry forged a kind of political settlement with the state on the basis of adherence to degeneracy theory, a settlement which benefited both parties, but particularly the material self-interests of mental medicine. Psychiatrists in the final third of the nineteenth century were crucial participants in the social organization of knowledge around the principle of degeneracy.

The history of degeneracy theory in French psychiatry is complex and warrants a fuller explanation than can be provided here, yet certain basic themes and developments can be identified. The first surge of interest in degeneracy theory occurred in the 1860s, following the publication of B.A. Morel's *Treatise on Degeneracy* in 1857. Morel, the founder of degeneracy theory, argued that there was a growing number of French men and women who were predisposed to a host of neurological and mental illnesses because of bad heredity. Most of those afflicted with hereditary degeneracy, Morel maintained, were members of the working or 'pauper' classes. Their mental instability and poor health could be traced to the 'immoral' lifestyle they pursued in the swelling urban and industrialized centres of France, a lifestyle characterized by alcoholism, indigence, crime and sexual profligacy. Medically unsound conduct, Morel contended, weakened and destabilized the nervous system. It was then common for these pathophysiological conditions to be handed down to offspring through inheritance, according to Morel. Heredity, as Morel and his colleagues came to believe, ensured that pathological characteristics would persist, change form, and actually proliferate from generation to generation.

Morel's formulation of degeneracy theory endorsed the continued existence of psychiatric asylums and institutional practice at a time when both were under heavy attack. According to his theory, the rising incidence of mental illness in French society – documented time and again by psychiatrists – was due to lower-class ignorance of proper morals, values, and hygienic principles. In other words, the insane poor were held to be responsible for their diseases. Degeneracy theory also neatly explained away the catastrophic overcrowding of insane asylums with chronically ill cases. These cases, Morel and his followers argued, were essentially due to heredity, the pathological extent of which limited the number of acute cases and hence the medical possibilities for achieving a cure. The asylum, according to Morel, became an important institutional site for the segregation, classification, and subordination of 'degenerate', lower-class persons: its presence guaranteed the isolation from society of 'tainted' and troublesome lunatics whose symptoms could only be identified consistently by an asylum-trained psychiatrist. Thus Morel's theory vindicated asylum psychiatrists for their increasing failure to cure their hospitalized patients. At a time when the usefulness of both psychiatrists and asylums was being openly questioned in the press, in the Chamber of Deputies, and in medical learned societies, Morel was telling his colleagues that far from being responsible for the acknowledged calamitous state of affairs regarding the public assistance to the insane, hospital psychiatry was in fact privy to expert knowledge of the national epidemic of madness.

Psychiatric interest in hereditarianism and degeneracy theory peaked in the 1880s. By this decade the new leader in mental medicine was Morel's follower, Valentin Magnan. Thanks to Magnan's persuasive talents, more and more of the psychiatric community swung over to the theory of degeneracy. Naturally enough, there was not quite unanimity among France's psychiatrists, even by 1890. However, even Magnan's foes had to admit that in criticizing degeneracy theory they were in a distinct minority within psychiatry.

The growth of interest in degeneracy theory in the 1880s and 1890s was still tied to a significant degree to the professional ambitions of psychiatrists to vindicate their roles as medically qualified hospital physicians. Yet other considerations surfaced in the last two decades of the century to compel them to accept degeneracy theory. Psychiatrists were now more than ever eager to appear as biologically and medically erudite practitioners. They wished to be seen as possessors of a body of formal and scholarly knowledge, knowledge that was important for establishing the academic credentials of psychiatry as a medical science with a place for itself in the reformed curriculum of university medical faculties.

The acceptance of degeneracy theory turned out to be a felicitous choice for the French psychiatric community, for it wove together a variety of themes that reflected late nineteenth-century trends in French culture, biology, and medical science. As Robert A. Nye (1984) has shown, *fin-de-siècle* French scholarship and official culture was punctuated with concerns about the apparently declining biological and reproductive fitness of the nation. Moreover, as biology developed into a prestigious science in the last half of the nineteenth century, mainstream medicine began to attribute more and more causal importance to heredity, especially in dealing with the chronic and constitutional diseases of the nervous system. It soon was conventional in late nineteenth-century French medicine to explain diseases of the nervous system as characteristics which the organism was forced to acquire and then transmit through heredity as it struggled to adapt to pathogenic environmental conditions, such as the domestic and occupational *milieux* of the working classes and the rural poor.

Therefore, in changing their professional discourse from the largely psychological terminology of the early nineteenth century to the rhetoric of degeneracy theory in the late nineteenth century, psychiatrists were able to appear biomedically and culturally up-to-date. The hereditarianism of degeneracy theory enabled psychiatrists to maintain that madness had an ineradicable biological component, that the otherwise bewildering plethora of psychological symptoms encountered in everyday asylum practice could be organized around and referred to a purely natural phenomenon like heredity. Doctors of psychological medicine could disguise their ignorance of the precise physiological and anatomical lesions responsible for the different categories of madness by basing their explanations of mental illness on the physical transmission of characteristics from one generation to the next. Finally, adherence to degeneracy theory as a seemingly coherent body of medical knowledge authorized psychiatrists to pose as trained specialists committed to the positivist ethos of order and progress through science. As institutional experts in the medical management of madness, psychiatrists could pose as prototypical Comtean scientists at a time – the early 1880s – when the French Republican state was attempting to reconstruct public subjectivity and consciousness through a flood of civil and educational legislation. In so far as their claims to academic and specialized knowledge were recognized as legitimate, psychiatrists could erase the stigma of social marginality and receive just remuneration as a professional group with unique contributions to the reconstitution of public morals and political order.

A sign that the psychiatric endeavour to make their knowledge claims appear more scientific was at least partially successful was the creation of a chair in mental pathology in 1877 at the Parisian Faculty of Medicine, one of the faculties of the centralized French university system. At one point early in the nineteenth century there had been a chair in mental pathology, yet during the Royalist purges of the university system in 1821–22 it had been abolished and never reinstated. The appointment of Dr Benjamin Ball to the chair in 1877 meant that there would be official courses in psychiatry delivered at the Faculty, addressing the long-standing complaint of asylum psychiatrists from the 1820s to the 1870s that there had been no formal university teaching in mental pathology. Before 1877 asylum psychiatrists themselves had to teach clinical courses in the subject if they wished to train young physicians for careers in mental medicine. After 1877 this would no longer be the case. The creation of the chair indicated that psychiatry was a genuine medical specialty with the prestige and resources that went along with this academic status. To cite Freidson again, prospective alienists could now receive instruction in 'a curriculum that includes some *special* theoretical content (whether scientifically proven or not)' which 'may represent a declaration that there is a body of special knowledge and skill necessary for the occupation' of psychiatry (Freidson 1970: 134–5). At the same time, the strengthened ties between asylum psychiatry and the state university system encouraged the trend in psychiatry theory towards more formalized and abstract bodies of knowledge.

This point constitutes a crucial link between the history of psychiatry and the history of school subjects in the secondary-school curriculum. While it is clear that university scholars have managed to impose a pattern of domination on the construction of knowledge, whether in the form of curricula or psychiatric theory, teachers and psychiatrists have been major participants in these patterns. In effect, psychiatrists, like their counterparts in teaching, were 'socialized' or disciplined by patterns of resource allocation and associated work and career prospects to legitimate high-status definitions of knowledge. These definitions largely derive from the pervasive influence exercised by scholars within the state university system. For late nineteenth-century French mental medicine, as for geography teachers in secondary schools, the hegemonic form of high-status knowledge stressed academic features that had less to do with the actual techniques employed by practitioners and the needs and wishes of clientele than with the material self-interest of professionals anxious to surrender solicitously to developing structures of power. By adopting the rhetoric of positivist science in their claims to scholarly, esoteric knowledge of insanity, French psychiatrists celebrated their liberation from what they perceived to be their original tutelage to their patients: as the occupant of the chair in the clinical study of mental illness argued in 1880, by shifting the 'axis' of psychiatry away from psychology and towards the study of organic and biological conditions, mental medicine would no longer be limited to the role of 'secretary' to patients, laboriously writing down everything their clients said.

To summarize, French psychiatric knowledge in the nineteenth century followed a distinct evolutionary pattern. The origins of psychiatric knowledge in nineteenth-century France were utilitarian and practical in nature. Psychiatrists devoted themselves to serving the 'clientele' of the burgeoning public asylum system. They adopted an individual-oriented form of psychotherapy predicated on the curability of most mentally ill patients. When asylums quickly filled up with chronically ill and incurable patients, psychiatrists lost much of their therapeutic optimism. As a result, they began to devote the bulk of their attention to asylum administration and patient management rather than activist therapy. This process was reinforced by the fact that the new generation of psychiatrists who replaced the talented amateurs of the previous generation did not share the same sense of philanthropic commitment to their patients and were more concerned with the pursuit of professional status. The disengagement of psychiatry from its original objectives was reflected in the social history of knowledge by the emergence of a new form of psychiatric discourse called 'degeneracy theory'. It represented the final break with the relatively humane and optimistic therapeutic approach to madness. It served the interests of psychiatry because it derived from a body of knowledge with great cultural, political, and medical resonance for a host of constituencies with their own interest in the management of deviance. Degeneracy theory symbolized the advent of university hegemony over the knowledge of occupational practice, the decontextualization and disembodiment of psychiatric knowledge fostered by its increasing definition according to standards set by scholars from the Faculty of

Medicine. Psychiatric knowledge thus became rigidified and virtually useless for psychiatrists intent on the delivery of effective medical care to their institutionalized patients; in effect, it 'disciplined' alienists by stifling innovation and directing their attention away from the therapeutic task endorsed by the original 'moral treatment'. Yet its advantages in other respects were considerable. It enabled psychiatry to win status and resources from the French state which were fundamental to its survival and growth as a profession. More ominously, it authorized the long-standing psychiatric treatment of the mental patient as an object to be classified and controlled rather than cured. In its desertion of its original clientele, psychiatry resembles the pattern of development we shall discern for school subjects.

SCHOOL GEOGRAPHY IN TWENTIETH-CENTURY ENGLAND

In 1976 Foucault was interviewed for the Marxist geographer's journal, *Hérodote*. The first question asked by the interviewers was about his work which, they argued,

> to a large extent intersects with, and provides material for, our reflections about geography and more generally about ideologies and strategies of space. Our questioning of geography brought us into contact with a certain number of concepts you have used – knowledge [*savoir*], power, science, discursive formation, gaze, episteme – and your archaeology has helped give a direction to our reflection. For instance the hypothesis you put forward in *The Archaeology of Knowledge* – that a discursive formation is defined neither in terms of a particular object, nor a style, nor a play of permanent concepts, nor by the persistence of a thematic, but must be grasped in the form of a system of regular dispersion of statements – enable us to form a clearer outline of geographical discourse. Consequently we were surprised by your silence about geography.
>
> (Foucault 1980)

As the interview progressed the imperial, military, and national aspects of geography were discussed and Foucault talked of power-knowledge in relation to geography.

> Once knowledge can be analysed in terms of region, domain, implantation, displacement, trans-position, one is able to capture the process by which knowledge functions as a form of power and disseminates the effects of power. There is an administration of knowledge, a politics of knowledge, relations of power which pass

via knowledge and which, if one tries to transcribe them, lead one to consider forms of domination designated by such notions as field, region and territory. And the politico-strategic term is an indication of how the military and the administration actually come to inscribe themselves both on a material soil and with forms of discourse.

(ibid., p. 69)

By the end of the interview Foucault was clearer about some of the content of geography and its relationship to the 'discourse of right'.

The longer I continue, the more it seems to me that the formation of discourses and the genealogy of knowledge need to be analysed, not in terms of types of consciousness, modes of perception and forms of ideology, but in terms of tactics and strategies of power. Tactics and strategies deployed through implantations, distributions, demarcations, control of territories and organisations of domains which could well make up a sort of geopolitics where my preoccupations would link up with your methods. One theme I would like to study in the next few years is that of the army as a matrix of organisation and knowledge; one would need to study the history of the fortress, the 'campaign', the 'movement', the colony, the territory. Geography must indeed necessarily lie at the heart of my concerns.

(ibid., p. 77)

But in the history of a school subject there is an interesting relation and interrelation between the subject as content and the subject as form. In both cases the subject continues to function as a maker of subjectivities. Most of the focus of the interview with Foucault remained, no doubt, because of the journal geographers' preoccupations with their subject's content, on aspects of geographical content. But the power–knowledge relation crucially relates to the form that the school curriculum espouses and embodies, because as well as serving to carry content to pupils, the school subject also serves many other constituencies – notably the state and the professional groups involved in schooling. By focusing on the history of school subjects in English schools in the twentieth century, it is possible to explore analogies between the foregoing history of psychiatry in France and aspects of schooling in England. School subject teachers composed professional groups that, as was the case with the French psychiatrists, were understandably concerned with the acquisition of status and resources. Again the state was an important sponsor and professional groups of teachers sought the rhetorics that would maximize state aid. In analysing the rhetoric employed in the promotion of school subjects we gain

117

insight into the agendas of schooling. As we shall see, there are a number of powerful analogies with the manner by which state aid was secured for psychiatrists. Central in these analogies is the relationship between the professionals and their clients/pupils/inmates; and alongside this the position of specialized knowledge as a central indicator and ingredient of this relationship and of the relationship between the professional groups and the state.

THE ESTABLISHMENT AND PROMOTION OF GEOGRAPHY AS A SCHOOL SUBJECT

In the late nineteenth century geography was beginning to establish a place in the curriculum of public, grammar, and elementary schools of Britain. The subject was emerging from its first stages in which it appears to have been little more than a dreary collection of geographical facts and figures which, one of the founding fathers of geography, H.T. MacKinder (1887) contended, 'adds an ever-increasing amount to be borne by the memory'. At this time this was a non-graduate subject, for geography remained outside the universities. It was partly to answer this problem that MacKinder posed the question in 1887: 'How can geography be rendered a discipline?' But MacKinder was aware that the demand for an academic geography to be taught in universities could only be engendered by the establishment of a more credible position in schools. Essentially, it was in the high-status public and grammar schools that geography needed to establish its intellectual as well as pedagogical credibility. In these schools, without full-fledged academic status, the subject's position as an established part of the curriculum remained uncertain.

In the elementary schools geography was rapidly seen as affording utilitarian and pedagogic possibilities in the education of the children of working people. Hence the take-up of the subject grew considerably in the period following the 1870 Education Act. In 1875 'elementary geography' was added to the main list of 'class subjects' examined in elementary schools.

Given its limited base in the elementary and secondary school sector, the promoters of geography began to draw up plans for a subject association. In 1893 the Geographical Association was founded 'to further the knowledge of geography and the teaching of geography in all categories of educational institutions from preparatory school to university in the United Kingdom and abroad'.[6] The formation of the Association in 1893 was well-timed and it rapidly began to operate as a vocal lobby for the subject. Two years later the Bryce Commission reported and its recommendations were built into the 1902 Education Act. Further, the 1904 Secondary regulations effectively defined the traditional subjects to be offered in secondary schools; geography's inclusion in the regulations was a major staging-post in its acceptance and recognition and in the broad-based take-up of external examinations in geography in secondary schools. The emergence of external examinations as a defining factor in secondary curricula around 1917 is clearly reflected in the sharp increase in the Association's membership around this date. At this stage geography was included in many Examination Board regulations both at School Certificate and Higher School Certificate as a main subject. Certain Boards, however, included geography only as a 'subsidiary subject'.

The founding of a subject association was only a first stage in launching the subject; also required was an overall plan aimed at establishing the subject in the various educational sectors mentioned in the constitution. At a discussion on geographical education at the British Association in September 1903, MacKinder (1903) outlined a four-point strategy for establishing the subject.

> Firstly, we should encourage University Schools of geography, where geographers can be made. . . .
>
> Secondly, we must persuade at any rate some secondary schools to place the geographical teaching of the whole school in the hands of one geographically trained master. . . .
>
> Thirdly, we must thrash out by discussion and experiment what is the best progressive method for common acceptation and upon that method we must base our scheme of examination.
>
> Lastly, the examination papers must be set out by practical geography teachers.

This strategy reads very much like trade union pleas for the closed shop. The geography teacher is to set the exams and is to choose exams that are best for the 'common acceptation' of the subject. There is not even the pretence that the pupils' interest should be the central criteria; the teaching of geography is to be exclusively in the hands of trained geographers and the universities are to be encouraged to establish schools of geography 'where geographers can be made'.

In the immediate period following this pronouncement, the Geographical Association continued the earlier rhetoric about the subject's utility; the changeover was slowly implemented. Thus in 1919 we learn that 'in teaching geography in schools we seek to train future citizens to imagine accurately the interaction of human activities and their topographical conditions.' Eight years later we hear that 'travel and correspondence have now become general; the British dominions are to be found in every clime and these facts alone are sufficient to ensure that the subject shall have an important place in the school time-table' (Hadlow Report 1927). Alongside these utilitarian and pedagogic claims the Geographical Association began to mount more 'academic' arguments. But the problems of the utilitarian and pedagogic emphases had by now surfaced. Thus in the 1930s the Norwood Committee was concerned with the way geography appeared to effortlessly change direction and definition, thereby intruding on the territory of other subjects and disciplines. Above all, they were concerned with the temptation afforded by what they called the 'expansiveness of geography' for 'environment is a term which is easily expanded to cover every condition and every phase of activity which makes up normal everyday experience'.

The results of such 'expansiveness' in school geography were later reported by Honeybone (1954), who argued that by the 1930s geography 'came more and more to be a "world citizenship" subject, with the citizens detached from their physical environment'. He explained this partly by the spread 'under American influence' of 'a methodology, proclaiming that all education must be related to the everyday experience of children'. Thus, through the work of these teachers untrained or badly trained in the subject, 'by 1939 geography had become grievously out of balance; the geographical synthesis had been abandoned; and the unique educational value of the subject lost in a flurry of social and economic generalizations'. The central problem remained the establishment of departments in universities where geographers could be made and the piecemeal changes in pursuit of pupil relevance and utility could be controlled and directed. To further this objective the Geographical Association began to promote more 'academic' arguments for the subject. Hence in 1927 we learn that 'the main objective in good geographical teaching is to develop, as in the case of history, an attitude of mind and a mode of thought characteristic of the subject' (Honeybone 1954).

The increasingly academic presentation of the school subject applied more pressure on the universities to respond to the demand for the training of geography specialists. As a recent president of the Geographical Association has noted, 'the recognition of our subject's status among university disciplines. . . could never have been achieved without [the] remarkable stimulus and demand injected from out of schools' (Garnett 1969). The contention, whilst correct, contains the origins of the status problems geography has encountered in universities. As David Walker (1975) recently noted, 'some senior members of our ancient universities can still be found who dismiss it as a school subject'. As a result, until recently geographers remained a frustrated university profession because of what Woolridge described as

the widespread belief among our colleagues and associates that we lack academic status and intellectual respectability. What has been conceded is that geography has a limited use in its lower ranges. What is implicitly denied by so many is that it has any valid claim as a higher subject.

(quoted in David 1973)

Woolridge, however, hints that acceptance at the lower level is the main threshold to cross: 'it has been conceded that if geography is to be taught in schools it must be learned in the universities' (*ibid.*).

The period following 1945 does seem to have been critical in geography's acceptance and consolidation within the university sector. Professor Alice Garnett explained in 1968 why this period was so important:

Not until after the Second World War was it widely the case that departments were directed by geographers who had themselves received formal training in the discipline, by which time most of the initial marked differences and contrasts in subject personality had been blurred or obliterated.

(Garnett 1969: 368)

By 1954, Honeybone could write a summary of the final acceptance and establishment of geography as a university discipline.

In the universities, there has been unparalleled advance in the number of staff and scope of the work in the departments of geography. In the University of London alone, there are now six chairs, four of them of relatively recent creation. Students, both graduates and undergraduates, are greater in number than ever before. Many of the training colleges and university departments of education are taking a full part in this progress; employers are realizing the value of the breadth of a university training in geography; and the Civil Service has recently raised the status of geography in its higher examinations. In fact, on all sides, we can see signs that, at long last, geography is forcing its complete acceptance as a major discipline in the universities, and that geographers are welcomed into commerce, industry and the professions, because they are well educated men and women.

(Honeybone 1954)

Thus, by the mid 1950s geography had progressed to the crucial stage in the acceptance of a subject. The selection of subject matter was 'determined in large measure by the judgments and practices of the Specialist Scholars who lead inquiries in the field' (*ibid.*). Of course, the final take-over of geography by the universities meant control of the definition of the subject was in the hand of specialist scholars. The context in which these scholars operated was substantially divorced from schools; their activities and personal motivations, their status and career concerns were situated within the university context. The concerns of school pupils, thereby unrepresented, were of less and less account in the definition of this well-established academic discipline. The implications within schools soon became clear. In 1967 the report on *Society and the Young School Leaver* noted that the student of geography felt 'at best apathetic, at worst resentful and rebellious to geography... which seems to him to have nothing to do with the adult world he is soon to join' (Report 1967). The report adds:

> A frequent cause of failure seems to be that the course is often based on the traditional belief that there is a body of content for each separate subject which every school leaver should know. In the least successful courses this body of knowledge is written into the curriculum without any real consideration of the needs of the boys and girls and without any question of its relevance.

The threat to geography began to be appreciated at the highest level. A member of the Executive and Honorary Secretary of the Geographical Association recalls that 'the subject began to lose touch with reality....[G]eography got a bad name.'[7] A college lecturer, David Gowing (1973), saw the same problem facing the subject and argued:

> One must recognize the need to take a fresh look at our objectives and to re-examine the role and nature of geography in school. It is not difficult to identify the causes of increasing dissatisfaction. Pupils feel that present curricula have little relevance to their needs and so their level of motivation and understanding is low. Teachers are concerned that the raising of the school leaving age and some forms of comprehensive reorganization may exacerbate the problems.

The increasing control of geography by the university specialists plainly posed problems for the subject in schools. To recapture the sense of utility and relevance of earlier days the subject would have needed to focus more on the needs of the average and below-average school student. However, geography still faced problems of academic status within some universities and also among the high-status sections of the secondary sector.

The advances in university geography after the Second World War partly aided the acceptance of geography as a subject suitable for the most able children, but problems remained. In 1968 Marchant noted: 'Geography is at least attaining to intellectual respectability in the academic streams of our secondary schools. But the battle is not quite over.' To finally seal its acceptance by the universities and high-status sixth forms, geography had to forever renounce its pedagogic and utilitarian intentions. The supreme paradox is that the crisis in school geography in the late 1960s led not to change which might have involved more school pupils but to changes in the opposite direction in pursuit of total academic acceptance. The final push for status centred around the 'new geography', which moved away from regional geography to more quantitative data and model-building. The battle for new geography was perhaps the final clash between those traditions in geography representing the pedagogic and utilitarian traditions (notably the fieldwork geographers and some regionalists) and those pushing for total academic acceptance.

Geography then achieved total academic acceptance both as a high-status, highly resourced school subject and, associated with this status passage, as a fully-fledged academic university 'discipline'. Control of the subject passed towards the detached scholars in universities. The pupils/clients in the school are faced with school subject knowledge defined by those divorced from their milieu and from the concern as to how learners learn. Not surprisingly, most school pupils react to such alien knowledge 'with passivity and resignation, a prelude to disen-chantment' (Marchant 1965). In geography, as with all other 'proper' subjects, the vast majority will leave school without the coveted A-level examination passes. In so doing they will be closing the door on the route to university for which, as we have seen, the whole subject had been avowedly restructured.

The processes and struggles that traverse the emergence of geography as a school subject in England point to salient features in the 'professionalization' and modernization of the subject. In the early stages of the subject utilitarian arguments about the subject as a hand-maiden to Empire prevail. The content of the subject reflects these national and imperial preoccupations. Children are being schooled into a particular version of national and economic identity. But geography still remains a marginal and low-status subject in the public and gram-mar schools where the upper and middle classes children are located.

The content of the subject therefore clearly serviced certain interest groups, but the form of the subject remained problematic. The geography of empire was a dreary collection of facts and figures, whether 'capes and bays' or 'homes in many lands'. The professionaliz-ation of geography demanded that MacKinder's four-point strategy was painstakingly followed. There had to be 'University schools of Geography where geographers could be made'. But once established, such university departments began to 'make geographers' not in the image of secondary schools, not in the image of the nation and empire, but above all in the image of themselves. The patterns of status and prestige within the universities became the major factors in the subsequent definition of geography. The discursive formation of geography from here on was derived from the prevailing patterns and symbolic drift of university scholarship. The subject was presented as a 'discipline', a coherent body of knowledge with the status and rigour of a scientific discipline. The culminating discursive formation in geography's status passage resonated above all with the status and prestige concerns of contemporary university professionals. Ultimately, geography, whether for secondary schools or for higher education, was driven by their needs and concerns. In the process of academic establishment, the geography profession accepted the hegemony of university scholars and the result was a particular content and form for the subject created in the image of those scholars.

The close connection between academic status and resources is a fundamental feature of our educational system. The origin of this connection is the examination system created by universities from the late 1850s and culminating in the school certificate system founded in 1917. As a result, the so-called 'academic' subjects provide examinations which are suitable for 'able' students whilst other subjects are not.

E.M. Byrne's work has provided data on resource allocation within schools. She discerned that

> Two assumptions which might be questioned have been seen consistently to underlay educational planning and the consequent resource allocation for the more able children. First, that these necessarily need longer in school than non-grammar pupils, and secondly, that they necessarily need more staff, more highly paid staff and more money for equipment and books.
>
> (Byrne 1974)

The implications of the preferential treatment of academic subjects for the material self-interest of teachers are clear: better staffing ratios, higher salaries, higher capitation allowances, more graded posts, better career prospects. The link between academic status and resource allocation provides the major explanatory framework for understanding the aspirational imperative to become an academic subject. Basically, since more resources are given to the academic examination subject taught to able students, the conflict over the status of examinable knowledge is, above all, a battle over the material resources and career prospects of each subject teacher or subject community.

The allocation of resources from the state government and the local authorities thereby sponsored university influence over school geography. The professional groups involved in the promotion of the subject had to accept the control of university scholars in the definition and academic establishment of their subject. The relationship between the professional body of knowledge and the clients in secondary schools has important analogies with the relationships discerned for psychiatric knowledge and its clients. The demands of professionals and of state sponsors would seem to have a great deal in common, certainly enough to warrant substantial further investigation.

CONCLUSION

The comparison of French psychiatry and psychiatric knowledge with English schooling and school knowledge reveals some remarkable similarities. These similarities cross centuries as well as cultures, yet they appear to point towards certain continuities of social purpose.

French psychiatrists made a clear bargain with the state. In return for status and resources, psychiatrists reneged on their original therapeutic optimism and utilitarianism. The development of a body of knowledge – degeneracy theory – underpinned a practice and institutional power which in the asylum allowed for the surveillance of patients and their moralization through the regulatory internalization of ruling-class values and attitudes. This psychiatric style of disciplinary 'treatment' was all the more effective because it seemed to be a humane and commonsensical alternative to letting the lunatics of the nation loose in the streets. It also constituted an important chapter in the French state's campaign to control and manage those social groups labelled as dangerous, not through coercive policing, but through the construction of docile and socially approved mentalities during the second half of the nineteenth century.

In the development of schooling, school subject knowledge evolved in a similar manner. The subject teachers, in the case of geography, reneged on their original social and pedagogic optimism in pursuit of status and resources. In the phase of successful academic establishment of the subject, when geography was defined as a high-status school subject with major resources and finance, the students were 'at best apathetic, at worst resentful and rebellious to geography'. At the high point of its political acceptance, the clients of school geography were clearly 'approaching passivity and resignation, a prelude to disen-chantment'. However, their alienation simply made them more deferential to the social hegemony and high-status definition of abstract subject knowledge, a process which reinforced the devaluation of practical/manual labour and the disqualification of the majority from the material rewards possible only through academic credentialism.

In some senses the history of psychiatry and geography may be seen as passing through three stages. The first was a period of professional optimism and systematic close engagement with the concerns and interests of the clients/pupils. The second stage was a period in which a body of professional/curricula knowledge was developed. In the case of psychiatry, this focused on degeneracy theory; in the case of geography, a body of knowledge focused on imperial and territorial concerns. These new bodies of knowledge began substantially to influence the nature of professional relationships with clients/pupils. Finally, in the third stage, a more systematically abstracted body of knowledge emerged in the universities where the subject becomes institutionalized. From this new detached site, future definitions of the professional body of knowledge are now produced and reproduced.

It seems then that psychiatry and education may have the same 'morphology of reform', to use Carl Kaestle's (1972) words, as public institutions, schools, and asylums have more in common than meets the eye. In both cases, knowledge implied the power of trained and licensed professionals to displace talented amateurs in institutional practice and fulfil state agendas of classifying and subordinating disadvantaged groups. Yet professionals, while gaining important advantages, underwent their own 'policing' and disciplinary process. In many significant respects, the conditions of their practice ceased to be defined by practitioners themselves and were instead formulated by specialist 'scholars' and administrators far removed from the sites of service. State tutelage replaced the relative flexibility and freedom to innovate which characterized the origins of public schools and asylum medicine. Teachers, for example, submitted to the increasing control exerted by examinations, syllabuses, text-books, and teacher training. We contend that until insights into the complex relations between professional power and professional knowledge are recognized and scrutinized widely, this two-dimensional process of disciplining subjectivity into 'docile bodies' will ensure that schooling never becomes true 'education' and psychiatry never becomes synonymous with mental health.

NOTES

1   The field of curriculum history has expanded considerably of late. See the I.F. Goodson (ed.), *Studies in Curriculum History* (London, Philadelphia, New York: Falmer Press) series that began in 1985 and comprises I.F. Goodson (ed.), *Social Histories of the Secondary Curriculum: Subjects for Study*; G. McCulloch, E. Jenkins, and D. Layton, *Technological Revolution? The Politics of School Science and Technology in England and Wales Since 1945*; B. Cooper, *Renegotiating Secondary School Mathematics: A Study of Curriculum Change and Stability*, B. Franklin, *Building the American Community: Social Control and Curriculum*; B. Moon, *The 'New Maths' Curriculum Controversy: An International Story*; I.F. Goodson, *School Subjects and Curriculum Change*; T.S. Popkewitz (ed.), *The Formation of School Subjects: The Struggle for Creating an American Institution*; B.E.

Woolnough, *Physics Teaching in Schools 1960–85: Of People, Policy and Power*; I.F Goodson, *The Making of Curriculum: Collected Essays*; P. Cunningham, *Curriculum Change in the Primary School Since 1945: Dissemination of the Progressive Ideal*; and P.W. Musgrave, *Whose Knowledge? A Case Study of the Victorian Universities Schools Examinations Board 1964–1979.*

2   For historical treatments of nineteenth-century French psychiatry, see Castel 1976; Goldstein 1987; and Semelaigne 1930-32. For general accounts of the history of nineteenth-century psychiatry, see Ackerknecht 1965; Postel and Quétel 1983; Scull 1981; and Bynum, Porter, and Shepherd 1985.

3   There are several sources for the institutional history of the insane and French psychiatry in the first half of the nineteenth century. See, for example, Bleandonu and Le Gaufey 1978; selections from the *Annales E.S.C.* 1978; Jones 1980; and Petit 1980.

4   For an expression of these psychiatric demands, see Lunier, Costans, and Dumesnil 1876.

5   For recent accounts of degeneracy theory, see Bing 1983; see also Bynum, Porter, and Shepherd 1985; and Shortt 1986.

6   Manifesto of Geographical Association printed on the inside cover of all copies of *Geography*.

7   Interview, 30 June 1976.

REFERENCES

Ackerknecht, E.H. (1965) *A Short History of Psychiatry*, translated by Sula Wolff. New York: Hafner.

Annales E.S.C. (1978) Translated by Elborg Forster and Patricia M. Ranum. Baltimore: Johns Hopkins University Press, pp. 180–212.

Bing, F. (1983) 'La théorie de la dégénéréscence', in J. Postel and C. Quétel (eds), *Nouvelle histoire de la psychiatrie*, Toulouse: Privat, pp. 251–356.

Bleandonu, G. and Le Gaufey, G. (1978) 'The creation of the insane asylums of Auxerre and Paris', in R. Forster and O. Ranum (eds) *Deviants and the Abandoned in French Society*, Baltimore: Johns Hopkins University Press.

Bynum, W.F., Porter, R., and Shepherd, M. (eds) (1985) *The Anatomy of Madness: Essays in the History of Psychiatry*, vols 1-2, London and New York: Tavistock.

———(1985) 'Degeneration and hereditarianism in French mental medicine 1840–1890', in Bynum, Porter, and Shepherd, *op.cit.*, vol. 1, *People and Ideas*, pp. 188–232.

Byrne, E.M. (1974) *Planning and Educational Inequality*, Slough: NFER, p. 29.

Castel, R. (1976) *L'ordre psychiatrique: L'âge d'or de l'aliénisme*, Paris: Editions de minuit.

Corrigan, P. and Curtis, B. (1985) 'Education, inspection and state formation: A preliminary statement', Canadian Historical Association, *Historical Papers*, pp. 156–71.

Curtis, B. (1983) 'Preconditions of the Canadian state: Educational reforms and the construction of a public in Upper Canada 1837–1846', *Studies in*

Political Economy: A Socialist Review 10 (Winter): 99–121.

David, T. (1973) 'Against geography' in D. Bale, N. Graves, and R. Walford (eds) *Perspectives in Geographical Education*, Edinburgh: Oliver and Boyd, pp. 12–3.

Dowbiggin, I. (1985) 'French psychiatry, hereditarianism and professional legitimacy 1840–1900', *Research in Law, Deviance, and Social Control* 7: 135–65.

Foucault, M. (1980) 'Questions on geography', in M. Foucault (ed.) *Power/Knowledge: Selected Interviews and Other Writings 1972–1977*, Brighton: Harvester Press, p. 63.

———(1979) *Discipline and Punish: The Birth of the Prison*, translated by Alan Sheridan. New York: Vintage, pp. 27, 137–8.

Freidson, E. (1970) *Professional Dominance*, New York: Atherton, p. 106. Cited in A.T. Scull (1979) *Museums of Madness: The Social Organization of Insanity in Nineteenth-Century England*, Harmondsworth: Penguin, p. 141.

Garnett, A. (1969) 'Teaching geography: Some reflections', *Geography* 54: 387.

Giroux, H.A. (1983) 'Theories of reproduction and resistance in the new sociology of education: A critical analysis', *Harvard Educational Review* 53: 257–93.

Goldstein, J. (1984) "Moral contagion': A professional ideology of medicine and psychiatry in eighteenth- and nineteenth-century France', in Gerald L. Geison (ed.) *Professions and the French State 1700–1900*, Philadelphia: University of Pennsylvania Press, pp. 181–222.

———(1987) *Console and Classify: The French Psychiatric Profession in the Nineteenth Century*, Cambridge: Cambridge University Press.

Gowing, D. (1973) 'A fresh look at objectives' in R. Watford (ed.) *New Directions in Geography Teaching*, London: Longmans, p. 153.

Hadlow Report (1927) *Report of the Consultative Committee: The Education of the Adolescent*, Board of Education. London: HMSO.

Honeybone, R.C. (1954) 'Balance in geography and education', *Geography* 34: 186.

Jones, C. (1980) 'The treatment of the insane in eighteenth- and early nineteenth-century Montpellier', *Medical History* 24: 372–90.

Kaestle, C.F. (1972) 'Social reform and the urban school', *History of Education Quarterly* 12: 218.

Lunier, L., Costans, A. and Dumesnil, E. (1876) *Rapport générale à M. le Ministre de l'intérieure sur le service des aliénés*, Paris: Imprimerie nationale.

MacKinder, H.J. (1903) 'Report of the discussion on geographical education', *Geographical Teacher* 2: 95–101, London.

———(1887) 'On the scope and methods of geography', *Proceedings of the Royal Geographical Society* 9.

Marchant, E.C. (1965) 'Some responsibilities of the teacher of geography', *Geography* 3: 133.

———(1968) 'Some responsibilities of the teacher of geography', *Geography* 3.

Nye, R.A. (1984) *Crime, Madness, and Politics in Modern France: The*

Medical Concept of National Decline, Princeton: Princeton University Press.

Petit, J. (1980) 'Folie, language, pouvoirs en Maine-et-Loire 1800–1941', *Revue d' histoire moderne et contemporaine* 27: 529–64.

Pinkney, D.H. (1986) *Decisive Years in France 1840–1847*, Princeton: Princeton University Press.

Postel, J. and Quétel, C. (eds) (1983) *Nouvelle histoire de la psychiatrie*, Toulouse: Privat.

Report (1967) *Society and the Young School Leaver*, Working Paper no. 11, London: HMSO, p.3.

Ritti, A. (1914) *Histoire des travaux de la Société médico-psychologique et éloges de ses membres*, vols 1–2, Paris: Mason.

Rothman, D.J. (1971) *The Discovery of the Asylum: Social Order and Disorder in the New Republic*, Boston and Toronto: Little, Brown.

Scull, A.T. (ed.) (1981) *Madhouses, Mad-Doctors, and Mad-Men: The Social History of Psychiatry in the Victorian Era*, Philadelphia: University of Pennsylvania Press.

Semelaigne, R. (1930–2) *Les pionniers de la psychiatrie française avant et après Pinel*, vols. 1–2, Paris: Baillière.

Shortt, S.E.D. (1986) *Victorian Lunacy: Richard M. Bucke and the Practice of Late Nineteenth-Century Psychiatry*, Cambridge: Cambridge University Press, pp. 100–9.

Walker, D. (1975) 'The well-rounded geographers', *The Times Educational Supplement*, 28 November, p. 6.

Young, M. (1971) 'An approach to the study of curricula as socially organized knowledge', in M. Young (ed.) *Knowledge and Control*, London: Collier MacMillan, pp. 19–46.

Part III

Discourse and politics

7 Deconstructing hegemony
Multicultural policy and a populist response
John Knight, Richard Smith, and Judyth Sachs

COMPETING TEXTS?

In recent years there has been an increasing interest in the nature of knowledge, its constitution, and the effects kinds of knowledge have on institutional practices. This interest has undermined assumptions of certainty by arguing that sets of foundational and methodological conventions ('disciplines') as well as the facts they produce ('knowledge') are themselves open to criticism ('deconstruction'). The notion of truth itself has been radically deconstructed so that its conditions of production and consumption are seen to be part of its definition. In turn, particular conceptions of truth about the condition of the world are seen to prevail over competing versions because of the peculiarities of time, space, and social conditions that provide the rules that specify truth and the economic and political role it plays (Foucault 1980: 132).

Nowhere is this interest more appropriate than in the critical appreciation of official state policies. Such policies attempt to represent the world in factual terms so that certain kinds of practices flow 'naturally' from them. They appropriate scientific methodologies and social science theory in order to create a reality that is rational, objective, seamless, and which taps into the sensibilities of national popular consciousness. In doing so, such policies tell stories which, once interpreted by audiences, are emptied of meaning and filled with available social myths (Barthes 1973). Competing stories are thus available as resources for decoding and recoding and otherwise clashing or collaborating with official policy.

These issues are exemplified in a major concern of the Australian Schools Commission era[1]: multicultural education, here considered as it was constructed in Queensland, an Australian state. We examine two competing versions of 'multiculturalism' and 'education': namely, the 1979 Queensland Education Department policy discussion paper, *Education For a Multicultural Society* (MS), and the 1981 response to it by the populist and fundamentalist education lobby, STOP/CARE (SC).[2]

Our concerns are to establish the truth claims over which these two texts engage in power-struggle and to identify the discursive mechanisms used to achieve a state 'policy' on multiculturalism and education. We go on to show the significant epistemic continuities in both texts (and the discourses in which they are embedded) that assume and support the material conditions of inequality and relations of power and subordination in the Queensland social formation. In that context, we juxtapose some themes in the texts which signal difference and struggle as well as epistemic continuity in policy formation. And, as Foucault (1970, 1972, 1977) has shown, apparently specific or parochial material and events illuminate more general discursive and structural features whose effects on the shaping and implementation of educational policy are largely unrecognized.

COMPETING TEXTS

Prior to 1978 the Queensland Department of Education had no policy on multicultural education. Federal initiatives provided a climate and funding appropriate for such development and in 1978 the Director General of Education set up a working party to develop policy and directions in multicultural education. Their report, which drew heavily on the current literature on multicultural education, was accepted as the policy basis for multicultural education in Queensland.

This policy was unacceptable to many Queenslanders. In late 1983 and early 1984, using previously successful tactics, the STOP/CARE organization co-ordinated a public campaign against multiculturalism and multicultural education. Meetings of 'concerned parents' and other 'interested citizens' were held around the state. Newsletters were circulated widely. *Pro forma* letters were mailed to state politicians. The director of STOP/CARE and her husband discussed their objections with the Minister for Education and the education ministerial committee. The Premier was reported as saying that the multicultural programme would be scaled down, adding that it should highlight cultures and religions traditional to Australia, and that it was time to 'stop giving our own culture and religion away'.

However, although some materials were reviewed, the programme was not removed. Given the success of prior attacks on other liberal or progressive materials (e.g., *Man: A Course of Study* (MACOS), the *Social Education Materials Project* (SEMP), peace studies, sex education, evolutionary science – see Smith and Knight 1978, 1981; Knight 1986) such failure begs explanation. We begin with the struggle between MS and SC over an appropriate policy on multiculturalism and education.

COMPETING IDEOLOGIES?

These two sets of texts, and the social forces they represent, are engaged in struggle centred on the production, control, and status of knowledge and truth in relation to multiculturalism and education. In the case of MS in particular, the text can be seen as an attempt to establish leadership in the field of education around an issue of intellectual and moral reform, namely, a new policy for Queensland schools. SC contests that policy in so far as it attempts to discredit the status of the truth presented by MS and to present an alternative set of assumptions around 'Australian' and 'Queensland' 'society'. We briefly rehearse their contrasting positions.

The central theme of MS is a multicultural Australia, and an education appropriate to that end. In the Australian society constructed in this document, tolerance and social harmony are predominant in the way in which differing cultural and ethnic groups are positioned. The strains and tensions inherent in such cultural diversity are recontextualized in a mythical process of 'social change' that elides discrimination, fragmentation, and social conflict. Thus Anglo-Australians, Aborigines, and the wide range of cultures and ethnic groups now in Australia are discursively linked so that a particular conception of 'national identity' is retained and its central political and social institutions are maintained. However, certain elements, namely, 'monocultural education', the 'White Australia policy', the outdated policy of assimilation, and the attitudes of traditional Anglo-Australians, are by definition excluded from this consensus.

Rejecting all such pluralist notions, SC asserts the necessity of a monocultural Australia. Two clearly identifiable and opposed forces (one good, the other evil) centre around multiculturalism and monoculturalism. The former is linked with MACOS and SEMP: 'humanistic Marxist socialism', 'republicanism', 'the United Nations', 'cultural and social disharmony', 'cultural relativism', 'social engineering', and so on. Opposed to this array is 'our monocultural society', 'our Australian way of life', 'our flag', 'our Christian and British heritage', 'the Royal Family', 'our legal system', 'patriotism', 'the family', and 'our school system'.

READING TEXT: DISCURSIVE ASSUMPTIONS

In previous work of this kind (e.g., Smith and Knight 1978, 1981; Freeland 1979; Scott and Scott 1980), texts such as these were therefore conceived of as encompassing two opposed ideological systems: liberalism and conservatism. The elements of each and their internal logical connections rendered them antagonistic and incommensurate. Further, 'conservatism' was identified with the state in so far as it was

135

preferred by the government of the day and was used to further dominant class interests in education. In this chapter we seek to break with that conception in a number of ways.

It is a commonplace that conflicts of class and social interests are also 'a battle of ideas which is integral to the course and outcome of the struggle' (Aarons 1987: 10). In that struggle, certain sets of ideas and practices are privileged over others, so that there is a dominant ideology which consists of a specified body of content and originates with a specific group – 'the ruling class' (cf. Marx, in Bottomore and Rubel 1963: 93, or Abercrombie, Hill, and Turner 1980: 1–4).

We have argued elsewhere (Knight, Smith, and Chant 1989) against the search for a set of coherent elements believed by a certain proportion of a given class. Rather, we propose a model of social life that is concerned with the way in which power, including systematically structured relations of domination and subordination, is maintained by the mobilization of meaning (Shapiro 1981; Thompson 1984; Laclau and Mouffe 1985), that is to say, discursively.

In such a framework, ideas and practices, including projects and apprehensions of possibilities, are co-joined as simultaneities (Bakhtin, in Clark and Holquist 1984: 87). In so far as they are incorporated within systems of domination, they are ideological in their effects. Ideology and discourse (and their manifestations in and through texts)[3] are therefore a site of struggle over a range of potential closures (Laclau and Mouffe 1985; cf. Gramsci 1981) rather than givens which flow from particular theories.

Such (necessary) 'evidence' of ideological struggle and contested domination (as above) privileges 'difference' over epistemic continuity. Materialist analyses have properly located such struggle in socio-historical and economic setting. But any adequate analysis of the production, reproduction, and contestation of the social relations of authority and power should attempt also to 'excavate' their epistemic foundations, that is, those largely unseen controls on discourse whose effect, within that specific epoch, is 'for permitting certain facts, opinions and ideas to be uttered while forbidding others' (Sturrock 1986; cf. Foucault 1970, 1972).

Within such bounds the denotation of discursive elements (e.g., family, multiculturalism, or education) is not fixed but can be connotatively linked to other elements to produce different meanings in different discourses. This absorption and appropriation of elements occurs in both the construction of the text and in its 'readings' by audiences. Similarly, the polysemic nature of signs and sign-based discourses means that ideological incorporation and contestation can occur at the point of reading as readers either become passive consumers or turn the text against its 'preferred' meanings. The outcome cannot be 'read off' from a knowledge of class position, for example, although, as Morley (1980: 173) notes, position in the social structure may structure and limit the repertoires of discursive or 'decoding' strategies available to audiences. Hence, while analyses of such text typically focus on their themes and issues *per se*, we are concerned with the manner and effects of their articulation (Laclau and Mouffe 1985). Here we draw particular attention to the discursive constructions through which both those who affirm and those who contest 'official' policy seek to define the field, articulate positions, and mobilize audiences. Thus, silently they set limits for the sayable and the possible (Burton and Carlen 1977; Donald 1979; Knight, Smith, and Chant 1989).

Discourses whose project is primarily establishing moral and intellectual leadership (Burton and Carlen 1977) attempt to establish a preferred reading across a variety of audiences by articulating different discursive practices to a shared ideological frame of reference. As society is characterized by a vast plurality of subjects who are themselves constituted by discourse, hegemony is thus a 'discourse of discourses' (Jessop 1982: 198–9). Responses to and interpretations of particular texts should not therefore be understood simply in terms of individual psychologies. Rather, individual readings will be framed by cultural formations and practices which are derived from the objective position of the individual reader in the social structure.

Therefore, while we focus on texts in this chapter, we conceive of the texts as situated within a complex of Queensland discourses that form their conditions of existence. That is, while we attend to the features of specific texts, we connect them to the broader Queensland social formation when we consider the effects of the projects inscribed in the texts.

Finally, we acknowledge a plurality (not an infinity) of readings. While certain readings are preferred, there is no final reading. Hence, as with the material it addresses, this study seeks to persuade, so that our text upon texts (the reading of MS and SC which follows) is contested within the epistemic framing of those whom it engages.

DE/CONSTRUCTING THE TEXTS

The project of both MS and SC is the construction of 'truth' around the central ideas of multiculturalism and education. This is what is at stake in the confrontation and debate between the texts. In both cases the 'speaker' in the text selects from a range of possible alternative courses of action in order to establish the status of what is said. The essential problem for the speakers in both texts is simultaneously to describe the material and ideal causes of multiculturalism so that a particular 'truthful' position is legitimated. The project is largely achieved by the sequential organization of the text and the meaningful connection of utterances. In particular, the speaker is positioned in the text by the mode of address which provides both an identification for the speaker and a coherent point of view that is the 'preferred', but not guaranteed, reading. We commence with MS and then move to SC.

Though 'only' a departmental discussion paper, MS is constructed from and within a particular institutionalized discourse, the discourse of state policy (formal, impersonal, technical, prescriptive, authoritative), a discourse of legitimate power. The intent of its title, *Education for a Multicultural Society*, is authorized by the subtitle, 'A discussion paper based on the Report to the Council of Directors of the Queensland Department of Education', which is in turn 'prepared by The Working Party on Multicultural Education'. That is, its power derives from its location in the properly constituted structure of authority of government and the superior and specialized knowledge of those who are authorized to speak on these issues.

MS further legitimates this official status by an historical account, rehearsing Commonwealth initiatives and resources, and establishing that Australian and Queensland communities, schools, and teachers have long been multicultural. Nevertheless, there is 'currently considerable attention' around the multicultural nature of Australian society and an 'upsurge of interest' in multicultural education. The dilemma is solved by the appointment of a committee 'in the interests of promoting further discussion of desirable directions'. The result is to be a theory of a 'broadly based multicultural education program', spelled out as principles for future policymaking. Note that the multicultural 'philosophy' is presented as a material *fait accompli*, yet MS is produced ideally to promote 'further discussion'. This contradiction is dissolved by invoking a liberal pluralist solution ('the Committee would not presume to make recommendations') and by nihilating competing points of view. Competing perspectives from beyond the text are acknowledged but are delegitimated by the dismissive 'advocated by particular interests groups'.

The 'broad' approach is established by invoking superior knowledge (most likely of success in the long term). This is the discourse of power and knowledge, of the sovereign state, acting on behalf of 'all schools, all teachers, all students and all school communities'. The state (the Minister for Education), in adopting a moral stance that distances the problems of teachers in accounting for multicultural backgrounds from the problematic set by the policy guidelines, completes a circle of control over teachers and parents. The policy, secured as morally sound, is one that 'involves all teachers' and indeed, the 'Committee commends these approaches to teachers in all Queensland schools'.

This concern for control over teachers emphasizes the way in which the state monopolizes the ground of multicultural policy. Thus while recognizing the history of social diversity, MS claims that past attempts to deal with the multicultural 'needs' of students have been 'largely *ad hoc*'; the absence of policy has 'not assisted schools'; there has been a lack of 'co-ordination' and resources. Moreover, the real lacks reside in the teachers, in human fallibility. Teachers have had good intentions but their *ad hoc* school-based curriculum development has been based on 'inadequate' and 'limited' understanding.

The proposition that such developments cannot ensure continuity establishes the legitimate state interventionist role which is guaranteed by an appeal to the stereotyped idea that the very cohesion of Queensland society is at stake. Thus the central point of discourse is set by the need of the state to oversee the reproductive function of education.

In that reproductive mode, all sectors of the social formation must be incorporated under the legitimate authority and superior knowledge of the Department (and hence of the state). Therefore the text attempts a preferred reading across a variety of readers, at the one moment addressing teachers in schools, at another parents and the community, at yet another, teachers and community. Hence, drawing upon a discourse of official policy, MS seeks to incorporate and legitimate difference (e.g., 'children of diverse ethnic backgrounds', 'cultural diversity', 'English and community languages') within the one social formation. Thus, working in what Laclau and Mouffe (1985: 127ff) describe as a 'discourse of difference', it creates an implied consensus of contrasting positions, blurring and dissolving, or even ignoring and creating silences on the contradictions of lived experience and social ideals. Hence while difference remains, it is effectively absorbed as an oppositional force to social stability and the core elements of Australian society.

There is therefore an inescapable ambiguity on the status of multiculturalism. The constructed history of the emergence of multicultural education clearly signals the dangers of the multicultural project, a danger MS attempts repeatedly to neutralize, as illustrated in this extract:

> All Queensland State Schools must help all children *cope* with the *realities* of living in such a (multicultural) society; *secure* in their own personal and cultural identities and *tolerant* of those of others; but *aware of the strains and tensions* implicit in multiculturalism and *conscious of their responsibility* to contribute to the *national identity* – the changing and growing 'common culture'.
>
> (section 1.4, emphases added)

Note that the extract begins with danger: 'cope with the realities of living in', and moves to a means of ameliorating that danger by creating children who are 'secure' personally and therefore (or yet) 'tolerant' of others. In other words, the problem is (as the policy statements later defines it) one of 'bias and prejudice' (that is, it is a problem located in individuals). It is therefore (as the policy statement also asserts) 'primarily affective, dealing with attitudes and dispositions'; that is, it is constituted as a psychological rather than a sociological problem. There is therefore a major silence on issues of social and structural inequality. It is a problem that can be dissolved by changing attitudes, removing discrimination. Yet MS does not stop at this point. Against children being made 'aware of the strains and tensions' (that is, aware of the dangers implied in the initial statement about coping with the realities of a multicultural society) 'implicit in multiculturalism' (that is, inherent in, and incapable of any final dissolution), it casts a further psychologistic imperative: children should be 'made conscious of their responsibility' to the 'national identity'. That is, if the multicultural society fails or collapses, it will be from their failure to accept that responsibility; the Department and the constructors of MS are absolved of responsibility. However, positively, being made conscious of that responsibility somehow implies a fulfilment or achievement of what it demands. To round off the statement, there is then that final positive attribution: the 'national identity' is equated with the 'common culture'. That is, the juxtaposition of opposites has dissolved the tensions and contradictions and we are left with what the paper elsewhere describes as 'not a oneness but a unity... a voluntary band of dissimilar people, sharing a common political and institutional structure'.

Such apparently dialectic attempts at reconciling oppositional positions and dissolving contradictions allegedly inherent in multiculturalism occur at critical points in the document. In each case, a section commences with a history which legitimates what it then develops, and moves on in a smooth and polished (inevitable?) progression that culminates in an upwelling of oppositions which it can no longer ignore and which must once more be dissolved into the text.

This is exemplified in section 4, which takes all that has been constructed thus far and applies it as education for a multicultural society. After a series of repeated and pious commonsense stereotypes, a key dilemma emerges and has to be faced: the difficulty of achieving a balance between the legitimate desire of minority groups for cultural maintenance between minority cultures, and the social necessity of their being equipped to operate within 'the mainstream culture' (section 4.2).

The dilemma is resolved in the next paragraph: multicultural education will be achieved when the school emphasizes 'both the intrinsic worth of all people and the contribution that differences between groups and individuals make to the whole society' (section 4.2).

So the school must resolve the impenetrable contradictions of liberalism and capitalism by reasserting them. The movement in the above section from a stress on individuals to an acceptance of the reality of groups or collectivities of people increases the difficulties of resolving contradictions when the contradictions are recognized as social rather than psychological.

Against this discourse of legitimate (bureaucratic) authority, SC draws on the discourses of populism, social conservatism, and fundamentalist Christianity to attack MS. It speaks for and with the authority of the Australian people, asserting the superiority of their 'traditional way of life' based on 'our British heritage', whose legitimacy is found in the absolute 'truths' and moral superiority of Christianity.

Nevertheless, in that it addresses 'multiculturalism' and 'education' as the problematic of the text, the agenda of SC is similar to MS. The form of the reader–text relationship, however, differs because the matrix of ideas that are prescribed by its operations draws on a range of discourses that lie beyond and around MS. Here it is assumed that there are sectors of Queensland society (social conservatives, fundamentalists, the Returned Services League,[4] the League of Rights etc.) who resonate to Anglo-Australian themes and share concerns about the social and political divisiveness of multicultural policy. What is at stake in SC is the definition of political stability, the *status quo*. The state, embodied as the fusion of 'the people' and the political executive, is the speaking subject of this text.

This can be seen in the use of 'shifters' (Donald 1979) that are definable only in relation to the speaking subject. SC alternates between the discursive 'here and now' ('I have received'; 'at *my* request'; 'I was most distressed to learn') and an historical 'then' when the speaker is suppressed ('*They* set about commissioning'; 'it is what *they*') (emphases added). It is important to unravel who is signified by these shifters. 'I' is quite clearly the spokesperson for SC speaking as the knowing expert with a much publicized track record of successful educational interventions. This connection is provided symbolically:

JANUARY 1978: This date is significant! It means that, IMMEDIATELY the Government banned MACOS [*Man: A Course of Study*] from primary school. . .
(*Stop Press*, 31 December 1983: 2)

Here 'they' signifies 'Education Directors – the same bureaucrats who had implemented and defended MACOS and SEMP'. These agents are explicitly acknowledged as relatively autonomous and therefore a threat to the reproductive functions of education ('the Education Directors began looking for another way to CONDITION AND SOCIALISE our children (and their teachers)!'). The contradiction within the state, thus uncovered, is resolved by invoking a notion of the overarching political state, centred on the premier and 'our society'. 'Our' in this context incorporates parents, families, Queensland employers, children, teachers, and the Queensland government who together have a duty to protect 'our social well-being', 'our policy of integration', 'the Australian lifestyle we presently enjoy', and 'the Anglo Saxon Christian culture':

> I trust, Mr Premier, that your government will see the vital need to have this programme eradicated before it wastes any more of the taxpayers' money and leads Queensland any further down the road to centralism in Education and ultimate Socialism.
>
> (*Stop Press*, 31 December 1983: 3)

The state is thus constructed and empowered to enact a leadership function for an unproblematic, division-less, mono-cultural society. The dissension in this co-operative monolith is isolated in the education bureaucrats.

This bureaucratic dissent is linked by SC with a range of 'external' elements that threaten social stability and security. Thus, working in what Laclau and Mouffe (1985: 127ff) term a 'discourse of equivalence', SC seeks to articulate and reduce ensembles of differences in the social formation into two irreconcilably opposed forces: an evil and conspiratorial multiculturalism, and a virtuous and necessary mono-culturalism. The intent is to mobilize its readers in active opposition to multiculturalism and the education bureaucrats.

INTERTEXTUALITY AND EPISTEMIC CONTINUITY

This struggle to define educational policy is thus a struggle for control of the productive and reproductive functions of schooling and hence for the legitimate definition of Australian society. Such attempts to mobilize meaning on the disputed discursive terrain of 'multiculturalism' thereby incorporate Queenslanders as subjects within systems and relations of domination and subordination. Thus they are ideological in their effects. But while contestation is a necessary prerequisite for hegemony, it is not sufficient.

The deconstruction of MS and SC brought to view certain shared concerns and foundational assumptions. They include the threat of multiculturalism to the national identity and common culture; the need to manage and control social change to maintain social cohesion and stability; the pre-eminence of English as a language common to all Australians; and a shared psychologistic construction of individuals. There is a mistrust of schools and teachers; a paternalistic concern for the protection and appropriate socialization of children; and a recognition of the centrality of the curriculum in shaping children's consciousness and hence of the need to maintain an external control upon it. These commonalities are indices of an epistemic frame in which the material conditions of inequality and relations of power and subordination in the Queensland social formation are taken for granted, and hence remain unaddressed, unspoken, denied. We briefly rehearse certain aspects of these continuities and their implications for curriculum development and educational policy.

SC and MS agree that multiculturalism threatens the national identity and common culture. To SC it is 'a dangerous socialist innovation', part of a UN-based international conspiracy to subvert 'the British heritage' and our loyalty to the Crown, destroy Christianity and patriotism, suppress traditional education, 'and cause the breakdown of home and family life'.

While MS avoids such flamboyant rhetoric, it too has been shown to be less than enthusiastic in its implementation of multiculturalism. As noted previously, schools and teachers are instructed to rely on the Education Department for a proper reading of multiculturalism. The text warns that there are '*strains and tensions* implicit in multiculturalism'; that 'the issue of *balance*... is not easily resolved'; that 'Anglo-Australian perspectives on historical and other events *should not be eliminated or denigrated*'; that children must be made 'conscious of their responsibility to contribute to *the national identity* – the changing and growing "*common culture*"'; that 'some educators are deeply concerned that cultural studies, by fostering cultural pride, might lead to *conflict* and to the *fragmentation* of Australian Society'; and that schools and teachers must follow the aims outlined in MS if 'cultural studies are [to be] likely to foster *constructive social change* and to reduce rather than exacerbate, *ethnic divisions*' (emphases added). It is clear, then, that such a dangerous development as multiculturalism must be tamed and processed by the Committee and the Department. The metaphor is that of the rawness, disorder and danger of the natural being processed and transmuted into a civilized, ordered, and safe form (Levi-Strauss 1970).

It follows that SC and MS concur in the necessity for a continuing Anglo-Australian hegemony. As noted above, SC upholds 'the traditional Australian way of life', which is centred around 'our Christian culture', 'our British heritage', and a 'judicial system, based solely on British principles'. Thus, logically, Australia 'has always been a monocultural society'.

A careful examination of MS indicates similar though more muted concerns. It rejects the elimination or denigration of 'Anglo-Australian perspectives'. While it denies 'the so-called "White Australia Policy"' and discards 'the earlier policy of assimilation' as now 'inappropriate',

MS is equally clear that there is and must be a 'national identity' and a 'common culture'. Moreover, we have noted the desire that 'minority groups will opt for preparation for life in the mainstream society as opposed to cultural maintenance', while the counter-positioning of 'ethnic and mainstream groups' clearly indicates that pre-eminence is accorded to the latter. And so we read that 'Queensland school programs should stress not a oneness but a voluntary band of dissimilar people, *sharing a common political and institutional structure*' (section 4.3, emphasis added).

Here is a shared concern that the central core of Australian society should be beyond challenge. While the signifiers differ, that which is signified has a certain commonality. Clearly, MS aims to 'reduce, rather than exacerbate, ethnic divisions'. It is our reading that such a position, rather than being 'multicultural', is a simple rephrasing of the prior policy of integration, and seeks a continuing Anglo-Australian hegemony. (Here see Lingard 1983; Henry and Lingard 1982.)

Such concerns for social cohesion and stability from both texts index the need to manage and control change. SC is openly opposed to change, except to an earlier (purer) way of life. The term 'innovation' has always a negative connotation, as in for example 'this dangerous Socialist innovation' (which is 'simply another way of getting the "MACOS and SEMP" ideology and aims into the classroom'). Here liberal or progressive claims that multiculturalism is creating a 'new society' are linked with the panoply of evil forces and events already reviewed in detail.

Previously cited statements from MS indicate a similar concern for managing change. Despite the overt concern for a multicultural society, the presentation of multiculturalism is such that it improves the 'self concept' of each student, giving 'a sense of identity and achievement' and thereby 'promotes his chances for becoming a productive, well-adjusted member of society'. But such a focus implies adjusting the individual to the *status quo* rather than changing society.

Indeed, both MS and SC embody unquestioned ideological assumptions of individualism in a decontextualized frame, that is, apart from the groups and communities in and from which individuals are constructed and take their identity. Linked with this is their common stress on the cultural dimension of society, to the neglect of its structural inequalities.

Thus much of the rhetoric of MS is cast in the language of psychologisms, in which 'all people should be presented as individuals', where culture is presented as a quality possessed by individuals whose cultural and ethnic identities contribute to their 'self concept'. Hence, 'multiculturalism allows an individual the freedom to support and maintain his (*sic*) own culture, while placing responsibility on him at the same time to contribute to the national identity'. While at critical points in the document the text shifts from the decontextualized individual to the language of social and ethnic groups or of society as a whole, the relationship of individuals to such groups is left undefined; indeed, the text specifically warns against adopting cultural 'stereotypes' for individuals. This psychologistic and cultural bent implies (ironically) social conformity, for rather than changing the unaddressed structural inequities that disadvantage ethnic minorities, we are told that 'above all, changes must occur *in people*, as the change in focus is primarily *affective*' (emphases added). Thus inequality is resolved through the elimination of discrimination, 'bias and prejudice'.

For SC this stress on individualism is necessary to oppose the collectivism of international socialism. The individual press for salvation extends from making the right choices in everyday life to being on the right side in the present conflict between good and evil. Hence, one of the SC texts concludes with a construction that clearly seeks to position and mobilize its readers:

> God has put you in possession of alarming facts – what are you going to do about what you now know? If you stand idly by and allow this to happen... how will you be able to explain your apathy to your children... when they find themselves in communist slavery.
>
> (*Stop Press*, 14 September 1981: 3)

For all of these reasons both documents recognize the centrality of teachers and the curriculum in shaping children's consciousness, hence their press to control the curriculum and policy processes. MS's reservations on teachers and schools, along with similar concerns about managing community input, have been noted. A major sector of the document addresses education as 'cultural transmission or enculturation', noting the role of the curriculum in 'the shaping and modification of human experience', its reproductive function in promoting beliefs, values, and the like, and stressing the importance of the 'hidden curriculum' so far as the appropriateness of its rules, routines, and procedures are concerned.

The vehemence of the SC attack on the content of multicultural education and the processes of schooling ('manipulating the minds of children', 'changing attitudes through a hidden curriculum', 'values clarification', and an ultimate intent to create 'a ONE WORLD SOCIALIST DICTATORSHIP, and a ONE WORLD NON-CHRISTIAN RELIGION') indicates its recognition of the central role of curriculum and school experience in shaping children who will become 'the citizens of tomorrow'.

Their major difference is more about who controls the curriculum.

SC sees the Education Department, under the direction of the 'bureaucrats' and the 'humanists', as failing in its task to socialize the young properly. It appeals to the Premier and to other politicians to control the Department and eradicate the multicultural course. That is, the Education Department, which should be part of the state, needs reincorporating into the state. Here it is significant that later developments, including the attempt in 1987 to amend the Queensland Education Act,[5] have effectively ensured that incorporation.

To MS, however, the Department is the proper source of curricular control, and is performing management and reproductive functions for the state from within the state. It sees no contradiction between the state's political function and its educative role. However, schools and teachers are more marginal, either upon or beyond the borders of the state, and need to be reincorporated into its intentions.

CONSTRUCTING HEGEMONY THROUGH CONTESTATION

We have argued that the contestation of truth around issues of multiculturalism, education, and Australian society constructs and masks significant continuities in the themes and assumptions of MS and SC. We have further sought the ground of such continuity in shared epistemic assumptions which constitute 'silence' on social structural inequalities and, in particular, the material conditions of Queensland and Australian society. This silence can be identified as a set of values that on the one hand deny social divisions and on the other hand celebrate them as being natural and inevitable.

That denial, inscribed in MS, is at the heart of policy formation and implementation. Such policy can be seen as an element of the steering mechanism of the state (Habermas 1976) in response to the effect of a multicultural society. Resistance to the assimilationist policies of successive federal and state governments by immigrant populations in the workforce, in social welfare provision, and in social movements in the last decade or so created problems of legitimation. As Dale (1982) and Weiler (1983) have argued, education in such circumstances becomes a key site for relegitimating the state by accommodating and nihilating contradictions. A new technology, a new industry is required to encompass and control the emergent reconceptualization of what constitutes education. The new 'truth' reconstructs education equally, for all teachers, all parents, and all students so that the potential of a radical relativism implied by 'multicultural' is neutralized by a centralized control network, the policy, and its implied practices. The attempt to perfect education, while society is left untouched, by the emphasis on cultural differences being individual differences is a hidden but prescribed system of power. The commonsense, populist, and moralistic stance of SC shares the anti-diversity tactics of MS.

It is this structuring continuity across the texts that constitutes the 'hegemonic principle' (Mouffe 1979: 178–95). In this sense SC and MS are representative of the same form of history that is operative in relation to the incorporation of multiculturalism across social, political, educational, and economic spheres of contemporary society. SC thus colludes with MS to ensure a silence about issues such as justice and power, and ultimately, the class interests of multicultural education policy, and in doing so assists in constituting them.

A curious paradox is inherent in these practices. The construction of 'truth' and 'lies' around multiculturalism and education and the 'debates' which it engenders ensures that the multiculturalist emphasis is increasingly lost. The interest in multiculturalism is coupled with a bourgeois hypocrisy which reveals 'multiculturalism' as a 'story' guaranteed by empiricist 'evidence' and codified in the interests of 'equality' while at the same repressing it. Such hypocrisy 'mingles ceaselessly the art of rectifying and the right to punish' (Foucault 1977: 303).

It is important, however, to locate the recontextualization of multicultural education within a broader historical framework of ideological transformations. The debate around multicultural education is part of a larger shift, from the mid-1970s, away from progressive and liberal curricula, texts, and resource materials. While the groups and lobbies (religious fundamentalists, social conservatives, employers) opposing such materials are well known, the nature and outcomes of the contest are contingent on its socio-historical context and its agonistic field, that is, the infrastructural organization of knowledge from which their assumptions are drawn.

The multiplicity of discourses available in Queensland society are produced in specific conditions created by geographical location, cultural and religious homogeneity, unique economic and political circumstances and particular histories around the provision of schooling, the operations of the urban and provincial media, health services, and race relations (Smith and Knight 1981). Social practices produce meaning so that Queenslanders and Queensland social relations are constituted, mediated, and reproduced in and through discourses (Jessop 1982: 196; Wuthnow *et al.* 1984: 148). To this extent there is a common nucleus of signifiers (Jessop 1982: 196) such as 'land rights', 'migrants', or 'education' which are differently accented in different discourses but nevertheless provide the ground on which both MS and SC are obliged to work if their political agendas are to succeed. To this extent also, they share the same epoch characterized by increasing state power. By emphasizing the relations between MS and SC, especially the common antagonism to structural realities that neither side wants addressed, let alone remedied, the dynamics of social inequality (that is, of class relations) are revealed.

These relations can be indexed in the political, social, and economic instability of the late 1970s. The Queensland economy was characterized by a falling demand for primary products, a declining manufacturing sector, rising levels of unemployment, and increasing foreign control. The restructuring of the economy towards a post-industrial era saw an increase in the deskilling of work and the adoption by employers of casual and part-time work. New Right concerns emerged with moves for contract labour, deregulation, and a restructuring of the wage-arbitration system. A wave of largely Asian migrants and refugees followed the earlier influx of (white) European migrants. There were renewed calls (e.g., from the League of Rights, sectors of the Returned Services League, the 'Blainey Debate'[6]) to halt these changes to Queensland's and Australia's ethnic composition and to maintain an Anglomorph identity.

At the same time, protests against repressive industrial legislation, and for land rights, civil rights, and personal freedoms increased. Unionists, Aborigines and Islanders, the unskilled, the young, the less educated, many women, and some ethnic groups were becoming marginalized. Large numbers of the petty bourgeoisie (small business people, farmers, entrepreneurs) also lost status and power. In this period, young people were scapegoated as a generation nurtured on 'permissive' lifestyles and the culture of consumerism, lacking commitment to work and traditional social structures. There was therefore a growing fear on the part of dominant political interests of the threat of social and political revolt from those alienated from the existing system.

New social groups added to this threat. Here we include the so-called 'new class' of educated professionals, bureaucrats, managers, for whom big business, big government, and big unions were natural and acceptable, and the new entrepreneurs, seeking quick wealth from speculative enterprises and for whom any ideal other than self-advancement was redundant.

As Wexler and Grabiner (1986) have argued, two distinct but contradictory discourses that represented these conditions coalesced on the question of public education. On the one hand, cultural 'restorationists' (here SC) sought to re-valorize a traditional way of life and to return to past educational principles and practices. On the other hand, free-market interests (represented here by MS) campaigned for social and political stability linked to 'choice' in curricular matters and private schooling, and sought changes in the governance of education so that it was tied more closely to the marketplace. In our view, such reforms provided for political stability and social cohesion in a period of possible crisis by articulating the concerns of influential but competing factions within the state.

Thus SC expressed views compatible with the interests of the old petty bourgeoisie, rural groupings, and fundamentalist religionists while MS represented newer fractions of the ruling elites, the state bureaucracies, transnational and out-of-state business interests. MS sought to incorporate a range of minority groups with the mainstream of Australian society for greater stability in a period of economic transition and social turbulence. SC, however, sought stability through the maintenance of traditional social and economic structures. Both sets of intentions were desirable for the decision-makers in Queensland politics and society. That is to say, hegemony is articulated by its contestation.

POLICY STUDIES IN EDUCATION

This conclusion raises a crucial issue for the study of educational policy construction and implementation. It underscores the significance of the distinction Bernstein (1986) makes between the relay and the messages of official educational discourse, and the relative importance of each. Whatever else the discussion has achieved, it has shown that the relay, or the principles by which multicultural messages are constructed, was decisive in determining what went to public schools as preferred orientations. The policy set the agenda for the practical implementation of curriculum development and pedagogical work, pre-service and in-service teacher education. As we have tried to show, the encoding of the social in MS is such that it divests the reader from its determinate conditions. For many teachers and school administrators, the text of MS reproduces what is already known because, as Belsey (1980: 128) proposes, the 'myths and signifying systems' represent experience as it is conventionally articulated in Queensland society. In this way, the principles of its construction connect the concerns of the state and the cultures of teachers.[7] A critical and productive educational policy studies, especially if it is for teachers to use, then has the task of producing new meaning around such policies that expands the multiplicity of voices in it (Barthes 1975). Only when the 'official' authority of the text as knowledge and its source as guarantor of its truth are transcended, can the construction of really useful knowledge begin.

SUMMARY

In summary, MS and SC articulated the same sets of subjects, themes, and issues (Australians, migrants, culture, children, education, teachers, curriculum, schools) to the definition of opposed positions: a multicultural or monocultural Australia. Asserting contrasting positions (monoculturalism versus multiculturalism), they engaged in ideological struggle for the production and status of knowledge and truth in relation to multiculturalism and education. In this struggle they used contrasting discursive mechanisms, to justify their 'policy' on multiculturalism and education.

Despite such apparent differences, they shared significant epistemic continuities such that their ideological contestation maintained and celebrated the material conditions of inequality and relations of power and subordination in the Queensland and Australian social formation.

NOTES

A cognate paper was presented at the 1984 conference of the Australian Association for Research in Education. See also *New Education* 10, 1988. This chapter is a modified version of a paper presented at the inaugural conference of the Institute for Cultural Policy Studies, Griffith University, 1988.

1 The Australian Schools Commission was established in 1973 to develop policies and programs for equality of educational opportunity for all sectors of Australian society. It was abolished in 1987.
2 STOP/CARE: The Society To Outlaw Pornography and The Committee Against Regressive Education.
3 In this framework, discourse is 'the social process in which texts are embedded, while text is the concrete material object produced in discourse' (Hodge and Kress 1988: 6).
4 The RSL represents all Australian military personnel who have returned from active service overseas.
5 The 1987 amendments to the Education Act sought direct control by the state over the structure, content, and processes of all areas (state, private and tertiary) of education in Queensland.
6 Blainey, a noted conservative Australian scholar and historian, articulated the concerns of many Australians over a perceived threat to social stability by a too-liberal policy on the migration of Asians, particularly Vietnamese refugees, to Australia.
7 Some evidence for this connection is discussed in Smith, Sachs, and Logan (1987), 'Transforming "knowledge" into school knowledge: teachers' use of the "culture" concept', unpublished paper, University of Queensland.

REFERENCES

Aarons, L. (1987) *Here Come the Uglies*, Sydney: Red Pen.
Abercrombie, N., Hill, S., and Turner, B. (1980) *The Dominant Ideology Thesis*, London: Allen & Unwin.
Anderson, D.S. and Vervoorn, A.E. (1983) *Access to Privilege: Patterns of Participation in Australian Post-Secondary Education*, Canberra: Australian National University Press.
Barthes, R. (1973) *Mythologies*, St Albans: Paladin.

————(1975) *S/Z*, London: Jonathan Cape.
Belsey, C. (1980) *Critical Practice*, London: Macmillan.
Bernstein, B. (1986) 'On pedagogic discourse', in J. Richardson (ed.),
    Handbook of Theory and Research for the Sociology of Education, New
    York: Greenwood Press, pp. 205–40.
Bottomore, T. and Rubel, M. (1963) *Karl Marx: Selected Writings*,
    Harmondsworth: Penguin.
Burton, P. and Carlen, F. (1977) 'Official discourse', *Economy and Society* 6
    (4): 377–407.
Clark, K. and Holquist, M. (1984) *Mikhail Bakhtin*, Cambridge, Mass.:
    Harvard University Press.
Dale, R. (1982) 'Education and the capitalist state: contributions and
    contradictions', in M. Apple (ed.) *Cultural and Economic Reproduction in
    Education*, London: Routledge & Kegan Paul, pp. 127–61.
Donald, J. (1979) 'Green paper: noise of crisis', *Screen Education* 30: 13–50.
Foucault, M. (1970) *The Order of Things: An Archaeology of the Human
    Sciences*, New York: Random House.
————(1972) *The Archaeology of Knowledge*, New York: Vintage Books.
————(1977) *Discipline and Punish: The Birth of the Prison*,
    Harmondsworth: Penguin.
————(1980) *Power–Knowledge*, edited by Colin Gordon, London:
    Harvester.
Freeland, J. (1979) 'Class struggle in schooling: MACOS and SEMP in
    Queensland', *Intervention* 12: pp. 29–62.
Gramsci, A. (1981) 'Antonio Gramsci', in T. Bennett, G. Margin, C. Mercer
    and J. Woollacott (eds), *Culture, Ideology and Social Process*, London:
    Batsford, pp. 191–218.
Habermas, J. (1976) *Legitimation Crisis*, London: Heinemann.
Henry, M. and Lingard, R. (1982) 'Multiculturalism: rhetoric and reality',
    New Education 4 (2): 75–89.
Hodge, R. and Kress, G. (1988) *Social Semiotics*, Cambridge: Polity Press.
Jessop, B. (1982) *The Capitalist State*, Oxford: Martin Robertson.
Kenway, J. (1987) 'Left right out: Australian education and the politics of
    signification', *Journal of Education Policy* 2 (3): 189–203.
Knight, J., Smith, R. and Chant, D. (1989) 'Australian new right discourse:
    the dominant ideology thesis revisited'. *Australian and New Zealand
    Journal of Sociology* 25(3): in press.
Knight, J., with Smith, R. and Maxwell, G. (1986) 'The right side': creation
    science in Queensland', *New Zealand Sociology* 1 (2): 88–103.
Laclau, E. and Mouffe, C. (1985) *Hegemony and Socialist Strategy*, London:
    Verso.
Lévi-Strauss, C. (1970) *The Raw and the Cooked*, London: Routledge &
    Kegan Paul.
Lingard, R. (1983) 'Multicultural education in Queensland: the assimilation of
    an ideal', *Discourse* 4 (1): 13–31.
Morley, D. (1980) 'Texts, readers and subjects', in S. Hall *et al.* (eds)
    Cultural, Media and Language, London: Hutchinson.
Mouffe, C. (ed.) (1979) *Gramsci and Marxist Theory*, London: Routledge &
    Kegan Paul.

John Knight, Richard Smith and Judyth Sachs

Scott, A. and Scott, R. (1980) 'Censorship and political education: the Queensland experience', *International Journal of Political Education* 3: 49–66.
Shapiro, M. (1981) *Language and Political Understanding: The Politics of Discursive Practice*, New Haven: Yale University Press.
Smith, R. and Knight, J. (1978) 'MACOS in Queensland: the politics of educational knowledge', *Australian Journal of Education* 2 (3): 225–43.
——(1981) 'Political censorship in the teaching of social sciences: Queensland scenarios', *Australian Journal of Education* 22 (1); 3–23.
Sturrock, J. (1986) *Structuralism*, London: Paladin.
Thompson, J.B. (1984) *Studies in the Theory of Ideology*, Cambridge: Polity Press.
Weiler, H. (1983) 'Legislation, expertise and participation: strategies of compensatory legitimation in educational policy', *Comparative Education Review* 27 (2): 259–77.
Western, J.S. (1983) *Social Inequality in Australian Society*, South Melbourne: Macmillan.
Wexler, P. and Grabiner, G. (1986) 'The education question: America during the crisis', in R. Sharp (ed.) *Capitalist Crisis and Schooling*, South Melbourne: Macmillan, pp. 1–40.
Wuthnow, R., Hunter, J.D., Bergersen, A. and Kurzweil, E. (1984) *Cultural Analysis*, London: Routledge & Kegan Paul.

8 Management as moral technology

A Luddite analysis

Stephen J. Ball

It is necessary to pass over to the other side – the other side from the 'good side' – in order to try to free oneself from these mechanisms that have made two sides appear, in order to dissolve the false unity of this other side whose part one has taken. That's where the real work begins, the work of the history of the present.
('Non au Sexe Roi', interview with Michel Foucault, *Le Nouvel Observateur*, March 1977)

In education circles the term 'management' now holds a particular and reverential place. The need for 'good' management in schools, colleges, and universities provides a point of massive agreement among educational practitioners of all leanings and persuasions. Management is firmly established as 'the one best way' to run educational organizations. Management training is becoming *de rigueur* for anyone who aspires to high office in educational institutions. The unchallengable position of management effectively renders discussion of other possibilities for organization mute. But the profundity of the effects of management on the practice of teachers and other education professionals is rarely fully appreciated. Management plays a key role in the ongoing process of reconstructing the work of teaching.

As the result of a whole series of political and economic changes affecting schools in England and Wales, culminating in the provisions of the 1988 Education Reform Act, the very nature of the school as an organization is being transformed. This transformation has begun to shift the governance of schools from professional/collegial in style to managerial/bureaucratic. In effect, control is to be exerted over teachers' work by the use of techniques of management and the task of schooling is increasingly subject to the logics of industrial production and market competition. Teachers are increasingly subject to systems of administrative rationality that exclude them from an effective say in the kind of substantive decision-making that could equally well be determined collectively. As Habermas (1984) suggests, this is a process

153

whereby subsystems of purposive-rational action encroach upon structures of intersubjectivity. Political, ideologically-loaded decisions are choked by bureaucratic-administrative systems and attempts are made to displace issues of moral and cultural identity with the imperatives of administrative efficacy. Our point here is that concepts like efficiency are treated as though they were neutral and technical matters, rather than being tied to particular interests. The question of 'efficiency for whom?' is rarely asked. Efficiency itself is taken as self-evidently a good thing. The costs involved for workers in achieving greater efficiency (intensification, loss of autonomy, closer monitoring and appraisal, non-participation in decision-making, lack of personal development through work) are rarely considered.

The training and professionalization of specialist managers structurally excludes others from decision-making processes. These others are to be managed; they are cast as lay persons, with at best a residual right of consultation. In this assertive process influence over the definition of the school is removed to a great extent from the hands of teachers. I am not here suggesting some kind of complex conspiracy against teachers, but rather taking account of the overall effect of the concatination of initiatives, constraints, changes in control and decision-making, and changes in conditions of work that are having their impact on teachers' daily lives.

In some LEAs (Local Education Authorities) management consultants have been brought in to make schools more efficient. They bring with them, as do training courses, the discourse and practices of industrial management. Within such a discourse the curriculum becomes a delivery system and teachers become its technicians or operatives.

In the restructuring of teachers' pay and conditions, in specialist training for school management, in central control over curriculum and the possibility of comparative testing (of students, schools, and teachers), the three basic elements of classical management theory are clearly in evidence. First, decision-making is formally lodged within the management team, separating policy from execution. Second, systems of quality control, time and motion study, and monitoring are brought into play through the development of teacher-appraisal schemes and the use of cohort testing. The development of graded assessment schemes also fits quite neatly into a system of performance comparison between teachers (and are employed for this purpose in the United States). Third, efforts are being made to link pay and promotion directly to performance. Thus we see the attempts by Sir Keith Joseph and the employers to link appraisal to pay and promotion within the negotiations in the 1985–86 teachers' industrial dispute, with progression through the main salary scale accelerated for those who could demonstrate outstanding performance (see Hartley and Broadfoot 1988). In all this teachers are likely to emerge more clearly than ever as alienated workers, with little or no control over their own work situation. It is certainly possible in the near future that managers of schools, as in the National Health Service, will become career administrators, specifically trained for management, part of a corporate management structure and owing direct loyalty to their line superior in the LEA. Just as the teacher is being reconstructed as a technician within such a system, headteachers are already being reconstructed as managers. (Andrew Rowe, Conservative MP for mid-Kent, has suggested the establishment of a staff college for training heads in management skills (*Times Education Supplement*, 18 July 1986, p. 4).) The gap between workers and management appears to be widening steadily and inevitably, while at the same time the paraphernalia of controls upon the work of the teacher is growing ever more sophisticated and oppressive (Harris 1982). Michael Apple (1986) sums up the situation:

> Currently, considerable pressure is building to have teaching and school curricula be totally prespecified and tightly controlled by the purposes of "efficiency", "cost effectiveness" and "account-ability". In many ways, the deskilling that is affecting jobs in general is now having an impact on teachers as more and more decisions are moving out of their hands as their jobs become even more difficult to do. This is more advanced in some countries than others, but it is clear that the movement to rationalize and control the act of teaching and the content and evaluation of the curriculum is very real.
>
> (Apple 1986: 12)

I want to suggest that this shift is part of a 'radical right' thrust to gain closer and more precise control over the processes of schooling, and that the discourse of management plays an essential role in achieving this shift and justifying these new forms of control. Certainly, recent government statements attribute a key role to management as a mechanism for the reform of schools and the disciplining of teachers.

> The employing authority can only be satisfied that each school is properly staffed if it knows enough about the skills and competencies of individual teachers. Such knowledge can only come from some form of appraisal systems. An appraisal system is also needed for the professional enhancement of the individual teacher. Other professions – and some schools – have found that appraisal interviews provide an opportunity to identify individual and collective training needs. To be fully effective an appraisal system would have to be complemented by better arrangements

for the individual teachers' career development – including induction, in-service training, guidance on possible teaching posts and promotion. When I refer to the management of the teaching force I have this whole range of positive activity in mind. I am frequently misquoted in terms that suggest that I am only concerned with the need to dismiss the very small number of incompetent teachers who cannot be restored to adequate effectiveness. That is not the case. I am concerned with the whole range of positive advantages that would flow from applying to the teacher force standards of management which have become common elsewhere.

> (speech by Sir Keith Joseph, North of England Education
> Conference, 4 January 1985)

It is clear that in the reference here to standards of management 'common elsewhere', 'elsewhere' refers to industrial management. This is the model that schools are being urged, indeed required, to emulate. It is from industrial organizations that the concept and procedures of appraisal are drawn. It is often through the use of models from industry that management training in education is conducted.

Management is, *par excellence*, what Foucault calls a 'moral technology' or a technology of power. It is a modern, all-purpose equivalent of Bentham's panopticon, 'a generalizable model of functioning; a way of defining power relations in terms of the everyday life of men' (Foucault 1979: 205). Management is an all-embracing conception of organizational control. It subsists both as a body of theory to be learned and internalized by managers, and as a set of practices to be implemented, encompassing managers and managed.

> The establishment of management as a separate function. . . with unique expertise and responsibilities, and with major and critical claims to authority. . . upon which the efficiency of the whole enterprise depends. . . is a crucial first step to control over the workforce. . . because once this conception of management has been accepted by workers, they have in effect, abdicated from any question of, or resistance to, many aspects of their domination.
>
> (Littler and Salaman 1982: 259)

> In this form of management, power is not totally entrusted to someone who would exercise it alone, over others, in an absolute fashion; rather, this machine is one in which everyone is caught, those who exercise power as well as those who are subjected to it.
>
> (Foucault 1977: 156)

Management is a professional, professionalizing discourse which allows its speakers and its incumbents to lay exclusive claims to certain sorts of expertise – organizational leadership and decision-making – and to a set of procedures that casts others, subordinates, as objects of that discourse and the recipients of those procedures, whether they wish to be or not. Like other professional discourses, management produces the object about which it speaks – organization. Here, however, the professional claims of management are set over and against those of teachers, and those of organization against autonomy.

Management is a theoretical and practical technology of rationality geared to efficiency, practicality, and control. It is a means to an end and its participants are also means. It represents the bureaucratization of the structure of control via job descriptions, line management relations and the establishment of fixed flows of communication, and committee-style decision-making. And it embodies a clear empiricist–rationalist epistemology. Organizational control and individual action are subsumed within a technical perspective. A view which contends that social life can be mastered scientifically and can be understood and organized according to law-like generalizations. The selection of appropriate courses of action rests upon and is limited to the expertise of those, the managers, who possess appropriate scientific knowledge and training. It is thus a closed system which separates policy from execution, and reserves policymaking to those designated and trained in its techniques. Furthermore, it presents itself as an objective, technically neutral mechanism, dedicated only to greater efficiency; the one best method. This is Weber's rationalist nightmare, the 'mighty cosmos of the modern economic order... the iron cage [in which] specialists without spirit, sensualists without heart [are] caught in the delusion that [they] have achieved a level of development never before attained by mankind' (Weber 1948: 182).

Management is also an imperialistic discourse. Management theory views the social world as locked into irrational chaos, as needing to be brought into its redeeming order. It constructs its superiority via a set of potent discursive oppositions; order is set over and against chaos, rationality against irrationality, sanity against madness, neutrality against political bias, efficiency against inefficiency, and meritocracy against personal influence. It is the linguistic antithesis of crisis and as such it has a central political role in the 1980s.

The language of management deploys rationality and efficiency to promote control; it is a regime of 'jurisdiction' and 'veridiction'. As a discourse, a system of possibility for knowledge, it eschews or marginalizes the problems, concerns, difficulties, and fears of 'the subject' – the managed. The management subject is the objectified product of organization, authority, and responsibility. The limits and possibilities of action and meaning are precisely determined by position and expertise in the management structure. Management intends and constitutes 'subjected and practicised bodies'. And it 'increases the forces of the body in economic terms of utility and diminishes these forces in political terms of obedience' (Foucault 1979: 130). It characteristically attempts 'the manipulation of human beings into compliant patterns of behaviour' (Bates 1985: 21).

As a counsel of perfection and as an epitome of efficient form, management stands in tension with its imperfect servants. The managed are fragile, prone to irrationality, atavistic practices, and surfeits of emotion. Opposition to control, to change, to methods of efficiency, are thus treated as the worker's problem, typically as a 'symptom' of personal dissatisfaction or unfulfilled needs. Psychoanalytic or psychological analyses are frequently mobilized in response to individual resistance. Dissensus or conflict are not necessarily totally ignored in this work but are regarded, within the logic of the paradigm, as aberrant and pathological. In this way oppositional activity within the organization is defined, in terms of the perspectives of the dominant groups, as inherently irrational. The 'subject', the individual worker or practitioner, is constructed in terms of sameness and individuality (Macdonell 1986). The 'problem' is taken to be 'in' the person rather than the system, and collective interests, other than those of 'the system', are in effect deconstructed. Collective opposition is systematically misrecognized. Solutions are offered in terms of personal counselling or one-off adaptions of the system. The resister is cast as social deviant, and is normalized through coercive or therapeutic procedures. By responding to discontent on an individual basis, and by imposing structural and hierarchical divisions, all are subjected. Management is both a totalizing and individualizing system.

'THE ART OF PUNISHING'

The specification of individuality rests upon the production of 'precise dossiers [that] enable the authorities to fix individuals in a web of objective codification' (Rabinow 1986: 22). The personal file and the personnel manager are key mechanisms in the moral technology of management. And the techniques and research findings of psychology provide models, norms, and procedures through which individuals can be compared and monitored. Hierarchical observation, normalizing judgments, and forms of examination are all part of the total web of management control. In particular, these are fused and focused in the development of techniques of teacher appraisal.

In Great Britain to date staff appraisal seems to be emerging in a different way to the USA. In addition to traditional assessment by LEA inspectors or advisers, schools are increasingly developing their own internal schemes, many of which seem to be influenced by industrial practice. The primary aim of such schemes is to be formative; they are designed to promote job satisfaction, indicate training needs and guide future professional development. The method most commonly used is that of an appraisal interview by a senior member of staff. So far the idea of competency-based teaching has not met with approval in Britain. Nevertheless, central government seems to be atte.npting to introduce systematic staff appraisal by employers for summative purposes. Legislation has been introduced into parliament to give the Secretary of State for Education powers to mandate the appraisal of teachers in accordance with a national scheme.

(Turner and Clift 1988: 21)

Appraisal has become one of the prime features of the political reconstruction and disciplining of teachers as ethical subjects in the 1980s. It extends the logics of quality control and performance indicators into the pedagogical heart of teaching. It brings the tutelary gaze to bear, making the teacher calculable, describable, and comparable. It opens individuals to an evaluating eye and to disciplinary power. In Foucault's terms, appraisal is a form of examination.

The examination combines the techniques of an observing hierarchy and those of a normalizing judgement. It is a normalizing gaze, a surveillance that makes it possible to qualify, to classify, and to punish. It establishes over individuals a visibility through which one differentiates and judges them.

(Foucault 1979: 175)

The appraisal interview is a formal ritual of power and ceremony of visibility, a technology of objectification. It links the formation of knowledge with the display of power. The appraisee is there to be known, and recorded, by the appraiser. Thus Foucault itemizes three bases of the examination:

1. The examination transforms the economy of visibility into the exercise of power. It is a 'space of domination', a process of inspection and review without favour or prejudice, a compulsory objectification. In closed rooms, in confidence, and in accordance with agreed procedures the appraisees are required to reveal themselves and account for their actions, absences, and personal development. 'The exercise of discipline presupposes a mechanism that coerces by means of observing: an apparatus in which the techniques that make it possible to see induce the effects of power, and in which, conversely, the means of coercion make those on whom they are applied clearly visible' (Foucault 1977: 170–1).

2. The examination also introduces individuality into the field of

159

documentation. A 'meticulous archive' is constituted. Files are kept, notes made, records updated for future reference, as a basis for decisions elsewhere. Decisions about promotion, reward, or dismissal, aptitudes and competencies, as well as weaknesses and foibles are committed to writing. Performances are measured, 'making it possible to classify, to form categories, to determine averages, to fix norms' (Foucault 1979: 178). It is the establishing of norms that allows for the 'art of punishing' – punishing, for Foucault, includes rewards and observation as well as punishment. Norms introduce 'the constraint of a conformity that must be achieved' (Foucault 1979: 183). The individual is thus subject to description and to comparison.

> The subject of recording appraisal interviews is one which, certainly in the early days of a scheme, seems to generate concern among teachers. Whilst many were of the view that there was little point in having an appraisal interview if no record was produced, the nature of the record, who has access to it and where it goes, are all matters over which teachers tended to agonize. In some schools, teachers were initially given the option as to whether a record was kept or not. This was one way of trying to entice them to volunteer to take part in the scheme.
>
> (Turner and Clift 1988: 88)

3. The examination surrounded by all its documentary techniques, makes each individual a 'case'. A chronicle of the person is compiled, in terms of advancement or decay, responsibility or foolishness, co-operation or difficulty. Lives are lived through the accumulation of documentation, careers are collated, 'pinning down each individual in his own particularity' (Foucault 1979: 180). The use of 'normalizing judgments' is crucial in this as individuals are assessed in terms of general and specific measures of performance and documented in relation to indicators of relative efficiency and efficacy.

> One result of the spread of industrial ideas and practice to schools has been the adoption of 'target setting' as a component of appraisal. The Industrial Society has been very influential in this respect with two booklets published in 1983. . . . The purpose of a target setting exercise is, having reviewed past performance, to set specific tangible goals which can be tackled over a defined period of time. This ensures that there is some *outcome* from appraisal interviews and that they do not become oriented solely to review.
>
> (Turner and Clift 1988: 87–88)

The techniques of appraisal have been developed and legitimated to the extent that they co-opt individuals, and established notions of professionalism, into their operation. The teacher is encouraged to view the procedures of appraisal as a part of the process of self-understanding and self-betterment – professional development – which Foucault calls 'subjectification': the active engagement of the subject in self-formation, 'operations on [people's] own bodies, on their own souls, on their own conduct' (Foucault 1980a).

> Whether the prime purpose of appraisal be career development or improving one's performance on the job, there is disagreement among teachers about what might be considered to be a subsidiary purpose; criticism and the passing of judgments.
>
> (Turner and Clift 1988: 67)

The appraisal interview has elements both of the confessional and the psychoanalytical encounter, both of which rely upon the dynamics of self-revelation. The appraisees are encouraged to display their shortcomings, to seek out or identify appropriate therapeutic procedures, and to judge themselves and award their own punishment. This then is a technology of the self that permits

> individuals to effect by their own means or with the help of others a certain number of operations on their own bodies and souls, thoughts, conduct, and way of being, so as to transform themselves in order to attain a state of happiness, purity, wisdom, perfection or immortality.
>
> (Foucault 1988: 18)

Appraisal seen as a form of confession is thus particularly potent. It embodies both revelation and redemption, and brings the personal and the organizational into intimate relation.

> The confession is a ritual of discourse in which the speaking subject is also the subject of the statement; it is also a ritual that unfolds within a power relationship, for one does not confess without the presence (or virtual presence) of a partner who is not simply the interlocutor but the authority who requires the confession, prescribes and appreciates it, and intervenes in order to judge, punish, forgive, console.
>
> (Foucault 1981: 61)

The secular confession is founded on the notion of normal as against abnormal, transposed from the religious opposition of sin and piety.

EFFECTIVENESS AND DISCIPLINE

However, the confessional technique and technologies of the self are being introduced into school organization in another, more general sense. The model of self-betterment employed in current definitions of professional development is also applied in general terms to the self-improvement of whole schools.

School-effectiveness research can be seen to have played a crucial role in laying the groundwork for the reconceptualization of the school within the management discourse. First, effectiveness studies and school-difference studies have recentred the school as the focus of causation in explanations of pupil performance and variations in levels of achievement. School-effectiveness research provides a technology for the possibility of 'blaming' the school. The work of Rutter *et al.* (1979) in particular fitted perfectly (in terms of theoretical unity) into the Conservative discourse of derision mounted against comprehensive and progressive education in the 1970s, and the political deconstruction of comprehensive education in the 1980s. It also articulates the commodification of education involved in notions like 'market forces' and 'consumer choice'. As two of the Rutter study researchers explain:

> outcome measures are increasingly used by parents and LEAs, as well as researchers, in comparison *between* schools. Schools are now required to publish their exam results, although the details of how this is to be done have been left to individual authorities. Inevitably this leads to comparisons between schools and permits the construction of league tables of more or less successful schools.
>
> (Ouston and Maughan 1985: 37)

Second, the effectiveness studies have developed a technology of power that enables the monitoring and control of schools (again, by applying to them 'neutral' performance measures).

The ideological work done by effectiveness research, linked to notions like accountability, school review, and school improvement, should not be underestimated. The cruder manifestations of the conservative political critique of schools have been reworked into versions of surveillance and monitoring that 'fit' into the preferred teacher discourse of professionalism. In effect, teachers are trapped into taking responsibility for their own 'disciplining' through schemes of self-appraisal, school improvement, and institutional development. Indeed, teachers are urged to believe that their commitment to such processes will make them more professional.

Effectiveness researchers both construct norms that allow the establishment of a concept of the ineffective or 'sick' school, and again draw upon 'the confessional technique' (an admission of transgressions and a ritual of atonement). The 'poor' school, the 'failing' school is to take responsibility for its ailments and its own cure – self-improvement. Self-improvement is achieved by the improvement of selves, by making people aware of their weaknesses and getting them to commit themselves to methods of redemption. The failure of the organization is the failure of the individual, the person. Thus:

> People are the key to successful improvement initiatives. . . . Phrased another way, 'the search for excellence in schools is the search for excellence in people'. Good results are not attained by merely adopting new technical gimmicks or incremental curriculum reforms. Significant progress requires re-examination and improvement of organizational basics: work norms, management practices, staff competence, classrooms standards and so on.
> (Wilson and Concoran 1988: 119)

Effectiveness is defined in terms of the possibilities of measurement. To recognize ineffectiveness is to become subordinate to the measures of the norm, and the excellent. Thus to a great extent the discourses of control and effectiveness have become totally enmeshed. For example, Gray and Jones (1985: 114) conclude:

> To date, studies of school and teacher effectiveness have tended to converge in their conclusions. It may be that there are, in reality, just a small number of models of 'effective' practice, but we also wonder whether this assessment doesn't result from some of the assumptions in which researchers to date have themselves tended to invest. One important consequence of adopting the approach discussed here would be that it would be possible to generate, both quickly and fairly cheaply, models of 'effective practice' for schools and teachers facing very differing circumstances.

Thus 'normalizing judgments' are turned upon whole schools; each school is set in a field of comparison. An 'artificial' order is laid down, 'an order defined by natural and observable processes' (Foucault 1979: 179). The definition of behaviour and performance embedded in the order and the norm are arrived at 'on the basis of two opposed values of good and evil' (1979:180): the good school and the bad school, effective and ineffective practice. Individual schools are differentiated from one another in a hierarchy, or 'league table'. The regime of disciplinary power thus created 'measures in quantitative terms and hierarchizes in terms of the abilities, the level, the "nature"' of individual schools. The norm 'introduces, through this "value-giving" measure, the constraint of a conformity that must be achieved' (1979: 183). But as the previous extract indicates, where there is illness there is also 'cure', models of 'effective practice'. If self-examination fails, the expert, the authority, the consultant, the moral disciplinarian is at hand to intervene. And in this role the scientific and the moral are tightly intertwined. In effect, given the logic of management, ineffectiveness is seen as a disorder of reason and as such susceptible to cure by the use of appropriate techniques of organization.

In a dramatic sense the language, concepts, and field of concern of effectiveness research imposes stringent limits to the possible ways of thinking and speaking about and studying schooling. Effectiveness reconstructs the school and the teacher as its subject, to be evaluated, monitored, and managed. Thus Young (1985: 85) writing on the implications of school-effectiveness research for management in education, argues:

> What these studies and others cited elsewhere in this chapter underline is the considerable autonomy that exists for the individual teacher that can in some instances deflect from the achievement of known and approved goals. They also point up the need for an effective headteacher to ensure that the school community as a group functions well and that known and agreed goals are reached to the satisfaction of all.

The centre of concern here is again the control of teachers, and the assumption of consensus is unequivocal. It is in these ways that effectiveness and management are linked to the political discourse of Thatcherism by a common positivity. Together they constitute a powerful 'interdiscursive configuration' which has thoroughly displaced the weakly articulated concerns of comprehensive education – equality, talent development, tolerance, and participation – with a strongly articulated concern with efficiency, the social and economic requirements of industry, competition, and national interests.

As noted already, management is a form of organization that celebrates rationality. It is also couched in an ideology of neutrality, but in practice it is a 'political technology'.

> Political technologies advance by taking what is essentially a political problem, removing it from the realm of political discourse, and recasting it in the neutral language of science. Once this is accomplished the problems have become technical ones of specialists. . . . In fact, the language of reform is, from the outset, an essential component of these political technologies. . . . Where there [is] resistance or failure. . . .this [is] construed as further proof of the need to reinforce and extend the power of experts.
>
> (Dreyfus and Rabinow 1982: 196)

The school-effectiveness movement is thoroughly implicated in the formation and establishment of the conditions for this kind of displacement.

Management and school effectiveness as specific discourses bring objects into being by identifying them. When management theorists discuss 'successful' schools or 'good' management practice, they are also engaged in 'dividing practices' and the systematic creation, classification, and control of 'anomalies', the 'poor' school and 'bad' management. These are then the objects of management therapies. In this way, 'objects of knowledge are defined in ways that converging practices can use' (Wolin 1988: 184). In effect, the discourses of management and research fields like school effectiveness are forms of professional job creation: 'Practices set the conditions for discourse and discourse feeds back statements that will facilitate practice' (Wolin 1988: 184). New disciplines, like school management, provide new discipline for schools and new work for the moral technologists.

CONCLUSION

Management theories are, for the most part, rooted in versions of systems theory and humanistic psychology. They are focused on individual participants on the one hand, as part of a complex, interrelated, interdependent structure on the other. Their emphasis is upon order, procedure, and consensus. The school as an institution is rendered as a system of shared meanings and common goals and values. But theories of management reflect the particular interests and needs of administrators. They are top-dog theories; they contain a view of the organization looking down from the position of those 'in control'. They are inherently biased and distorted by this partiality. Management both intends itself as the real world of organizational life and acts to exclude other versions. As a discourse with a scientific status, as a 'regime of truth', management empowers the manager and objectifies and subjects the managed. As ever, as Foucault suggests, knowledge, power, and the body are interrelated in the achievement of subjugation.

All of this is evident in the current application of management theories to schools. Management is a 'micro-physics of power'. Its basis is disciplinary and it is a 'fundamental instrument in the constitution of industrial capitalism and the type of society that is its accompaniment' (Foucault 1980b: 105). The primary instrument is a hierarchy of continuous and functional surveillance. It is in this way that managements, as localized practices, are micro-power structures and power relations that touch every aspect of organizational life and are serially related. They are practical applications of power. They embody very specific mechanisms, procedures, and techniques with particular economic and political utility. The worker, the technician, the teacher is constituted (or reconstituted) in this network of discourses, roles, aspirations, and desires.

Stephen J. Ball

REFERENCES

Apple, M (1986) 'Mandating computers: the impact of new technology on the labour process'. Paper presented at the International Sociology of Education Conference, Westhill College, Birmingham.

Bates, R.J. (1985) 'Changes in educational administration necessary to cope with technological change', *Educational Administration Review* 3 (1): 17–37.

Cousins, M. and Hussain, A. (1984) *Michel Foucault*, London: Macmillan.

Dreyfus, H.L. and Rabinow, P. (1982) *Michel Foucault: Beyond Structuralism and Hermeneutics*, Brighton: Harvester Press.

Foucault, M. (1977) 'The eye of power', in C. Gordon (ed.) (1980) *Power/Knowledge*, New York: Pantheon.

——(1979) *Discipline and Punish*, Harmondsworth: Penguin.

——(1980a) 'Howison Lectures', Berkeley, 20 October 1980.

——(1980b) *Power/Knowledge*, edited by C. Gordon, New York: Pantheon.

——(1981) *The History of Sexuality : An Introduction*, Harmondsworth: Penguin.

——(1988) 'Truth, power self: an interview', in L. Martin, H. Gutman, and P. Hutton (eds) *Technologies of the Self*, London: Tavistock.

Gray, J. and Jones, B. (1985) 'Combining quantitative and qualitative approaches to school and teacher effectiveness', in D. Reynolds (ed.) *Studying School Effectiveness*, Lewes: Falmer Press.

Habermas, J. (1984) *The Theory of Communicative Action*, vol. 1, London: Heinemann.

Harris, K. (1982) *Teachers and Classes*, London: Routledge & Kegan Paul.

Hartley, L. and Broadfoot, P. (1988) 'Assessing teacher performance', *Journal of Education Policy* 3 (1): 39–50.

Littler, C. and Salaman, G. (1982) 'Bravermania and beyond: recent theories of the labour process', *Sociology* 16 (2): 251–69.

Macdonell, D. (1986) *Theories of Discourse*, Oxford: Blackwell.

Ouston, J. and Maughan, B. (1985) 'Issues in the assessment of school outcomes', in D. Reynolds (ed.) *Studying School Effectiveness*, Lewes: Falmer Press.

Rabinow, P. (ed.) (1986) *The Foucault Reader*, London: Peregrine.

Reynolds, D. (ed.) (1985) *Studying School Effectiveness*, Lewes: Falmer Press.

Turner, G. and Clift, P. (1988) *Studies in Teacher Appraisal*, Lewes: Falmer Press.

Weber, M. (1948) *The Protestant Ethic and the Spirit of Capitalism*, New York: Scribners and Sons.

Wilson, B. and Corcoran, T. (1988) *Successful Secondary Schools*, Lewes: Falmer Press.

Wolin, S. (1988) 'On the theory and practice of power', in J. Arac (ed.) *After Foucault*, New Brunswick: Rutgers University Press.

Young, P. (1985) 'Do schools make a difference?', in D. Reynolds (ed.) *Studying School Effectiveness*, Lewes: Falmer Press.

9 Education and the Right's discursive politics
Private versus state schooling

Jane Kenway

INTRODUCTION

The Educational Right and the private school lobby have all but colonized popular thinking and government policy on education in Australia. My concern in this chapter is to identify the key features of their discourse in order to suggest why this is so. Essentially I will examine the construction of a hegemonic discourse within a particular field of social relations and indicate how the discourse of this loosely linked, but mutually beneficial, political amalgam serves the interests of educational and social privilege. Clearly, then, I am looking at hegemony within a localized field as well as hegemony within broader Australian society. Foucault's discussions of discourse and of power–knowledge inform my analysis of the discursive ensemble under scrutiny. However, I have found it useful to supplement his generally rather narrow social lens with that of Gramsci who is much more concerned with the ways in which society as a whole is structured in dominance. After introducing the New Right and the historical context, I will explain the theoretical premises that inform my analysis. I will then focus in detail on an historical incident which powerfully exemplifies the discursive politics of the private school lobby and the Educational Right.

In Australia in the 1980s there has been a shift in popular thinking and government policy on education away from the social democratic settlement that characterized the early 1970s towards an explicitly right-wing position (see Young 1987; Johnston 1987: McWilliam 1987). While a number of sources of this movement may be identified, ultimately, as the edited collection by Sharp (1986) indicates, changes in the economy and the deepening crisis of contemporary capitalism seem to provide a root cause. The economic crisis has been accompanied by changes in the labour market, technology, and social life. These, amongst a range of factors (see Kenway 1987b), constitute upheaval and produce uncertainty in many people's daily lives. The grim prospect and/or reality of unemployment, or shifting temporary employment, haunts the social landscape of parents and their offspring and has it own dislocating side effects.

The implications for education of economic crisis, social change, and dislocation are unclear and sectional interests have for some time been engaged in struggle at the ideological and political levels to define the ways in which education is to be related to these changes. Such struggle has involved a strong offensive from the New Right, one component of which has been the intense promotion of private schooling and an attack on Australian state schools. Both have resulted in a crisis of legitimacy for public education. This ideological offensive is the subject of this chapter.

THE NEW RIGHT

The New Right is conducting very vocal moral surveillance over an increasing number of aspects of civil, economic, and political society in Australia and clearly, the ascendency of the Right in education cannot be divorced from its ascendancy in other fields of public commentary. Its agenda dominates media discussions of matters as diverse as taxation policy, industrial relations, welfare, and the privatizations of public services (see Aarons 1987; Coghill 1987; Sawer 1982). Increasingly, the Australian Labor government is dancing to the New Right's private tune (see Barnett 1988). As a social movement that conducts ideological work of consistent benefit to the socially powerful and privileged, the New Right is provoking disquiet. Those who identify with the Left in diverse political and academic arenas, in Australia and elsewhere, are coming to recognize the damage the New Right is doing and the urgent necessity for a comprehensive understanding of its political project in order that its tide may be turned. While some academics and political commentators seek to clarify what is new and distinctive about the New Right (and, indeed, explore the use of other, more explicit, titles), others seek to identify and elucidate its various ideological strands. Still others search for an adequate explanation of its apparent discursive monopoly on a range of economic, social, and political fronts. Although modes of analysis and theoretical frameworks and interpretations vary, there is none the less some agreement that the New Right consists of a loose amalgam of different sets of interests, that its organizing theoretical ideology includes an uneasy blend of many, sometimes contradictory, strands of political thought, and that it demonstrates a ready capacity for developing political rhetoric which both produces and taps contemporary popular concerns and discontents (Cohen *et al.* 1986;

Levitas 1986; Elliott and McCrone 1987; Hoover 1987; Miliband *et al.* 1987).

The New Right movement in Australia has a number of defining features. Briefly, these include highly visible judges of normality who tend to be 'corporate chiefs' (Aarons 1987: 4) and whose ideas are developed and clarified by a range of corporate-sponsored 'think tanks'. These include the Institute of Public Affairs, the Centre for Independent Studies, Australian Institute for Public Policy, and the National Civic Council consisting mainly of the Catholic Right. These think tanks are composed of academics, business people, former public servants, and politicians. New Right thinking is promulgated by such journals as the *IPA Review, Quadrant*, and *Newsweekly (NCC)*, by sympathetic journalists, and by *The Australian* newspaper and *The Bulletin* magazine. Aaron's (1987) study shows the way in which the think tanks, their journals, their journalists, and these two major news outlets are interconnected and operate a circuit of mutual citation and promotion. For instance, think tank members are often columnists for *The Australian*, whose journalists often cite their articles in think tank publications.

The organizing theoretical ideology of the New Right includes amongst its many strands an uneasy blend of conservatism and liberalism extending into libertarianism. As Dwyer, Wilson, and Woock (1984) argue, the former manifests itself in concern for the preservation of authority, traditional institutions, and values and in an expectation that strong governments will exert appropriate control in this regard. The latter, with its emphasis upon competition and self-reliance, is opposed to any mechanisms that interfere with the 'freedom, prosperity and progress' guaranteed by the market. Within New Right logic, the government's role is neither to promote social justice nor to develop public monopolies, but to, as Sawer (1982: ix) says, 'hold the ring for a free market system which will operate efficiently as long as it is not interfered with'. Privatization is a key concept and the central ethic is 'possessive individualism', in which individual freedom is interpreted as the right to accumulate private property and power unimpeded by the state. Privilege is equated with government power, not private wealth, and the New Right presents itself as protecting the 'little people' from public sector privilege. In the words of John Hyde, director of the Australian Institute for Public Policy:

> The market place is the ultimate 'consensus'. It is transaction by agreement among little people. The only alternative to the market economy is the command economy in which an elite – the privileged – make decisions and compel, with police backing, ordinary people to accept transactions which are not their

preference, and in which the privileged elite can. . . look after one
another with government and State patronage.

(Letters to the editor, *West Australian* 1 February 1986)

Broadly, for the New Right, ethics are a private matter of individual
choice, and the state is not responsible for implementing the social
conscience. A new morality is asserted and democracy is redefined.
Despite the social changes that have made public welfare a significant
concern of the state, the libertarian strand of thought is opposed to any
use of the state for egalitarian purposes. Any state- supported schemes
that seek to ameliorate the worse effects of a fundamentally unjust
society are regarded as an attack on 'enterprise and endeavour', on
self-reliance, individual effort, responsible management, and personal
sacrifice. Welfare, in any form, is construed as the responsibility of that
most valued of institutions, the family, and hence access to welfare
becomes dependent upon the ability of a family to pay for it. That such
conceptions of the family have implications for women's social roles
has been highlighted by many feminist observers of the New Right in
Australia and elsewhere (e.g., Webley 1982; David 1986). In her
collection of articles on the *New Right in Australia*, Sawer (1983: xi)
recognizes that the Right's

> ideological offensive represents an attack on what ever progress
> towards social justice has occurred. . . in favour of a restoration of
> 'freedom to choose'. . . . The reinvigoration of ideologies
> proclaiming the virtues of inequality and selfishness threaten not
> only those who are unable to compete on the job market but also
> the general moral standards of the community.

It will become clear as I proceed that these central tenets constituted the
basis of the thinking of both the private school lobby and the Educational Right during the historical period under examination. It is thus not
too fanciful to suggest that these two groups may be loosely identified,
in some ways at least, with the New Right.

THE HISTORICAL CONTEXT

Education is an important terrain upon which the New Right conducts
its political work. It is my contention that its strategies and effects in this
regard may best be scrutinized through the close examination of specific
rather than general educational struggles, that is, of critical historical
incidents. These are key moments in the direction of policy, times in
which political effort is intense and concentrated and thus particularly
amenable to analysis. The critical incident which I have selected for the
purposes of such an examination arose when the Australian Labor Party

(ALP) led by Bob Hawke returned to federal government in 1983 after nearly eight years of conservative reign by the Liberals under Malcolm Fraser. Historically, the ALP has opposed the more obvious forms of educational privilege, and, according to its restricted conception of social justice, sought to promote equal access and opportunity. None the less, it has concentrated on economic more than ideological matters, as demonstrated in the early years of the Schools Commission inspired by Professor Karmel (Marginson 1985). The dismantling of the 'Karmel settlement' and the movement towards the Right in education has been underway since Fraser came to power in 1975. But when Hawke replaced him and Susan Ryan took the education portfolio, many supposed that this movement would be arrested and those whose interests education best serves feared a frontal attack upon their educational privilege.

When, in its 1983 Education (policy and funding) Guidelines to the Schools Commission, the new Labor government announced, amongst much, that it intended to reduce funds to Australia's best 'resourced' private schools, the worst fears of the educationally and socially privileged were 'confirmed'. Further dismantling was predicted by the private school lobby (even, surprisingly, by the Catholic system, which had been offered a 3 per cent increase in funding) and by others speaking on behalf of privilege – namely, the Educational Right. At the same time, the state school lobby failed to predict the force of the rightist backlash and, by and large, withheld support for the Guidelines. A bitter, well-publicized debate between supporters of private and state schools ensued: the 'state aid war', as the media constantly called it. On the surface, each party sought merely to influence the 1984 Guidelines, which would determine funding policies for some time to come. However, at the debate's centre were issues concerning the relative place and impact of private and state schooling in Australian society, the extent to and manner in which public money should support private educational concerns, and, more broadly, the nature and purpose of schooling and what and whose interests it should serve.

This debate provided the Right with an opportunity to defend and even extend educational privilege. The state school lobby, thrown on the defensive, fought a rear-guard struggle seeking to protect the social-democratic advances made in state education. The Labor government initially entered the fray and offered its version of a socially just educational future for Australia. However, swayed by the force of the Right's attack, it soon detached itself from the ideological field and constructed for itself the image of neutral arbiter between competing and equal sectional interests. Eventually, when the Guidelines for 1984 were announced, it was clear that despite the 'educational consensus' the government claimed to have achieved, it had shown particular receptiveness to the discourse of the Right and the private school lobby, adopting much of their language and concern.

Clearly, many reasons for this shift can be identified (Kenway 1987a, 1987b). However, the case I wish to put here is that the Right displayed a particular facility for ideological work. Operating in the widest of discursive fields, it sought to establish closure around certain key concepts to have its definitions of value accepted as universally valid and its sectional interests defined as the general interest. To a large extent it achieved these aims and shortly I shall demonstrate how. First, however, some discussion of the theoretical premises that inform my analysis is required.

SOME THEORETICAL BACKGROUND

In considering the politics of the Educational Right I have found it useful to respond to Foucault's following invitation: 'What I say ought to be taken as "propositions", "game openings" where those who may be interested are invited to join in: they are not meant as dogmatic assertions to be taken or left en bloc' (Foucault 1981: 4). There is much within the theoretical apparatus developed by Foucault which helps to clarify the workings of the Right's discursive politics. However, in seeking an understanding not only of the operations of the Right's discursive ensemble but also of its broader social consequences, a Foucauldian analysis has its limitations. It is my contention that, in this instance at least, Foucault is usefully complemented by a post-structuralist reading of Gramsci and it is therefore my intention here to draw from both in analysing this particular historical moment.

Before proceeding further on this point, I want to make it clear that I recognize the contentious nature of what I am about to do. There is a certain irony in using Foucault to examine the Right when a number of social theorists are claiming that Foucault and post-structuralism more generally are useful for the Right (e.g., Benton 1984: Chap. 8; Giddens 1982: Chap. 15). Second, I also acknowledge that the Foucault/Gramsci combination may appear incongruous. Certainly those observers who locate Gramsci within the neo-Marxist trajectory and Foucault outside it will probably find this combination discomforting if not downright reprehensible. Indeed, Foucault himself 'rejects' Marxism. None the less, as my analysis proceeds I will, if only tangentially, address myself to such concerns and so hope to reduce the possible disquiet that such theoretical mischief may generate. At this point, though, I must emphasize that I am not attempting the ambitious exercise of synthesizing the two writers' work (see, however, Smart 1986; Mercer 1980). Neither am I seeking to address either modernist/post-modernist or Marxist/post-Marxist debates. Rather, I seek simply to demonstrate the benefits of combining their different foci for the analysis of the incident under scrutiny.

Foucault, discourse, knowledge and power

Given that the focus of the chapter moves from the specific to the general, it is apt that I begin by looking at Foucault's conception of discourse, a concept that is central to his preoccupation with the relationship between forms of power and knowledge. In fact, Foucault uses the term 'discourse' to designate the conjunction of power and knowledge (Foucault 1976). Prior to exploring this, and as a means towards explaining it, I shall mention Foucault's interest in knowledge which in a sense preceded his more overt examination of power–knowledge. In his early work, Foucault seeks to make clear the structures, rules, and procedures that determine the different forms of our knowledge, those aspects of knowledge so fundamental that they remain 'unvoiced and unthought' (Young 1981: 10). He calls this an 'archaeology of knowledge', a study of the rules that determine what can and cannot be said within a particular discourse at a particular time. These rules include such procedures as prohibition, exclusion, and the opposition between true and false. In discussing how different disciplines are constituted, he shows that knowledge can fix meaning, representation, and reason; that the very organization of the discourse can be an exercise of power, controlling and restraining what can be said as well as the right to speak. For Foucault, discourses are 'practices that systemically form the objects of which they speak. . . . Discourses are not about objects; they do not identify objects, they constitute them and in the practice of doing so conceal their own intervention' (1977b: 49). It is through discourse, then, that the social production of meaning takes place and through which subjectivity is produced and power relations are maintained.

Suggested in this outline is a proposition which Foucault went on to develop in his 'genealogies': his later studies of the historical and social conditions of the emergence of discourses and their relationship to institutional powers. The proposition is that knowledge and power are inseparable, that forms of power are imbued within knowledge, and that forms of knowledge are permeated by power relations. In order to suggest that power and knowledge are two sides of a single process, he coins the term 'power–knowledge', and says:

> Power produces knowledge. . . . Power and knowledge directly imply one another. . . . There is no power relation without the correlative constitution of a field of knowledge, nor any

knowledge that does not presuppose and constitute at the same time, power relations.

(Foucault 1979: 93)

Knowledge, he argues, is not a reflection of power relations but is immanent in them.

Foucault links the technologies of power with the emergence of the human sciences, arguing that the human sciences take people as both their object and their subject. They not only study practice, but effect it. For Foucault, the power–knowledge couplet (arising through the use to which institutions and governments put the human sciences) exists beneath the judicial and political structures of society. The 'judicio-political', according to Foucault, formally guarantees an egalitarian system of rights. The 'disciplines', however, run counter to such law, constructing inegalitarian technologies of power and regimes of truth.

Foucault discusses the totalizing and individualizing forms of power employed by institutions and governments via systems of power–knowledge relations. These individualization techniques may be seen in Foucault's discussion of the three modes of the objectification of the subject (see Rabinow 1984). That which warrants most attention for my purposes is what he calls – 'dividing practices'. This concept refers to those procedures which, through classification and categorization, distribute, contain, manipulate, and control people. Such methods divide people from each other and within themselves, giving them an identity which is both social and personal. In *Madness and Civilization* (1967), *The Birth of the Clinic* (1975), and *Discipline and Punish* (1977), Foucault shows that 'dividing practices' interconnect with the growth of the social sciences, that they relate historically to humanitarian rhetoric on reform and progress, that they became increasingly efficient and widely applied, and that they were usually applied to dominated groups.

The totalization procedures identified by Foucault arose as governments came to accept responsibility for economy, order, and the lives of people through all aspects of society. This resulted in centralized administrative apparatuses and a 'will to knowledge' about people's everyday lives and the state's resources. Through an ever-expanding archive containing intricate statistical details of individuals, the state developed an administrative grid which provided a means of both surveillance and regulation of everyday life. The human sciences assisted in this process through the provision of methods, plans, programs, data, and knowledge. The objectification of the human body via the combination of knowledge and power resulted in what Foucault calls 'disciplinary technologies'. The aim of such 'technologies', as Foucault says, was to develop a 'docile body which may be subjected, used, transformed, and improved' (Rabinow 1984: 179–88).

The rationality accompanying these disciplinary technologies is interested primarily in efficiency and productivity through a system of 'normalization' (Foucault in Gordon 1980: 104–8). This normative rationality has, Foucault claims, become an integral part of such state apparatuses as medicine, law, and education. Matters of values, justice, right, and wrong have been superseded by concern with the 'norm' and deviation from it. Normalizing technologies function to identify deviations. Other, accompanying, technologies provide corrective and disciplinary mechanisms. Such technologies include a vast apparatus for testing and documentation. Methods provided by the social sciences facilitate diagnostic and prognostic assessments and hierarchization, normative judgments to be made about the individual. The 'objective' knowledges produced as a result of such inquisitions becomes part of the 'web of control' of the state bureaucracy. Thus, Foucault argues, a characteristic feature of modern power structures is its capacity to both totalize and individualize the 'subject'.

Foucault makes a distinction between general and specific intellectuals (Rabinow 1984: 67–75), although his use of the latter term is somewhat ambiguous. A specific intellectual, as Poster (1982: 139) observes, is 'a creature of the twentieth century with its fragmentation of knowledge, its multiplication of disciplines, its infinite expansion of research centres, its explosion of the printed word, its professionalization of discourse'. The 'expert', the 'specialist', and the 'professional' produce, promote, and service 'regimes of truth'. They act as 'judges of normality' and endorse and benefit from the splintering of knowledge and the disempowerment of the unknowing. Specific intellectuals have, according to Foucault, superseded the 'universal intellectual', who spoke on behalf of the universal, for truth, justice, reason, and humanity (Rabinow 1984: 29). However, given Foucault's localized view of politics, the specific intellectual may also be equated with those who conduct counter-hegemonic work within their own discursive field (see Foucault in Gordon 1972: 129–33).

Knowledge is not regarded as neutral, pure, or, in itself, true or false. In considering 'rationality' historically and politically, Foucault points to the 'politics of truth telling', the manner in which social and self-government proceeds through the production and institutionalization of 'regimes of truth' (Foucault, in Gordon 1980: 108–33). Through genealogical analysis, Foucault suspends questions of truth and falsity and examines the institutional field over and through which a discourse gains and assigns power and control. He consider 'regimes of truth' as they have effects through apparatuses of power (Benton 1984: 177). As Foucault says, he is concerned to examine 'how forms of rationality inscribe themselves in practices or systems of practices and what role they play within them' (1981: 8) suppressing a plurality of alternative discourses and reducing their credibility. Regimes of truth may also be accompanied by or be the same thing as regimes of morality or moral technologies. These proselytize a form of morality, claim its higher status, and at the same time exercise a relationship of power (Minson 1980).

Unlike many critical theorists, Foucault avoids totalizing the concept of rationality. He talks about particular rationalities, in particular institutions, in particular power relations and generally refuses to make connections between diverse phenomena. According to Foucault, analysis should begin with the 'micro-   physics' of power (power–knowledge configurations), with localized mechanisms, histories and trajectories, techniques, and procedures. From here, he says, analysis should ascend to reveal how these have been colonized or appropriated by various forms of macro domination. Connections to a dominant state apparatus or a ruling group cannot be generalized; they must be reached through analysis (Smart 1983: 83–4).

For my purposes here, Foucault's 'game openings' are useful in the following ways. First, his discussion of the constitution of a 'regime of truth' is pertinent and my interest is in pointing to the themes, emphases, and omissions of the discursive regime under scrutiny and in exposing some of its governing rules and procedures. Second, however, rather than following Foucault's focus on the institutionalization of certain rationalities and their 'dividing practices', I will show how such rationalities are employed as part of the political strategy of the private school lobby and the Educational Right in their own 'dividing practices', and how the media and the Right developed their own power–knowledge apparatus. Further, I will demonstrate the manner in which both groups seek to encourage the political apparatus to use its disciplinary technologies, again, in their own interests. Now, while a Foucauldian analysis is useful in the manner outlined, it is less so in accounting for the range of 'non-governmental' discourses which, along with institutionalized rationalities, form part of the discursive ensemble of social movements such as the New Right and which help to constitute both people and governments as subjects. Further, while certainly recognizing the complex array of discourses which make up any 'regime of truth', Foucault is not as helpful as others on the matter of inter-discursivity or on the relationship between discourses and broad intersecting social structures of dominance. It is for these reasons that I seek to complement him by turning to Gramsci's work on hegemony.

Gramsci and the discursive constitution of hegemony

Gramsci has a wider focus than Foucault, as his interest is in the processes through which hegemony in society as a whole is achieved, sustained, adjusted, and challenged. He is particularly concerned with the forms of domination associated with social class, with the ways in which ideology binds together classes and class fractions in dominance and subordination. However, he offers a mode of class analysis that recognizes the importance of culture and emphasizes particularly the dynamic and open nature of class formation and class relations. Gramsci refuses the economic a sole causal primacy and his view of ideology moves beyond the notions that each class has its own fixed and closed ideological paradigm, that all ideology is class-related, and that social dominance is wrought through ideological distortion, mystification, and imposition. Gramsci asserts that there is no such thing as a pure class ideology; rather, he sees a universe of different ideological elements from which different classes 'selectively articulate in different ways to produce their own class ideologies' (Jessop 1982: 193). In Gramsci's view, then, class hegemony is achieved through ideological struggle on many fronts and it is this that has led a number of social theorists to use Gramsci as the touchstone for theorizing the discursive constitution of hegemony – discourse being understood here in a Foucauldian sense.

Gramsci sees ideology as providing the 'cement' upon which hegemony is built. It is the 'terrain' upon which people 'move, acquire consciousness of their position, struggle'. Rather than being given, subjects are seen to be the result of social practice, products of history, which has 'deposited' an 'infinity of traces without leaving an inventory' (Gramsci 1971: 324). Ideology, then, is social practice or action that embodies what Gramsci variously refers to as 'systems of thought' or 'conceptions of the world'. These, essentially, may take the highly developed and systematic form of 'philosophy' or the simpler, spontaneous, and contradictory form of 'common sense', this latter being understood as accumulated popular knowledge, or the thought which is embodied in everyday living.

Central to the development of class ideologies are those whom Gramsci calls intellectuals. He defines intellectuals according to their 'functions in dominance', that is, in the formation of the state, the constitutions of classes, and the organization of 'spontaneous consent' to the dominant interests that structure the social formation. Accordingly, intellectuals are divided into two groups: 'traditional' and 'organic'. It is this latter group that functions in such a way as to give the fundamental class to which it is organic an awareness of itself, not only in economic but also in social, cultural, and political fields (Gramsci 1971: 5). Organic individuals may, therefore, be seen to encompass any who have the effect of providing or challenging the hegemonic 'cement' of civil and political society, including civil servants, teachers, journalists, and pressure group leaders.

Intellectuals operate in conjunction with the 'ideological structure', that complex network of material and institutional structures throughout the social formation which, according to Gramsci, includes churches, trade unions, the family, schools, the mass media, and political parties. These organize culture and propagate ideologies in ways related to the class struggle. The 'private' terrain upon which such ideological endeavour occurs is what Gramsci calls 'civil society' (Jessop 1982: 148–9) and for Gramsci 'civil society' stands between the economic structure and the political apparatus and overlaps both (Gramsci 1971: 265). These areas of overlap indicate why Gramsci sees civil society as the primary terrain of class struggle. It is seen to make up the 'system of fortresses and outworks' that protect the 'outer ditch' – the political apparatus which he sometimes calls the state (Gramsci 1971: 238).

Gramsci's concept of the state goes beyond his narrower conception of what he variously calls the 'political apparatus', the 'state apparatus', or 'political society'. As Jessop (1982: 142–52) claims, when Gramsci talks of the state or state power, he is focusing upon the modalities of class domination within the whole social formation: 'the entire complex of practical and theoretical activities with which the ruling class not only justifies and maintains its dominance but manages to win the active consent of those over whom it rules' (Gramsci 1971: 244).

Hegemony

Let me return now to Gramsci's conception of hegemony, which has developed to include first, the offering of political leadership and the promotion of class allegiances within both the proletariat and the bourgeoisie; and second, the achievement of a position of dominance by a fundamental social class in alliance with other social groupings whose allegiances have been gained, and are maintained, through the process of ideological incorporation. One means by which this is achieved is through the construction of a mobilizing discursive ensemble that takes into account the interests of allied groups; recognizes and appropriates the concerns of those social groups which have not formed around class interests; makes some sacrifices of a corporate nature; and then welds together the interests and values of these disparate groups into a 'higher synthesis' – a fusion that generates a 'collective will'. Ideology provides the 'cement' that maintains this fusion and is generated through 'intellectual and moral leadership'. However, the achievement of class domination is seen as essentially fragile, in constant need of struggle and renewal, and always, ultimately, rests on the 'unstable equilibria of compromise' (Jessop 1982: 150).

Gramsci's term for such ideological struggle is 'war of position', and according to Mouffe (1979b) this is best understood as the struggle between two fundamental classes to articulate to their unifying principle, ideological elements coming from other social groups in order to form the higher synthesis mentioned above. The class struggle, then, is 'therefore equivalent to the work of articulating/disarticulating discourses from their previously secured position in an ideological field' (Hall 1980: 175), and class ideologies may be regarded as resulting from the reworking of a range of discourses in order that they may be organized and articulated so as to become a class discourse. Ideological elements are not seen, therefore, to necessarily belong to one class or another, as, across an ideological field, discourses may be formed and reformed. In the process of debate and persuasion, social groups and movements all seek to absorb and appropriate elements of the other's discourse. Such interdiscursive practice is seen to be possible due to the belief that a common nucleus of meaning may produce connotative differences depending upon the discursive ensemble into which it is inserted (Volosinov 1973; see also Salamini 1981). The fact that certain ideological elements may be equated with certain social classes or their agents, is, then, to be seen as the open result of political work. (Clearly, such a view has implications for the claim that Foucault has been irredeemably colonized by the Right.)

Clearly, interdiscursive skill is one factor amongst many that contributes to the achievement of class hegemony. Mouffe (1979b) asserts that Gramsci's concept of the 'national-popular' (i.e., any ideological expression of the people-nation) is particularly important in this regard. Laclau (1977: 106–9, 158–60) has developed a similar term: the 'popular/democratic'. According to Laclau, the popular/democratic terrain is one in which the people/state, rather than the capital/labor, contradiction is dominant. The people/state, oppressed/oppressor contradiction is exemplified in the ideological oppositions between 'big' or 'central' government and individuality and freedom. To Laclau, the field of the national-popular is the terrain *par excellence* of ideological struggle, as, rather than interpellating individuals as class members, it interpellates them as 'the people' (Laclau 1977: 106–9, 158–60). Gramsci also asserts the significance of 'common sense' as a primary site of ideological struggle. As common sense is open and receptive to a range of thought – always in a state of becoming – those involved in ideological work can intervene in popular thinking either to further reduce its capacity for liberating thought and practice or to recompose its elements and add new ones as a movement towards liberation. Such intervention capitalizes upon the contradictions within common sense arising through the absorption of world views that serve the interests of different fundamental classes (Hall, Lumley, and McLennan 1979: 50).

Hegemony and 'difference'

In their more recent writing, Laclau and Mouffe (1982, 1985) have developed Gramsci's notion of hegemony, elaborating more fully on the notion that hegemony is constituted through interdiscursive articulation. In order to account for the force of those current social movements that draw their inspiration from non-class issues, they refuse to privilege class analysis in their discussions of discursive politics. Instead, they recognize a plurality of social struggles and therefore a vast plurality of discursive subjects. The fact that certain ideological elements may be equated with certain social groups or sections, be they racial, sexual, or class groupings, must therefore be seen as a consequence of political struggle and meaning construction. Further, class subjectivities, rather than being determined by the subject's position in the relations of production with equivalent political and ideological dispositions, are actually only produced through interpellation. As Jessop (1982: 96) concludes, 'this suggests that class struggle is first of all about the *constitution* of class subjects before it is a struggle between class subjects' (emphasis added).

The social field, then, is seen to be constituted by difference, and the political project of any social movement is the discursive articulation of these different subjects, that is, the transformation of subjectivities in order to constitute new political subjects around a hegemonic principle which is possibly, but not necessarily, that of a fundamental class groupings. Political struggle is still defined as the politics of articulation and occurs through deconstruction and reconstruction, but this term now refers more widely to a struggle between discourses of difference.

Given that present in one individual are different and often contradictory subject positions, it must be recognized that the political constitution of subjects is not an easy task. In fact, in Laclau's (1983b: 118) words, 'the cleavage of the subject is the terrain and starting point for political action: hegemony is nothing other than the attempt – by definition incomplete and open-ended – to perform an impossible suture'. Accordingly, hegemony becomes a 'discourse of discourses' and is defined as the process of constructing politically the subjectivity of the masses (Laclau 1983b: 118), the formation of diverse subjects into a collective will.

This brings me back to Foucault, and to a pertinent point of convergence between this particular reading of Gramsci and Foucault. Power is not seen to be localized in a central apparatus; neither is it seen to emerge from an essential essence. Rather, for both writers it is seen to exist as a relationship at all points in the social totality. Therefore non-reductionist analysis is a central and shared feature of their work. Power for Foucault, like hegemony for Gramsci, is not simply imposed from the top down, but is regarded as complex and diffuse. While Gramsci talks of 'active consent', Foucault too moves beyond understanding power as the 'effects of obedience'. For Foucault, power is 'a complex strategical situation... and is exercised from innumerable points in the interplay of non-egalitarian and mobile relations' (quoted in Mercer 1980: 123).

The hegemonic effect, according to Foucault, is a consequence of the multiplicity of micro-powers – the 'proliferation of discourses' that produces consent. Each discourse has its effects in the construction of subjectivity and each exists in a complex matrix of intersection and connotation. For Foucault:

> Discourses are tactical elements or blocks operating in the field of force relations: there can exist different and even contradictory discourses within the same strategy: they can, on the contrary, circulate without changing their form from one strategy to another, opposing strategy.
>
> (1976: 21–2)

As I have indicated, Gramsci's conception of hegemony can also be understood to suggest a 'proliferation of discourses' which involve us 'as subjects in the most "spontaneous", "unnoticed", "natural" and "obvious" areas of our experience' (Mercer 1978: 22).

This reading of Gramsci helps to explain the political importance of the private school lobby's and the Educational Right's activities in civil society for both the political apparatus and the construction of common sense. Further, it provides a way of contextualizing the discursive politics of this political partnership within the wider ongoing processes of class formation and relations. The post-structuralist emphasis on the political strategy of discursive articulation/disarticulation and on the constitution of subjectivity through the appeal to 'difference' offers, in my view, a particularly convincing explanation of the power of the discourse of the Right in education.

Let me return now to the critical historical incident that I mentioned in the introduction. In what follows I will first give some indication of the nature of the discourse of the private school lobby as it struggled to reconstruct Labor's educational agenda; second, place this discourse in the context of that of the Educational Right; and third, explore the reasons that this discursive ensemble was so effective in constructing common sense, in influencing the federal Labor government's education policy and in serving the most socially powerful. My data are drawn largely from Australia's print media which, as I have shown elsewhere (Kenway 1987b) provided considerable ideological support for the above group's political project.

Jane Kenway

THE DISCOURSE OF THE PRIVATE SCHOOL LOBBY AND THE EDUCATIONAL RIGHT

The private school lobby

During 1983–84 the political strategy of the supporters of private schooling was to marshal and promulgate an arsenal of argument against the Labor government's policies on funding. While different lobby groups within the sector may have drawn selectively from this (for instance, Catholics feared integration with the state system, while highly resourced private schools feared the 'hit list') there was a strong tendency for all groups to posit and repeat much the same arguments. At their most sober and 'reasonable', private school supporters levelled criticism at the particular mechanisms employed by the Schools Commission in allocating funding. The method for identifying the 'hit list' schools was variously labelled as 'deficient', 'arbitrary', 'random', and as developed in 'haste and secrecy' (e.g., *Australian*, 5 August 1983, p. 3). The government's proposition that funding should be based upon 'need' was described as 'unclear' and even 'anachronistic and discredited' (e.g., 'Letters to the editor', *Canberra Times*, 5 August 1983, p. 2). It was pointed out that, according to Schools Commission projections, 'non-government' schools would soon be educating 28 per cent of the population and yet would only be receiving 16 per cent of total state and federal funds. This was perceived as a gross injustice that would only be rectified when these schools received 28 per cent of education money (*Canberra Times*, 26 July 1983, p. 11). Some school principals proffered other 'correctives', as did the headmaster of Canberra Grammar in his speech night address: 'If more money is needed, government schools could charge fees as they do in Japan. If the nation's education bill is too large, then relieve it in this way with all parents contributing, not by dividing the community as this government has done' (*Canberra Times*, 10 December 1983, p. 2).

Another cluster of arguments within this apparently pragmatic strand of rhetoric was to do with taxes. One claim was that those parents supporting private schools saved other tax-paying parents money, as governments were spared the cost of educating private school children in government schools. Such assertions contained the veiled threat that reduced funds would result in private school students returning to the state system *en masse*, causing an additional financial burden on the public. Some private school enthusiasts took this point further, as did one correspondent to the *Age* (17 August 1983, p. 15). It was 'bad economics', he asserted, 'not to encourage the easing of public costs through private investment'.

The discourse of democracy, particularly the concepts of rights, justice, and choice, inspired another set of arguments. The claims went as follows: parents have a right to choose private schools, and also have a right as taxpayers to have that choice supported by public money. As the NSW AIS (Association of Independent Schools) claimed, 'the proposals ignored parents' rights to choose schools as guaranteed by international convention and Australian law' (*Australian*, 27 April 1984, p. 2). They must pay twice, it was said: once for the education of other children and then for the education of their own (e.g., 'Letters to the editor', *Canberra Times*, 5 August 1983, p. 2). Some private-school supporters protested that it was no longer a matter of money but one of principle. For example, in a letter to the *Age* (17 August 1983, p. 15), the Roman Catholic Auxiliary Archbishop of Melbourne asserted: 'State aid is not the issue; this is about liberty, justice and high standards of education for all'.

There were three strong but often unstated implications in this particular argument. One was that a government that opposed funding therefore opposed choice and thus democracy. It was also held that private schools stood for diversity and that such diversity suggested a healthy democracy. The state system was depicted as monolithic and bureaucratic and, by implication, unhealthy. Again, not to fund was to oppose democracy. A third implication was that opposing 'choice' was the same as opposing the rights of parents and that this was, in fact, anti-family. As one correspondent in a letter to the *Age* (17 August 1983, p. 15) asked, 'Is it the parents who beget, nourish and mould the children or is it the state?'

Aligned to this appeal to democracy was an injured stance that invoked the language of the oppressed. To single out 41 schools for funding reductions was depicted as 'discriminatory'; it was to impose a 'means test' which was not only an 'invasion of privacy' but penalized self-help and attacked financially 'sacrificing' parents. Along this vein, there was a very determined denial that either the schools or parents were wealthy (e.g., *Australian*, 21 November 1983, p. 11; *Weekend Australian*, 12 May 1984, p. 18). As certain AIS spokesmen were fond of saying, 'Our schools represent a broad cross-section of the population' (*West Australian*, 2 April 1984, p. 16). Of course, collectively they may have included a cross-section but where the populations were concentrated was a matter excluded from discussion. An often-repeated ingredient of the wealth-denial argument was the claim that the withdrawal of government funds would make these expensive schools 'more elitist and exclusive' or 'havens for the rich', as, due to 'forced' fee rises, many 'struggling' parents would be compelled to withdraw their children. This wealth denial was often accompanied by the image of struggle and sacrifice, one form of 'sacrifice', depicted as somehow more pitiful than any other, was that of the mother forced into paid labour in order to pay school fees.

Prohibited was any recognition of the relativity of perceptions of wealth. Most parents interviewed by the print media described themselves as comfortable, 'forgetting' that to be comfortable, to choose to work, let alone to choose to sacrifice is, for many, a privilege. Notions of 'sacrifice' are also relative, but perhaps not to the headmaster of Knox in Sydney, whose students' parents 'forsake home improvements' and 'sell off valuables' in order to give their children a 'good education' (*West Australian*, 5 December 1983, p. 43).

The 'sacrifice' argument took a number of unexpected turns in the 'Letter to the editor' pages of Australia's major papers. One was that parents of high or dual incomes should not 'sponge on the state system' (*Age*, 10 December 1983, p. 12); another was that parents connected with private schools should not be expected to subsidize those uncaring parents who were not prepared to make the same 'sacrifices' as they had (*Australian*, 8 December 1983, p. 6).

Another element in this private school supporters' discourse found inspiration from the long-running educational standards debate. The claim was that if the government reduced funds and the schools chose not to raise fees, then they would be forced to lower their educational standards. The government, therefore, was implicitly anti-excellence, penalizing the schools for their success and trying to drag them down to the level of the state schools (e.g., *Canberra Times*, 5 August 1983, p. 2). As a bursar from a 'victim' school claimed, 'the government has somehow got the word "quality" mixed up with "wealthy".... We are being punished for our success in attracting parents' (*Weekend Australian*, 13–14 November 1983, p. 16). According to this logic, state schools could not compete in the 'educational market place'. The 'drifts', 'swings' or 'surges' from state to private schools so often described in the press were drawn upon as evidence of this.

Eventually, having 'fixed' meaning and reason, the private school lobby came to assert that parents actually had no choice. Only private schools, it seemed, could give children a good education. Rather than attacking the private school system, the government should rectify the deficiencies in its own schools and let the private schools get on with the business of providing good schooling (*Advertiser*, 7 November 1983, p. 6). Of course, such logic did not end the calls for funds and herein several contradictory strands of persuasion emerged. One was that the state schools did not need more money because money alone did not produce excellence (e.g., 'Letters to the editor', *Daily News*, 25 January 1984, p. 25). Another was that money should not be poured into a system which had so blatantly shown its inability to use it wisely. A common 'truth' was that the government would show better business sense if it directed more funds to those who knew best how to spend them. However, if private schools were to lose funds and therefore be unable to retain their students, the government would then have to fully fund those students in state schools and standards would be further depressed. The Schools Commission's suggestions for increased accountability were countered partly with this standards logic. Also, increased accountability was labelled an 'intrusion into the legitimate privacy of non-government schools' (*Sydney Morning Herald*, 18 April 1984, p. 4). Anything beyond the current levels were deemed 'excessive', 'threatening', and 'unnecessary'. It was argued that despite state aid, such schools should only be accountable to parents (*Sydney Morning Herald*, 25 March 1984, p. 3).

Much invective was directed at Education Minister Susan Ryan, who, to her opponents, as the *Sydney Morning Herald* (10 November 1983, p. 8) suggested, 'represented the unacceptable face of modern womanhood, assertive, single and threatening to old ways'. She was said to be attempting to split the private school sector by discriminating against Protestants and in favour of Catholics; she was believed to be discriminating against both in order to pay back election debts to the teachers' unions; and further, she was discriminating against religion in favour of secularism (e.g., *Australian*, 9 November 1983. p. 2; *Age*, 16 August 1983, p. 12; *Sydney Morning Herald*, 7 November 1983, p. 2). As Father John Fleming argued in the *Advertiser* (7 November 1983, p. 6), 'Opponents of aid usually but not always are opponents of religion in general and the Christian religion in particular'.

A domino theory emerged suggesting that the attack on the 'top' schools was preliminary to attacks on the Catholic sector. For example, a state aid campaigner from the Catholic sector said: 'We must care for parents in wealthy schools because our turn will come' (*Australian*, 9 November 1983, p. 2). Finally, in a style of rhetoric similar to that of the Cold War warriors, 'sinister' forces were seen to be at work. To Independent Senator Harradine, 'One advantage of private schools is that they keep children away from teachers from the teachers' federation which is run by communist party members bent on winning the battle to win the hearts and minds of Australian school children.'

B.A. Santa Maria, a long-time opponent of the Australian Labor Party and radical campaigner for Catholic education, emerged from a long silence on matters of schooling in two full-page spreads (*Australian*, 30 August 1983, p. 7; *Sunday Independent*, 14 August 1983, p. 24), depicting the ALP as dominated by 'Marxist, secularist teacher unionists, education intellectuals and highly paid public servants'. The government's intention was to 'divide and rule', and to integrate the Catholic system within the state. Catholics, he felt, were being duped by the 3 per cent increase. Similarly, the Roman Catholic Auxiliary Archbishop of Melbourne in his letter to the *Age* (17 August 1983, p. 5) said: 'I challenge any school to accept this Judas money'.

There is no doubt that on the matter of government policy on school funding, the private school lobby developed, through the media, a decisive and dominant regime of truth. Essentially, it was its capacity to weld disparate ideological elements into a coherent, unified, and distinctive discursive ensemble that contributed to its ideological and political ascendancy. However, this is not to overlook the flaws and weaknesses in the discourses of the other contending parties – the state school lobby and the Left – as it is these, too, which assisted the private school lobby's ascendancy and eventual victory (see further Kenway 1987b). What I shall discuss now, however, is the discourse of the Educational Right, emphasizing particularly its articulation with that of the private school lobby. In order to indicate its contemporary nature, I shall discuss the discourse to follow in the present tense.

The Educational Right

The term 'Educational Right' is not unproblematic. What I call the Educational Right is not a single, homogeneous entity, either socially or ideologically. The two strands of thinking which I identified earlier in the New Right may also be found in the thinking of the Educational Right. One set of ideas, rooted in economics, contains perceptions about individuals, the virtues of the market, and the evils of state intervention, and leads to the promotion of privacy and efficiency in education, the elevation of the role of the family, and the denigration of the idea that education may be employed as a means to effect social change. Accompanying this logic is a contradictory line of reasoning that wishes the state to assume greater responsibility for developing both 'basic skills' and vocational training. Education is to become more accountable to employers, and is to adjust its content to the demands of the labour market and changing technology. A second body of thought is based upon ideas about tradition, authority, and hierarchy. This conservative wing of the Educational Right calls for a return to the traditional form and content of schooling, and for the revived authority of the 'disciplines' and of teachers. The individualism of the libertarian wing is eschewed in favour of a notion that education should produce social cohesion and stability. This wing is anti-egalitarian and culturally elitist.

Clustered uncomfortably together under the title 'the Educational Right' are different social groupings and different 'intellectual and moral leaders'. The 'vanguard' of the conservative wing of the Educational Right is the Australian Council for Educational Standards (ACES), a group of 'specific intellectuals' comprised primarily of conservative academics. The Council's foundation in 1973 was marked by the publication of *ACES Review* which, along with the journal

186

Quadrant, has since provided an outlet for the views of conservative educational commentators. This group of academics makes regular media appearances, and the media reports in detail the texts of their public addresses. The media not only amplifies these educational commentators' voices, it also provides powerful echoes via the efforts of journalists such as Greg Sheridan (*The Australian*), Michael Barnard (*The Age*), Alan Fitzgerald (*Canberra Times*), and often via editorial support. The media also seek and air the views of spokesmen from industry, employer groups, and the New Right think tanks. Such people constitute the vanguard of the neo-liberal wing of the Educational Right.

Despite their contradictory positions, the groups that constitute the Educational Right have synthesized a new ideology of education under the 'mobilizing myth' (Levitas 1983: 8) of educational 'crisis'. State schooling is seen to have disintegrated into chaos; it is both disordered and demoralized. Further, it is not catering for the intellectual or employment needs of students. It is causing massive disquiet amongst parents, and it is not serving the needs of either the workforce or society. The Right's critique of current educational practice centres on the following areas: the curriculum and its assessment, and teachers and educational policymakers. While certain sections of the Right may emphasize one area rather than another, it is unified in its proclamation that standards have declined so alarmingly that not only students' futures but also Australia's future are at risk. The term 'standards' has become the Educational Rights' central slogan. The popular expression 'declining standards in Australian schools' now conjures up images not only of an innumerate, illiterate student population but also of a breakdown in the authority of the school, the 'disciplines' and the teachers. In the words of Lachlan Chipman, a professor of philosophy, education is experiencing a 'crisis of confidence; Australia is in danger of a new barbarism in education' (*Australian*, 30 May 1983, p. 3).

It must be made clear before proceeding further that the Educational Right does not believe all schooling to be in crisis. Its comments are directed at government, not private, schools. In most instances, when government schools come under attack, the private schools are brought forward as the exemplification of the standards towards which state schools should strive. There is almost no recognition of the differences existing within both the state and the private sectors. The debate is constructed on simple binary oppositions, with state schools always at the negative end of the pole and private schools at the positive. Class antagonisms are dressed up in a 'new' language of educational quality and democracy.

Jane Kenway

Standards

Within the Educational Right, the term 'standards' has three overlapping but essential connotations. It may refer to literacy and numeracy, to the extent to which schools prepare students for the work force, or to the content of the curriculum. The most common connotation relates to levels of literary and numeracy. The educational crisis is characterized, in these arguments, by a devastating drop in its levels. The most shrill notes of despair in this regard emanate from employment agencies, their employer authorities, and certain university academics, those whom Hannan, an educationalist (1985: 234–37), calls the 'illiteracy alarmists' and whose cries reverberate constantly through various media outlets.

A second way in which standards have been defined employs a technocratic, instrumentalist logic that asserts that schools must serve the needs of the economy. Within this logic, state education is seen to be in crisis in two major ways. The first draws a strong connection between Australia's economic problems, particularly unemployment, and the schools' failure to educate students to meet Australia's economic needs. In some instances, the schools are blamed for unemployment while in others it is argued that if schools were to revise their curricula in appropriate ways, certain economic problems would be ameliorated. Second, the public schools are 'in crisis' because they have failed to keep pace with the changing technology of the workplace; they are failing to produce sufficient qualified people for an increasingly 'high tech' labour market. This particular problem is promulgated by such groups as the Chamber of Commerce and various employers' federations and it is given considerable credibility and support through media discussions of the purposes of education and the solutions to the educational 'crisis'. It has become accepted (in many quarters) as common sense – its truth is fixed.

In Australia, an emphasis upon vocationalism and reemphasizing the 'skills', rigorously testing students' 'skills' competence, and reintroducing sorting and streaming tend to be defined as one solution to the problems of unemployment and the lack of correspondence between school curricula and the workplace. Another solution is through the diversion of funds in order to permit schools to teach technical and specialized skills. A third solution favoured by this wing of the Educational Right is to involve industry more in educational decision-making. Indeed, according to the *Australian* (26 January 1984, p. 3), the National Chamber of Commerce is unhappy with the government's education system as it is too much under the authority of the Department of Education and the Teachers' Federation. Apparently, 'education policy is too important to be left to professionals'.

The third wing of the Educational Right, the conservative wing,

188

regards this position as 'narrow pragmatism' (e.g., Kramer 1983: 5). Its understanding of 'standards' is reflected in the following quotation from Chipman:

> The debate about standards is as much to do with the standard of what is offered and of what is demanded from pupils as it is to do with standards of achievement. It goes as much to curriculum content and behavioural demeanour as it does to performances in literacy and numeracy tests.
>
> (*Age*, 7 June 1983, p. 16)

The decline in standards is seen to be reflected in the declining status of the 'disciplines'; however, which subjects comprise the 'disciplines' is not always clear. Barcan, an educational historian (*Canberra Times*, 7 May 1984, p. 3) seems to reflect the view of many members of this faction of the Educational Right when he says that schools should offer the 'humanist curriculum consisting of literature, languages, history and science'. According to Chipman, the purpose of schooling is to 'strengthen the intellect' and the disciplines are seen to provide the means by which this is achieved. They 'develop skills which are portable and applicable to wide and unforeseen variety of problems' (*Age*, 14 June 1983, p. 15). For Kramer, a professor of literature (1984: 8), 'education is about individual awareness, fulfilment, and learning how to work for the common good'. And to Barcan (*Canberra Times*, 7 May 1984, p. 3), 'progressive education must be blamed for the collapse over the last decade of the humanist tradition that education was to improve humanity'. Lumped under the general rubric 'progressive education' appears to be any approach which does not emphasize 'the authority of teacher and text' (Hannan 1985: 29), content, and general knowledge. Any emphasis upon such things as self esteem, creativity, personal development, inquiry methods, child-centered learning, or group work is regarded as a threat to standards (e.g., Chipman 1982a, 1982b).

Seen to be accompanying the declining standards of knowledge is a decline in standards of behaviour. According to the Right, the climate of government schools is now characterized by 'turbulence and disorder'. Barnard's (*Age*, 7 June 1983, p. 13) call for the state schools to be what they once were illustrates well this form of nostalgia and the search for scapegoats to blame for the end of the golden age,

> before radicalized teachers' unions and the advent of new thinking with all its accompanying jargon about the 'democratic curriculum' and the like were to envelop the education landscape like a stupefying fog.

Education policy under scrutiny

All factions of the Educational Right come together in their opposition
to the changes that have occurred in Australian education over the last
decade or so prior to 1987. The foci of much of the Educational Right's
invective are the various state and federal government reports and
reforms that promote and have led to the broadening of the secondary
and upper secondary school curriculum. They are all characterized as
'arbitrary', the outcomes of 'muddled' or 'shoddy' thinking, and as
'anti-intellectual' or as 'anti-academic'. The philosophy and purposes
underpinning such reforms, although depicted in various ways, are
always trivialized. To some (e.g., Partington 1984: 1), they are the
outcome of a 'Left ascendancy' in educational bureaucracies, which has
suddenly 'politicized' schooling. Witness the words of Barnard (*Age*, 26
June 1984, p. 13) speaking of an alternative Year 12 curriculum: 'a
hotch potch of anti-intellectualism and educational dilution', supported
only by 'militant teacher unions and a handful of trendy academics'. The
'disciplines' have been 'watered down', 'emasculated', and 'trivialised'
and such 'dilution' has led to much more than a crisis for the disciplines.
For example, Dr Rob Leckey, chairman of the Victorian Branch of the
Australian Institute of Physics, asserts: 'The drift in the standard of
science education poses a threat to Australia's status as an advanced
nation' (*Australian*, 29 February 1984, p. 12).

It is constantly asserted that state schools now offer a 'smorgasbord'
of knowledge comprised of 'Mickey Mouse' courses that reduce
students and the curriculum to the 'lowest common denominator' (see
Barnard in *Age*, 26 June 1984, p. 13; Chipman 1984: 39; Harrison-
Mattley 1983). Attempts to broaden the curriculum are either belittled
or treated as a conspiracy. 'They show no understanding of the current
realities of Australian society' (Kramer 1983: 5) and provide 'depres-
sing evidence of the bankruptcy of educational thought' (Barcan 1982:
14). Such attempts seek simply 'to amuse and titillate the young for a
short period' (Conway 1985: 3), and to ensure teachers' job security as
well as to reduce the numbers of unemployed youth (Chipman 1984:
40). Those curricula that focus on social issues are condemned as
politicizing schooling by moving away from the 'traditional'
curriculum, which is depicted as value-free (e.g., Barcan in the
Canberra Times, 7 May 1984, p. 3; *Sydney Morning Herald*, 22 January
1983, p. 9). As Conway (1985: 6) laments:

> Alas, schools are becoming increasingly enmeshed in the 'Mickey
> Mouse' curriculum – media studies, so called 'sex education' –
> even 'women's studies' (why not for men?) – and most recently:
> 'Peace Studies'.... The susceptibility of these new hybrid
> courses to ideological kite flying and propaganda is obvious.

The concern is about curriculum content and style but also assessment, and here we find universities constantly threatening to set their own assessment procedures if their wishes are not heeded (e.g. *Australian*, February 1984, p. 12). Moves in a number of Australian state systems away from external exams and towards school-based assessment are, like curriculum changes, treated with ridicule. The arguments used in support of such moves are incorporated into a discourse of derision and accompanied by the continued construction of a 'crisis'. The following quotation typifies the discourse, characterizing such moves as a

> trendy, no competition, no accountability, everyone's-a-winner philosophy that fails to distinguish between man's God-given individuality and 'elitism' and threatens to engulf education in soul-destroying medocrity.
>
> (Barnard in *Age*, 21 June 1983, p. 13)

Predictably, members of ACES strongly supported the Australian Education Council's national scheme testing numeracy and literacy which began in 1975, was repeated in 1980, and abandoned in 1983. This abandonment is described as 'a scandalous decision when public concern was mounting' (Chipman in the *West Australian*, 17 January 1984, p. 16). Members of ACES regularly complain that Australia now lacks any measure to show fluctuations in literacy and numeracy standards. For example, Chipman argues that the end of testing is a cover-up to protect state schools. He claims that it is a consequence of state teachers' fear of the results, their wish to protect their weaker colleagues, and their unwillingness to be compared with their private school counterparts. According to Chipman, this is yet another means by which state school teachers may keep parents in ignorance of 'what really goes on' (Chipman 1984: 39; Chipman in the *Age*, 7 June 1983, p. 16).

This refusal by the Right to engage in any serious way with the issues raised by recent educational reforms is well exemplified in an article by Alan Fitzgerald (*Canberra Times*, 23 December 1983, p. 2).

> Too much time is still taken up in classrooms devoted to basics like reading, writing and maths and not enough to the discussion of the evils of capitalism, the family and heterosexual behaviour. Much more time should be spent on the study of social role playing, street theatre, sexual liberation, and the wonders of Marxist-Leninist finger painting and slogan chanting.
>
> We can never hope to eliminate difference or discrimination between individuals and groups till we abolish standards that set the criteria by which difference is measured. Down with

standards. Up with ignorance and equality! Thank Karl Marx for the teachers' federation that can lead us into the brave new world of tomorrow.

Teachers

Accompanying the panic about declining standards and the production of unemployable youth is a sustained attack upon state school teachers and their unions, teacher education, educational reformers, and bureaucrats. Educational politics is seen to be dominated by the 'left-wing ideologies' with their 'left-radical egalitarian orthodoxy' (Conway 1985: 1). Conway (1985: 1) asserts that 'riding high both in Canberra and in at least three key States, radical New Establishment forces in education are now at the zenith of their power – with even Ministers of the Crown, as ex-teachers, available to serve their ends'. The activities of teachers' unions are widely reported in the media in the language of condemnation and censure. Teachers' unions are 'militant', 'politically motivated', and 'extremist'. Governments are portrayed as constantly bowing to their pressure. However, attacks on teachers are not always generalized. In some instances, the bulk of the 'responsible professionals' or 'passive majority' is separated from the 'trendy', 'progressive' or 'militant' visible and powerful minority (e.g., Barcan 1984a: 17). And thus divisions within the teaching profession are at once proclaimed, produced and reinforced.

Modes of teacher selection and preparation also come under attack. The strength of neo-Marxism in teacher education institutions is constantly alluded to (e.g., Barcan 1984b: 60) and decried as 'producing confusion about the status of knowledge and the role of the teacher' (Partington in the *Advertiser*, 16 May 1984, p. 16). 'The degree', Chipman (1984: 39) insists, 'should be built upon the study of primary disciplines and does not include "Education" as a constituent subject'. Geoffrey Partington asserts that 'many teacher training institutions are plague bearers rather than medical centers to deal with the "epidemics" which have afflicted educational thought in recent years' (*Advertiser*, 16 May 1984, p. 16). The quality of student teachers is also brought into question; they are described by Chipman as repeating, barely passing, and cheating their ways through universities (*Australian*, 27 June 1983, p. 3; Chipman 1982a: 17, 19).

According to the Educational Right, teachers have lost public respect as a consequence of their misguided attempts to democratize their class-rooms and the curriculum. Their movements away from authoritarian and traditional approaches to teaching and their undermining of the authority of the disciplines has lost them credibility and brought the state education system to a condition of crisis.

The 'truth' about private schooling

Within the discourse of the Educational Right, private schooling (especially high-fee church schooling) is depicted as everything the state system is not. The private schools exemplify the best in standards, discipline, and teacher dedication and quality; they symbolize educational 'excellence' and success. As I have indicated, much of the Right's rhetoric includes an appeal to traditional approaches to schooling with regard to the curriculum, assessment, and teachers' style. Tradition is equated with standards and both are equated with private schools. The inadequacies of the state system drive parents to private schools in the search for standards and 'some hope of excellence' (Conway 1985: 1). The state school system has, according to the Right, disillusioned, mystified, and confused parents by refusing to be accountable to them and keeping them uninformed. The 'anti-academic' 'anti-elitist', 'anti-accountability', 'anti-assessment', 'leftist' approaches, which the Right believes characterize state school teaching, are absent from private schools. They have not been 'unionized and politicised', says Partington (1984: 3). Further, private schools do not have 'a dislike of anybody being outstanding', points out the head of the University of West Australia's medical school (*Sunday Times*, 21 August 1983, p. 26). Neither do they believe that competition is unhealthy, asserts the executive director of the West Australia Chamber of Commerce. He explains: 'We live in a competitive environment yet children are not being prepared for it. . . . Many people prefer to send children to independent schools where competition is encouraged, (*Sunday Times*, 21 August 1983, p. 26). The private school lobby draws one of its principal sources of strength from its location within the 'standards' strand of the Educational Right's discourse; hence the power of its claims that to withdraw funds is to 'attack educational excellence'. Further, as a consequence of the common sense constructed by the 'specific intellectuals' of the Right, it is also able to show private schools to be in popular demand due to their standards and hence to justify claims for 'choice' and for funding.

The instrumentalist section of the Educational Right tends to exclude private schools from its polemic because, in contrast with state schools, a much smaller proportion of private school students move directly into the labour market, tending, rather, to proceed to some form of tertiary study. This exclusion has its ideological effects. State schools come to be seen as providing an uncertain route to anywhere, and the private schools to almost guarantee educational success, tertiary entrance, and employment. Again the private school lobby is able to find legitimation for its cause. To reduce funds is to attack the schools that are doing precisely what the state schools are not: producing employable youth,

fulfilling the demands of the labour market, and therefore serving the
national interest.

Just as the Right attributes the 'collapse' of standards in state schools
to teachers' union policies, so it attacks state teachers' unions for
discriminating 'on irrelevant political grounds against schools of the
highest pedagogical standards in favour of these schools which are
urged to practice a useless form of titillating custodialism' (Conway
1985: 4). Motivating such anti-private school behaviour is the 'politics
of envy and resentment' (Morgan 1984: 9). As Barnard (*Age*, 3 July
1984, p. 13) makes clear,

> the continuing and sometimes vicious campaign spearheaded by
> 'progressive' thinkers in militant teacher unions and Labor
> administration [seeks] to cripple the non-government sector, one
> of the few remaining means of providing any comparative
> measure of teacher performance in the State System. So far as
> union militants are concerned this drive towards a uniform
> greyness in which the cultivation of academic excellence is
> banished as 'elitism', may be summed up in a word: monopoly.
> Teacher monopoly.

The Right also constructs a dichotomy between state teachers as
teachers, and such teachers as parents. While many government school
teachers and 'university trendies' may 'march in the vanguard of new
education' (Barnard in the *Age*, 7 June 1983, p. 13), they will not have
their children 'suffer' the state system. As parents, we learn that they
'would not be pleased at the prospect of seeing their sons and daughters
consigned to some government schools where notions of excellence and
teacher accountability have long been regarded as expendable'
(Conway 1985: 2). The subtext of this line of reasoning is obvious: if
those inside the system don't trust it (and who would know better than
they?), how can parents outside the system do other than not trust it as
well?

Certain of the Educational Right's solutions to the 'education crisis'
have already become obvious: a return to the traditional form and
content of schooling, and/or a closer correspondence between certain
sections of schooling and the workplace. Another solution arises from
the liberal tenets of New Right thinking. Private schooling is located
firmly at the centre of liberal thought, and once more the private school
lobby has gained strength from the Right's positioning. Within this
logic, market forces are regarded as more likely to promote quality
education than is state 'intervention'. It is accepted that the private
schools exemplify the best in education and their 'excellence' is
believed to be a consequence of the free play of market forces. The state
should only 'intervene' through assistance with funds but otherwise

should leave the schools free to continue the job that they do so well. Within this liberalist thinking, accepting public money does not imply that the schools should be accountable to the government or the public. Taxpayers' rights do not extend so far. State support is encouraged only in so far as it permits the educational market to operate; beyond that, private schools must be private in order to operate effectively. To require accountability has, in the common sense of the debate, become an affront against privacy, a bureaucratic intrusion upon the rights of those who are managing their schools more efficiently than state governments are managing state schools.

Here we see the private schools contrasted with the government in their capacity to spend money wisely. Taxpayers' money is recklessly distributed by a spendthrift state, throwing good money after bad into the state schools. As Chipman (1984: 43) argues of the 1983 funding cuts, 'It is a classic example of government interference in the market place to give special preference to its own failing investment.' The discursive opposite of the spendthrift state is the private school, cautiously spending money and seeking not to extract any more than is necessary from the 'struggling' parents. A second discursive distinction is made between private schooling and the oppressive, centralist bureaucratic state seeking to produce a 'uniform greyness' and to thwart the educational freedom, enterprise, and initiative of the private system. In both of these binary oppositions, Rightist ideology draws upon the people/state contradiction theorized by Laclau.

Within Rightist thinking, education is regarded as a family, not a state, responsibility. Private schooling is seen to provide the means by which the family may accept responsibility for the child's schooling via the mechanism of choice; families are defined as the 'education consumers'. Rightist calls for the introduction of the voucher system and for dezoning also arise from within this logic (e.g., Harrison-Mattley 1982: 1–3). Were state schools subjected to market pressure, they might lift their standards. Witness Morgan's (1984: 10) comments on the voucher system:

> The teachers and parents as inheritors of the state schools would then have to compete, on equal terms, with the existing non-government sector. Competition and the role of the marketplace encompassing 100 per cent of our school population, rather than just 24 per cent, would provide a solution to the politics of envy. It would blunt the pursuit of conformity and mediocrity by bureaucrats, and it would broaden the sense of participation of parents in the education of their children.

For the Right, as Johnson (1983: 13) argues, 'education is a consumer good, acquired and regulated through the market according to demand in the shape of parental choice'. Further, as Hall points out (1980: 180), through the mechanism of choice, parents can now help to restore authority, discipline, standards, and traditional values. They can become agents in educational reform. Although both Hall and Johnson are referring to the British situation, the points which they make are particularly apt in Australia. The following comment from Chipman (*Age*, 7 June 1983, p. 11) exemplifies right-wing perceptions of the 'educational market-place': the 'second largest investment decision (after a house) which most families are called upon to make. . . is whether to send their children to non-state schools'. And, as Morgan (1984: 9) says, private schools are more 'responsive to consumer demands'.

Central to this discourse is the family, and two types of families are depicted. The first is the tight-knit nuclear family, guardian of popular morality, and central to our social system. Parents within this type of family care about the education of their children, and wish to exercise their parental responsibilities and rights by opting out of a system that can offer nothing to their children. The second type of family, the 'split', 'broken', single-parent or two-income family is a symptom of social breakdown and moral decay. The possibility that women may want paid work is never recognized in this discourse, and women in the workforce are regarded as both cause and effect of social decay. It is because of such families, and such women, that state schools, in particular, must increase their custodial functions at the expense of their academic. Teachers thus become child minders and social workers (e.g., Chipman 1982: 21–23; Partingon 1984: 8).

Within this discursive strand, private schools score a double victory. 'Caring parents' choose such schools; non-caring parents do not. Private schools not only have a strong academic emphasis, but are also strong on pastoral care. For those families who have suffered marital break-down or who have been forced by the deficiencies of the state system to become two-income households, the private school can help to supplement the family. Students and their parents become part of the 'school family' and the 'church family'. Those who oppose 'choice', as the Right has defined it, are represented in a particular way that sets them in opposition to parents and their needs, feelings, and aspirations. Teachers' unions are clearly constructed in this manner, as the following quotation illustrates:

> The office bearers of principal teachers' unions. . . have made no secret of their implacable opposition to any Federal or State policy that would seek to fund families and children instead of school systems, lest the power over public education be taken from

bureaucrats and returned to the parents and taxpayers to whom it fundamentally belongs.

(Conway 1985: 1)

Again the people/state contradiction is successfully employed. Popular needs are juxtaposed against the bureaucratic distant state, which is seen as unable and unwilling to respond to these needs.

Through its focus upon the family's right to choice in education, the Right has successfully expropriated the social democratic themes of choice and equality of opportunity and has used them in support of extra funding for private schools. As Chipman (1984: 43) argues, 'Current funding arrangements severely restricts choice for many, especially the disadvantaged'. To reduce funds to high-status, high-fee schools limits the opportunity of attending such schools to the children of the wealthy. Choice and educational excellence should not, the Right believes, be restricted to the wealthy. They should be available to the worthy; those who have worked hard, shown self-reliance, and made sacrifices – they are therefore open to anyone. Governments may best facilitate equal opportunity by facilitating choice. Teachers' unions and educational bureaucrats, it is argued, 'have confused equality of opportunity with equality of outcomes' (Barnard in the *Age*, 3 July 1984, p. 13). The former is equated with choice and diversity, the latter with compulsion and uniformity.

CONSTRUCTING A HEGEMONIC DISCOURSE

So far I have illuminated the major premises of the Educational Right's discourse, showing how the interdiscursive practices of the private school lobby and the Educational Right operated in such a way as to assist the private school lobby in its political project with regard to funding, and hence ultimately to assist the sectional interests that this lobby and the Right serve. There is clear evidence that the Right has taken on the role of policing the education system. It constructed a regime of truth and, together with key organic intellectuals in the media, developed an apparatus of power–knowledge that sought to establish the boundaries within which 'normal, moral and socially responsible' education is defined and outside of which all else may be regarded as deviant. It has not only assumed the mantle of moral arbiter; it has also, again in conjunction with the media, conducted a programme of surveillance, identifying, and publicly denouncing, and exposing 'deviant' knowledges, teachers, and schools. In developing this moral technology the Right appealed to three groups of people. It sought, first, to confirm and reconstitute the subjectivity of private school clients, to attach them more firmly to the discourse of private schooling, and to unify them as a common 'subject'. Second, it attempted to construct subjectivity in a wider discursive field, directing itself particularly to the parent and voter. Third, it sought to make docile a government that would carry forward a revised 'social justice' agenda while none the less reactivating the state's individualizing and totalizing apparatus. This strategy clearly sought to revive modes of knowledge and schooling which, historically, have classified and regulated populations in such a way as to anticipate and subsequently to confirm class and gender identities. In what follows I shall identify the major features of these overlapping ideological ensembles of the Right in education and the ways in which they achieve their hegemonic effects. In so doing, I will further demonstrate the merits of drawing upon both Foucauldian and Gramscian theoretical premises.

Both right-wing thinking on education and arguments used in support of private schooling deploy interdiscursive practices very effectively. They conjure up a field of other discourses in which, in Hall's (1980: 179) words, 'the interpellations of one summon up and condense a series of others'. Many aspects of the discourses under review here intersect and replicate many of the positions built up elsewhere. They had particular resonance with the themes, moods, and concerns of other national popular discourses using their conceptual apparatus, and drawing credibility and authority from what was already established as credible and authoritative. I have shown how the private school lobby is inserted within the ideological ensemble of right-wing educational thinkers, and vice versa. I have also indicated how both draw upon the popular New Right notions about social change, economics, the market, and consumption, as well as upon minimalist privatization arguments about the role of the state *vis-à-vis* private effort and the family. Further, I have suggested the way in which a common sense about standards, excellence, and so on has been constructed which draws upon a nostalgic myth about the 'golden age' of education. In this mythical era, families were all intact, children accepted the authority of parents and teachers, people were self-reliant and not dependent upon the state, and everyone could spell and use correct grammar.

Such interdiscursive practices are particularly effective because they capitalize upon the feelings that have been generated by the economic and social changes that I mentioned earlier. Confused, disaffected, frustrated, and anxious people are particularly responsive to the interpellations of the discourses I have described. Hall (1980: 80) points out that at the centre of the Thatcherite Right in Britain is the 'worried parent, facing the harsh realities of a competitive world'. Such parents are at the centre of the interpellative structure of the discourses in question here. As Hannan (1985: 28) says, the Right has 'sniffed a genuine fear'; it has recognized the sincere and warranted concern of parents for their children's futures. Second, the discourses in question have allocated blame and provided scapegoats in ways that reflect less upon the children or the parents (the victims) than upon the system they have 'suffered'. These discourses also offer seemingly unproblematic solutions ('illusory solutions', says Sharp (1984: 28)). Unlike those offered by the 'democratic curriculum' educational reformers, these have the comfortable ring of the familiar, and are firmly located in an already constructed myth system that includes notions about the neutrality of education and the infinitely expandable 'cultural capital' of private schooling.

The current social context provides a fertile bed in which to sow the seeds of a range of 'panics' through the language of crisis. The nation, employers, and industry are in crisis because schools are not responding to changing technology or producing employable youth. Further and very importantly, state schooling is depicted as both symptom and cause of a crisis in standards, authority, and moral values. The Educational Right and the private school lobby have intervened in the field of popular morality with particular perspicacity and have done so in part through the construction of a series of ideological oppositions. As Hall (1980: 179) points out, during periods of social upheaval and change, popular morality 'has the power to map out the world of problematic social reality in clear unambiguous polarities. . . it provides a moral reference point which both grasps experience and sorts it into evaluative categories', and so displaces 'political issues with conventional moral absolutes'. Further, as Green (1986: 20) argues, binarism is 'a practice that is both powerfully generative and profoundly restrictive and regulatory in terms of how thinking and discourse proceeds'.

The construction of binary oppositions with positive and negative poles has been a central organizing mechanism within the discourses under review. We have seen children's rights juxtaposed against those of teachers; teachers' unions and bureaucrats constructed in opposition to parents and taxpayers; and the responsibility of 'intellectuals' on the Right compared with the morally reprehensible behaviour of 'intellectuals' on the Left. Tradition, authority, discipline, and the 'disciplines' have been equated with quality education and with excellence, while in contrast, progressivism and alternative curricula have been constructed in such a way as to signify chaos, and educational, social, and economic decline. Educational Rightists have aligned themselves alongside parents through their joint concern about the future of Australia and its children, and have aligned themselves in opposition to teachers with their 'radical, irrelevant' theory and practice. In every polarity, state schooling occupies the negative end of the spectrum and private schooling the positive. These sets of oppositions point quite clearly to those responsible for the educational 'crisis', as well as to directions towards enlightenment. The unequivocal implication is that responsible parents may best secure their children's futures through private schooling, and that governments may best secure Australia's future and their own political survival both by underwriting such parental 'choice' and by encouraging state schools to emulate private schools.

I have already indicated certain ways in which the discourses of the Educational Right and the private school lobby deployed the people–power bloc distinction. Powerless individuals were juxtaposed against a 'self serving, unresponsive bureaucracy' (Burchell 1986). This distinction was a particularly powerful means by which the unity of the private school sector was constructed and maintained despite differing sectional interests. The sector united in its opposition to funding cuts to the highly resourced schools despite significant differences within the sector's schools with regard to resources and clientele. In addition, despite the fact that poorly resourced private schools benefited substantially under the Labor government, such schools placed loyalty to the sector above the amelioration of their own disadvantage. This unity was achieved partly through the scare tactics employed in an Australian version of the Cold War domino theory, partly through a discourse about the value of privacy in education, but also through the facility of the 'hit list' schools to tap into a popular conservatism similar to that which had led many Roman Catholics to break away from the ALP to form the Democratic Labor Party in the 1950s. The binarism constructed here opposed Catholic schooling to an 'interventionist' Labor state dominated by 'radical Marxist secularists' and was a particularly powerful 'dividing practice'.

This is a classic instance of the discursive construction of hegemony. The working class was divided and sections of it incorporated through a discourse that identified its interests with those of the ruling groups'. Disparate and contradictory interests were activated and welded into a common position. All other aspects of people's lives were relegated to the boundaries and private schooling became the means of mobilization, with 'choice' the unifying, hegemonic principle. The least affluent schools were persuaded that their long-term best interests were served by joining the wealthy schools in opposing the government's guidelines. The Catholic system has, for instance, since the establishment of the Schools Commission, benefited enormously under Labor governments. The fact that it continues to be suspicious of such governments is in part a testimony to the ideological force of the high-status, high-fee sections of the private school sector. These sections increasingly recognize the value of association with the powerful Roman Catholic educational bureaucracy, and also the danger that a split within the sector could leave them at the margins.

Another significant feature of the discourses under discussion is their development of a very effective slogan system characterized by key concepts that included choice, rights, excellence, standards, authority, self-reliance, and so on. As Laclau points out, such terms do not have a historically fixed class or sectional meaning; in fact each has a range of possible connotations. Again, the Right and the private school lobby have demonstrated their facility for interdiscursive work as, through a process of disarticulation and rearticulation, they inserted these traditional themes into their own discourses and in the process achieved closure around the meanings that they chose to employ. With regard to education, it is accepted as common sense that most parents believe that they have rights as parents, endorse a concept of choice, and wish for good quality teaching and high educational standards for their children. However, the crucial point :n public educational polemics in Australia is that, with the prolonged and intense assistance of the media, the Right has come to define what 'choice', 'standards' and such like mean. It is now their discourse that has a significant and insistent truth effect, which inspires loyalties and cultivates demand. The Right's ideological labours have achieved their ends, and sectional interests have become universalized – defined as the interests of the majority. This is precisely the action of hegemony.

A second highly effective aspect of the slogan systems of the Educational Right and the private schools has been the development of a discourse of derision. By focusing on the worst or the most problematic or contentious features of some aspects of the government system, by exaggerating these features through the use of ludicrous images, ridicule, and stereotypification, it has undermined both the image of the state system and the stature of leftist educational discourse. Naturally enough, differences in schools and philosophies are conflated and consequently misrepresented. A caricature has been developed and presented to the public as an accurate depiction of the 'real'.

A final feature of the discourses under consideration relates again to their interdiscursive capacities. The organic intellectuals of privileged sections of society have dismantled much of the social-democratic educational thinking which characterized the Karmel era. Many of the key concepts of that time have been redefined and reconstituted into the new logic of the Educational Right's discourse. As I have shown, those concepts, previously intended to serve the interests of the disadvantaged and oppressed, have been deployed to serve the interests of privilege. Those concepts that have not been rearticulated within rightist thinking have taken their place within the discourse of derision. Their content has been made to look foolish and misguided, and consequently they have lost their credibility and force.

The effect of both discourses has been to move educational common sense to the Right. In conjunction with this, and as a consequence of the power of rightist ideology generally, people have, as Sawer (1982: xii) says, undergone a 'revolution of decreasing expectations'. With regard to social justice, less is demanded and expected of the state's representative institutions, which nevertheless remain and retain active popular consent: 'authoritarian populism', as Hall (1980: 16) calls it. None the less, the cruel ironies within the discursive ensemble under scrutiny should not go unnoticed. The Right is clearly demanding that the state mobilize a definition of educational democracy in which (in Tawney's words), 'freedom to the Pike' will be 'death to the Minnow'. While on the one hand the state is reviled as an intrusive restraint on freedom, on the other it is seen to have been negligent in disciplining the state school population and is called upon to reassert its technologies of power so as to regulate schooling in ways appropriate to the economy, capital, and the class interests of the patrons of expensive private schools.

CONCLUSION

Since the critical period of 1983–84 the federal Labor government has further pushed its education policy up the New Right's road, and in a manner that increasingly resembles Thatcher's policies in Britain (see Quicke 1988; Stockley 1987; Hextall 1988). It has replaced the Department of Education with the Department of Employment Education and Training and the 'soft egalitarian' (Hextall 1988: 66) Susan Ryan has been removed as Minister to make way for the economic pragmatist, John Dawkins. Dawkin's instrumentalist, interventionist, and privatizing approach to education is reflected particularly in the radical restructuring of the tertiary sector currently underway (see *Australian Universities Review* 1988) but he also has a vision for Australian schools that includes national policies on discipline and curriculum, with special attention paid to maths, science, and technology and the needs of employers. It is clear that this approach to education represents a major triumph for the Educational Right, especially for its technicist/instrumentalist wing. Its 'policing' of the system through the intensive propounding of educational and social 'truths' has had the desired effects. Schooling and school knowledge, now harnessed securely to national economic restoration, are to be reaffirmed in their selective and differentiating functions. Yet we, the people, are assured that this is for the common good.

Foucault continually reminds us that knowledge is central to power relations. He talks of a new politics of truth, saying, 'the problem is not changing peoples' consciousness – or what's in their heads – but the political, economic, institutional regime of the production of truth'; to detach 'the power of truth from the forms of hegemony, social, economic and cultural within which it operates' (in Rabinow 1984: 74–5). For Foucault, oppositional politics should take the form of critique, beginning with a suspicion of universal truths. He suggests that 'maybe the target nowadays is not to discover what we are but to refuse what we are' (in Rabinow 1984: 22) and argues that

> the real political task in a society such as ours is to criticize the workings of institutions which appear to be both neutral and independent; to criticize them in such a manner that the political violence which has always exercised itself obscurely through them, will be unmasked, so that one can fight them.
>
> (in Rabinow 1984: 6)

In standing 'offside' in relation to certain knowledges, Foucault shows the value of refusing to think and act in accordance with the 'rules' of knowledge. In order to unmask the political violence of the Educational Right and the private school lobby, it is essential that those of us who are 'organic' to the educationally and socially disempowered also take such a stance. For, as I have suggested throughout, particular discourses are inseparable from general relationships of power. Therefore, to challenge the particular is to challenge the general. Further, as Gramsci reminds us, discursive hegemony is fragile and dynamic and thus open to reversal through sustained ideological work.

NOTE

The author wishes to acknowledge Bill Green, Lindsay Fitzclarence, Leonie Taylor, and Peter Watkins for their help with this study.

REFERENCES

Aarons, L. (1987) *Here Come the Uglies: The New Right, Who They Are, What They Think, Why They are Dangerous*, Sydney: Red Pen Publications.

Australian Universities' Review, The Green Paper Issue (1988) 31 (1).

Barcan, A. (1982) 'Attacking the academic curriculum', *ACES Review* (August/September): 14.

———(1984a) 'The future of secondary education in N.S.W.', *ACES Review* (November): 16–19.

———(1984b) 'Marxism, neo-Marxism and humanist culture', *Quadrant* (October).

Barnett, D. (1988) 'Taking the right's road', *The Bulletin*, July 12, pp. 32–5.

Benton, T. (1984) *The Rise and Fall of Structural Marxism: Althusser and His Influence*, London: Macmillan.

Burchell, D. (1986) 'The fire next time: the New Right is on the march', in the New South Wales Regional Magazine of the Sydney University

Postgraduate Association. Reprinted in *Graduate Post*, Murdoch University Postgraduate Association Newsletter, pp. 3–7.

Chipman, L. (1982a) 'Stopping the rot in Australian schools and colleges', *Quadrant* 26 (19): 52–60.

——(1982b) 'The children of cynicism', in R. Manne (ed.) *The New Conservatism in Australia*, Melbourne: Melbourne University Press, pp. 17–40.

——(1984) 'Failing Australia's children', *Quadrant* (January–February): 36–43.

——(1985) 'To hell with equality', *Quadrant* (January–February): 44–51.

Coghill, K. (ed.) (1987) *The New Right's Australian Fantasy*, Victoria: McPhee Gribble/Penguin Books.

Cohen, G. *et al.* (1986) *The New Right: Image and Reality*, London: Runnymeade Trust.

Conway, R. (1985) 'The new establishment in education', *ACES Review* (May): 1–8

David, M. (1986) 'Moral and maternal: the family and the Right', in R. Levitas (ed.) *The Ideology of the New Right*, Cambridge: Polity Press.

Dwyer, P., Wilson, B., and Woock, R. (1984) *Confronting School and Work: Youth and Class Cultures in Australia*, Sydney: Allen & Unwin.

Elliott, B. and McCrone, D. (1987) 'Class, Culture and morality: a sociological analysis of neo-conservatism', *The Sociological Review* 35 (3): 485–515.

Foucault, M. (1967) *Madness and Civilization: A History of Insanity in the Age of Reason*, London: Tavistock.

——(1975) *The Birth of the Clinic*, New York: Vintage Books.

——(1976) 'Politics: the study of discourse', *Ideology and Consciousness* 3: 7–26.

——(1977a) *Discipline and Punish: The Birth of the Prison*, London: Penguin Press.

——(1977b)*The Archaeology of Knowledge*, London: Tavistock.

——(1981) *History of Sexuality*, vol. 1, Introduction, Harmondsworth: Pelican.

Giddens, A. (1982) *Profiles and Critique in Social Theory*, London: Macmillan.

Gordon, C. (ed.) (1980) *Michel Foucault, Power/Knowledge: Selected Interviews and other Writings 1972–1977*, Sussex: Harvest Press.

Gramsci, A. (1971) *Selections from the Prison Notebooks*, edited and translated by Quintin Hoare and Geoffrey Nowell Smith, New York: International Publishers.

Green, B. (1986) 'Reading reproduction theory: on the ideology and education debate', *Discourse* 6 (2): 1–13.

Hall, S. (1980) 'Popular-democratic vs. authoritarian-populism: two ways of taking democracy seriously', in A. Hunt (ed.) *Marxism and Democracy*, London: Lawrence and Wishhart, pp. 157–85.

Hall, S., Lumley, B. and McLennan, G. (1979) 'Politics and Ideology', in M. Barrett *et al.* (eds) *Ideology and Cultural Production*, UK: Hutchinson and Centre for Cultural Studies, pp. 45–75.

Hannan, B. (1985) *Democratic Curriculum: Essays on Schooling and Society*,

Sydney: Allen & Unwin.

Harrison-Mattley, P. (1982) 'Zoning of our schools over parental freedom of choice', *ACES Review* (August/September): 1–3.

———(1983) 'Our Mickey Mouse Schools', *Quadrant* (December): 71–3.

Hextall, I. (1988) 'Educational changes in England and Wales: The impact of the New Right', in E.B. Gumbert (ed.) *Making the Future*, Atlanta: Georgia State University.

Hoover, R. (1987) 'The rise of conservative capitalism: Ideological tensions within the Reagan and Thatcher governments', *Comparative Studies in Society and History* 29 (2): 245–68.

Jessop, B. (1982) *The Capitalist State: Marxist Theories and Methods*, Oxford: Martin Robinson.

Johnson, K. (1987) 'Popular discourses and schooling: Cultural and ideological analysis'. Paper presented at the joint AARE/NZARE Conference, University of Canterbury, Christchurch, New Zealand.

Johnson, R. (1983) 'Educational politics: the old and the new', in A.M. Wolpe and J. Donald (eds) *Is Anyone Here From Education?* London: Pluto Press, pp. 11–28.

Kenway, J. (1987a) 'Left right out: Australian education and the politics of signification', *Journal of Education Policy* 2 (3): 189–203.

———(1987b) *High Status Private Schooling and the Production of an Educational Hegemony*, unpublished Ph.D. dissertation, Murdoch University W.A.

Kramer, L. (1983) *Aces-looking forward'*, *ACES Review* (October/November): 5.

———(1984)'The ABC of higher education', *ACES Review* (June/July): 7–8.

Laclau, E. (1977) *Politics and Ideology in Marxist Theory*, London: New Left Books.

———(1983a) '"Socialism" the "People's Democracy": The transformation of hegemonic logic', *Social Text* 7 (Spring/Summer): pp. 115–9.

———(1983b) 'Transformation of advanced industrial societies and the theory of the subject', in S. Hanninen and L. Palden (eds) *Rethinking Ideology: A Marxist Debate*, New York and Bagnolet, France: International General/IMMRC, pp. 39–44.

Laclau, E. and Mouffe, C. (1981) 'Socialist strategy – where next?' *Marxism Today* (January): 17–22.

———(1982) 'Recasting Marxism: hegemony and new political movements', *Socialist Review* 66 (2): 91–113.

———(1985) *Hegemony and Socialist Strategy: Towards a Radical Democratic Politics*, London: Verso.

Levitas, R. (1985) 'New Right utopias', *Radical Philosophy* 39 (Spring): 2–9.

———(ed.) (1986) *The Ideology of the New Right*, Cambridge: Polity Press.

McWilliam, E. (1987) 'The challenge of the New Right: its liberty verses equality and the hell with fraternity!' *Discourse* 8 (1): 61–76.

Marginson, S. (1985) 'The collapse of the 1973 Karmel consensus', *Australian Teachers' Federation Research Papers*, issue 9.

Mercer, C. (1978) 'Culture and ideology in Gramsci, *Red Letters* 8 (19): 19–40.

———(1980) 'Revolutions, reforms or reformulations?' in A. Hunt (ed.)

Marxism and Democracy, London: Lawrence and Wishhart, pp. 102–37.

Miliband, R., Panitch, R. and Saville, J. (eds) (1987) *Socialist Register, 1987, Conservatism in Britain and America: Rhetoric and Reality*, London: Merlin Press.

Minson, J. (1980) 'Strategies for socialist: Foucault's conception of power', *Economy and Society* 9 (1): 1–43.

Morgan, H.M. (1984) 'Private schools and the mining industry', *ACES Review* (April/May): 8–10.

Mouffe, C. (1979a) 'Introduction' in C. Mouffe (ed.) *Gramsci and Marxist Theory*, London: Routledge & Kegan Paul, pp. 1–18.

———(1979b) 'Hegemony and ideology in Gramsci' in C. Mouffe (ed.) *Gramsci and Marxist Theory*, London: Routledge & Kegan Paul, pp. 168–203.

Partington, G. (1984) 'Problems afflicting state school', *ACES Review* (November): 1–4.

Poster, M. (1982) 'Foucault: a new kind of history', *Social Research* 49 (1): 116–42.

Quicke, J. (1988) 'The 'New Right' and education', *British Journal of Education Studies*, 26 (1): 5–20.

Rabinow, P. (ed.) (1984) *The Foucault Reader*, New York: Pantheon Books.

Salamini, L. (1981) 'Gramsci and Marxist sociology of language', *International Journal of the Sociology of Language* 32: 27–44.

Sarup, M. (1984) *Marxism, Structuralism and Education*, Sussex: Falmer Press.

Sawer, M. (ed.) (1982) *Australia and the New Right*, Sydney: George Allen & Unwin.

Sharp, R. (1984) 'Reclaiming the agenda: Socialist directions', *Radical Education Dossier* (Autumn): 25–9.

———(1986) *Capitalist Crisis and Schooling: Comparative Studies in the Politics of Education*, Melbourne: Macmillan.

Smart, B. (1983) *Foucault, Marxism and Critique*, London: Routledge & Kegan Paul.

———(1986) 'The politics of truth and the problem of hegemony', in D. Couzens Hoy (ed.) in *Foucault: A Critical Reader*, Oxford: Basil Blackwell, pp. 157–73.

Stockley, D. (1987) 'In darkest England', *Arena* 80: 11–18.

Volosinov, V.N. (1973) *Marxism and the Philosophy of Language*, New York: Seminar Press.

Webley, I. (1982) 'Women who want to be women', in M. Sawer (ed.) *Australia and the New Right*, Sydney: George Allen & Unwin, pp. 135–51.

Young, R. (ed.) (1981) *Untying the Text: A Post Structuralist Reader*, London: Routledge & Kegan Paul.

Young, R.E. (1987) 'The New Right and the Old Left: A plague on both their houses', *Discourse* 8 (1): 48–60.

Index